the use & misuse of computers in education

the use & misuse of computers in education

Allan B. Ellis

President, Educational Research Corporation
Newton, Massachusetts

McGraw-Hill Book Company
New York
St. Louis
San Francisco
Düsseldorf
Johannesburg
Kuala Lumpur
London
Mexico
Montreal
New Delhi
Panama
Rio de Janeiro
Singapore
Sydney
Toronto

Library of Congress Cataloging in Publication Data

Ellis, Allan B date
The use and misuse of computers in education.

Bibliography: p.
1. Computer-assisted instruction. I. Title.
LB1028.3.E44 371.39'445 73-11238
ISBN 0-07-019236-7

THE USE AND MISUSE OF COMPUTERS IN EDUCATION

1234567890KPKP7987654 3

This book was set in Caledonia by Black Dot, Inc. The editors were Robert C. Morgan and Phyllis T. Dulan; the designer was Perez Kaminsky; and the production supervisor was Bill Greenwood. The drawings were done by John Cordes, J & R Technical Services, Inc.
The printer and binder was Kingsport Press, Inc.

To Carole,
Leslie,
and Douglas
with love

Contents

Foreword

The possibility that computers will be used in schools seems to turn otherwise reasonable men and women into either implacable Luddites or doomsday zealots. To some the machine is the symbol of inhumanity, a blinking, rigid monster devoted to the dehumanization of the school. To others the computer is the route to new pedagogical sophistications, a device to free the child from the clutches of the biased, smothering teacher. The former think the latter are bloodless technicians. The latter find the former fearful reactionaries. Both Luddites and zealots are wrong, of course, and both are perversely right.

The computer is but another vehicle to employ in helping people learn, a cousin of books, films, blackboards, chalk, gerbils, abacuses. Like each of these devices, it can be well used or misused. It is a particularly sophisticated device, which makes it both promising and difficult. It requires careful preparation for use—as much or more as do some films—and it is as yet costly to operate. It requires teachers and administrators who can master its strengths and weaknesses, experts who are neither Luddites nor zealots. Their tribe is small indeed. The purpose of this book by my colleague Allan Ellis is to help it increase.

Rarely can one productively start in educational reform with *things*, whether they are books, films, or computers. One starts with a consideration of the *ends* of instruction, and employs things only as each of these emerges as the most efficient approach to meet, or to help meet, these ends. One uses a book or a computer only if a particular situation with a particular goal uniquely calls for one or the other. Effectiveness, economy of time, and the extent of financial outlay govern the choice.

The zealots' mistake has been to start with the thing. We've got this marvelous machine, now how can we use it? They have backed into the question of ends, sometimes virtually creating them to serve the machine's purpose. They have all too often ignored the commonsense realities of American schools, and have tried to market ridiculously expensive devices to meet trivial ends. In recent years the marketplace has cut many of the zealots down to size.

The Luddites gloat at the zealots' current discomfiture. However, as Ellis points out, there are few applications of computers that can serve to undercut their bias. The Luddites seem to control the field. As he says, "the promise of the computer in education is not a simple promise. . . [however] the computer can be our excuse and our mechanism to rethink and reformulate the very procedures we automate" and, later, "thinking about the computer's role in instruction does not mean thinking about computers. It means thinking about instruction." Such is thin gruel for hungry, doubting schoolmen, but it is an honest assessment of the state of computing art in education. The machine, Ellis asserts, is yet "incomplete." And the work to be done is not engineering or technological development. Until we substantially rethink and recast the programs of our schools, there will be little call for new devices. The task is, in the first instance, a philosophical and psychological one. Our current curriculum, born in the 1890s, is comfortably encumbered with an equally historical pedagogy, one which most teachers, students, and parents (in spite of the noisy complaint of a small minority) find quite satisfactory. There is no need for computers, as there is little call for the sophisticated new goals which computers alone could efficiently meet.

Therefore, this book about computers starts and ends with a call for new thoughts about instruction writ large. Only a revolution of educational ends and means could create an appropriate place for the misunderstood machine. That such a revolution is seriously overdue is appallingly obvious. That a reconstructed curriculum, which probably would be sited outside of schools as well as within them, would require computers is highly likely. Against the arrival of that day, a new group of educators, who are neither Luddites nor zealots, needs to be formed, and serious inquiry on the purposes of instruction and the place of computer technology in reaching them must be pressed.

THEODORE R. SIZER
Headmaster
Phillips Academy
Andover, Massachusetts

Preface

For the uninitiated educator this book provides an introduction to computers. For the educator who already uses computers this book encourages a second look at the opportunities that accompany such use. More specifically, the book identifies and examines some of the more critical central issues educators confront as they attempt to cope with the presence—and presumably the promise—of computers in their lives and in their work.

The book has two purposes. The first purpose is to pursue with the reader a line of reasoning which begins with the careful definition of computer, followed by a look into three implications of this definition which are of particular importance to people in education and are usually ignored by almost everyone who uses computers in schools. The discussion ends with a consideration of how computers enhance our ability to address complex educational problems. The second purpose is to provide information about computers and their role in education so that the reader will have sufficient background to follow the argument of the book, to become a knowledgeable reader of other books and articles in the field, and to become a skeptical viewer of attempts to automate education. These two purposes combine into an attempt to develop in the reader—be he naïve or sophisticated—a point of view about computing which will convince him to play a more critical and yet a more active role in the use of computers in education.

The book consists of three parts. Part I proceeds from the premise that computers are consistently misused in schools because in the final analysis educators are unclear and confused about what computers are.

By clarifying the relationship between procedures and the machines that execute them, Part I establishes a firm and sturdy definition of computers. Part II looks into certain implications this definition holds for the proper use of computers in schools, showing how these implications have been missed in almost all the work done thus far. Finally, Part III presents a case study of the major steps involved in building a computer into an education machine by capitalizing upon the three implications of what computers are. Part III also documents the relevance and the usefulness of the point of view about computers established in earlier parts of the book.

Aside from some very technical works suitable for engineers and logicians, it is not possible to write a book just about computers. Books that use "computer" in their title usually boil down to being books about *people* who use computers. Sometimes these books tell what people have done, and other times they deal with what people are doing or propose to do. More than anything else this book is about the things people *ought* to do with computers, and by implication, therefore, about the things most people whom we call educational technologists have failed to recognize about their efforts.

To help the reader follow and assess its general arguments, this book cites many examples. Since, as with all examples, they are drawn from a larger set of possible instances and do not exhaust the full range, the reader should seek out other cases that fit the arguments. Moreover, many of the examples are time-bound even though the arguments they support are not so perishable. Thus some of the examples, such as the references in the Appendix to RCA computers which have since been purchased by and renamed UNIVAC, have already become out-of-date. Yet their strength as supports for the assertions of this book are not appreciably diminished.

Acknowledgments usually begin with the apology that it is impossible to list all the people who affected the author's professional life and, therefore, contributed to his capacity or his need to write a book. It is impossible as a practical matter, of course, since there are not enough pages. But it is impossible in the truer sense that none of us can be aware of all those who have shaped our interests or our thinking. Yet always there are a few people whose contributions to the specific act of writing a book are so direct, so important, and so far beyond any reasonable expectation that mentioning them slights no one.

Foremost among the people who contributed to the writing of this book is F. Andre Favat, who tried with a special patience, through many drafts, to teach me that thinking is never more precise than the language it uses. To whatever extent this book is written clearly and well, both the author and the reader have him to thank. Another person for whose kind and considerable assistance I am especially grateful is Marietta Haley, who typed, retyped, designed, drew, secured permissions, obtained photographs, read, proofread, and generally managed the logistics of putting all the pieces together. Nothing even vaguely resembling a coherent work would now exist were it not for her constant help.

Among my other colleagues and friends who offered criticism and encouragement I wish in particular to thank Richard Willard, David Engler, William Cooley; also Marc Belth, Anna Doring, Karl Ellis, Robert Emmet, Donald Murray, Bernard O'Donnell, Alice Scates, Shoji Shiba, Margarita Sureda, John Williamson, and Karl Zinn.

I am also indebted to Harold Borko, who convinced me that the book should not be just another collection of articles; to Jacqueline Hargrove and Nona Strauss, who helped with the typing; and, of course, to my wife and children, who put up with all the inconveniences that go with having a writer in the house.

Finally, I wish to thank Seymour Papert, who, through his work and his writings, showed me what is truly possible with computers in education.

ALLAN B. ELLIS

1: what is a computer?

"That's a great deal to make one word mean," Alice said, in a thoughtful tone.

Lewis Carroll
Through the Looking Glass

CHAPTER ONE: common conceptions about computers

Remove every computer and every application of the computer from all the school districts in the country, and the schools will not shut down. Certainly there will be inconvenience, but this will be administrative inconvenience mostly, forcing some schoolmen to take on again the clerical chores associated with scheduling schools, keeping attendance, writing teachers' salary checks, printing grade reports, and such. Nor will the quality of the students' educational experience appreciably diminish. Some students—the few who take a high school course in computer programming—will have to wait a year or two until they get to college to learn about computers, but otherwise there will be little effect.

But this is not the impression we receive from the educational technologist. In conferences and symposia, presidential study commissions and congressional hearings, and books, articles, and project reports on the role of computers in education, the educational technologist encourages us to believe that the computer is indispensable to the life of the school. For example, the 1971 annual meeting of the Association for Educational Data Systems—the largest collection of people working on the use of computers in schools—opened with the assertion that "we can't do without the computer in education."[1]

The origin of this belief in the indispensability of the computer is not

[1]Convention Reporter, *Highlights of the 1971 Annual Meeting of the Association for Educational Data Systems*, Lubbock, Tex., 1971.

difficult to find. People have heard or read that the computer holds great *promise* for education and that it will have as revolutionary an effect upon schooling as did the Gutenberg press. Should this promise be fulfilled then surely the computer would be vital to education. But since, as this book will show, the computer's promise has not yet been fulfilled, the educational technologist has no basis to assert that the computer is right now "no longer a gimmick or a frill [but] an integral part of the [educational] programs that are being mounted today.[2] Only when its promise is fulfilled can the computer be indispensable.

Nor is the promise of the computer in education a simple one. Indeed the full power of this promise remains unclear, although the purpose of this book is to suggest that in education, as in other endeavors, the computer's promise rests in being both our excuse and our mechanism to rethink and reformulate the very procedures we automate. Thus it is we, and not the computer itself, who must fulfill the computer's promise. As we shall see, this is a very delicate matter. The computer's promise is complex, often disguised and misleading, and we must not interpret what it offers too literally.

Most educators have been too literal about computers and, as a result, they are overconfident that they know what computers are. Take, for instance, the meeting in November 1970 of the National Association of Users of Computer Applications to Learning, convened "to formulate a national policy statement by addressing the *critical issues* facing the use of computers in education." At the very bottom of their list of important concerns (they gave it a "priority weight" of zero) was the matter of developing "a better definition of computer technology in education." When asked by an outsider why this issue had been placed so low, the Chairman explained that the members had been involved with data processing for some years and that "we all know what computers do."

Ironically in their security about what computers do, such educational technologists miss the most important point of all about computers: anyone who knows what computers *do*, knows nothing about computers. Speaking about what computers *do* is a logically deviant enterprise. The whole point about the computer, as will be seen later, is that, unlike toasters or cigarette machines or snow blowers, it is not designed, in the ordinary sense of the word, to *do* things. Because the typical educator who uses computers has missed the distinction between computers and ordinary machines, he has been satisfied to look to ordinary places for his definition of computers. The result is a common sensical definition of computers which does not stand much scrutiny and which, as we shall see, leads to erroneous implications.

How this is so will be the concern of Chapter One. The subsequent pages of Part I will then attempt to build a strong, unshakable definition

[2]Ibid.

of computers. With this definition in hand, Part II will explore the principal implications for education of what computers are. Finally, Part III will show in detail what is involved in using a computer to address a complex educational problem, examining one such effort from its inception through to its completion four years later. Taken together the three parts of this book will endeavor to show, first directly and then through examples, that whatever chance there is for us in education to realize the promise of the computer depends almost entirely upon our coming to understand what computers are.

Common Belief

The situation in the final moments of Euripides' *Electra* is so involved and so utterly complicated that there is no hope of resolution. Suddenly a metal crane attached to the top of the scenery is lowered onto the stage. Suspended from the metal crane is a dummy, and everyone in the audience knows that this dummy represents a god and that by one godly act he will set everything right, freeing the heroine and her brother from their fate.

This literary device of *deus ex machina* is no longer considered good drama, of course, but for some modern men, faced with intellectual and scientific problems as intricate as any Greek tragedy, the idea is still in vogue. These men do not expect miracles any more from metal cranes and gods who ride upon them; these have been replaced by a more complicated machine which they call a computer. The intention, however, remains much the same: to somehow rescue *man* from his otherwise inextricable problems and puzzles.

In intellectual and scientific investigation, as in modern drama, this point of view is out of place. Yet it is not entirely unreasonable that most people see the computer as a twentieth century *deus ex machina* because, certainly, there are ways in which computers so exceed human capacities that they seem godlike.

Of all the things they are supposed to be, for example, everyone agrees that first of all computers are fast. Indeed, few men would be surprised to learn that in the time it takes an average person to read this sentence an ordinary computer performs one million six hundred thousand operations. They have become used to hearing that whenever NASA launches a rocket to the moon, computers figure from minute to minute where the missile is heading, correcting its flight, and standing by to look even deeper into the trip the missile has yet to make. It is unusual to no one that computers are used at places like the Cambridge Electron Accelerator to keep up with miniature atomic particles as they approach the speed of light. Even on election night—although politicians may worry about the effects upon the electorate—voters take it in stride when computers announce the various winners well before the polls across the country have closed. People have come to expect such things of computers.

But speed is not the only thing we take for granted about computers. Like gods we expect them to be infallible as well. When a computer writes a payroll check for $20,000 instead of $200, for example, it invariably makes the evening newspaper because computers are not supposed to make mistakes. Airlines that use computers to quickly locate vacant seats on a flight, do not expect the computer to assign the same seat to two travelers. Astronauts who do not have the luxury of extra time to make up their minds rely on computers to navigate them through space, where even minor errors are quickly magnified. Scientists, educational researchers, applied mathematicians, economists, even businessmen have come to rely on the computer's accuracy much the way we depend upon electricity in our homes, expecting neither delay nor error and being considerably inconvenienced by either. Thus speed and accuracy go hand in hand, and, in reality, what people mean when they say computers are fast is that they are fast at getting the right answer.

Just as expectations about the computer's speed involve its accuracy, so too do they involve its capacity to handle large amounts of data. Businessmen describe computers that search entire files of inventory, keeping check on sales and placing new orders when stock is low; librarians speak of using computers to store their bibliographies; and policemen in Los Angeles tell how their computerized files on crimes and criminals help them maintain peace and order. A frequent topic of the conversations of politicians, housewives, college students, and commuters concerns the dangers of such computer files made up of dossiers on each one of us available for instant retrieval and scrutiny. Thus, the handling of otherwise unmanageable amounts of data stands prominent among the things people fearfully, or hopefully, expect of computers.

According to common belief, then, the computer is a device for processing large quantities of information, not only at great speeds but with unfailing accuracy, and indeed there seems little reason to question the view of the computer as the present day "god from the machine." Nor does there seem to be cause to question the common belief upon which this view is based since surely computers are fast, accurate, and able to store large amounts of data.

Yet even a cursory second look at these three characterizations of computers will reveal that common belief stems from a hasty use of words. Philosophers have known for some time that the hasty use of words is at the root of most philosophical problems and that it is the breakdown of language that yields most of our faulty conclusions. This notion is true for us as well, as we attempt to understand computers. Because the world of computers is so often a world of half-truths and oversimplifications, much of our common belief about computers loses its force once we are clear about the words we use.

For instance consider the computer's speed. When Paul Siegel says that a computer can multiply two ten-digit numbers in the time it takes a jet plane to fly one inch, he is speaking about a special kind of time.[3] Given that a computer program to perform this multiplication has been written by someone, and translated to computer language, and tested, and revised, and transported to the computing center, and given that the two numbers involved have been put in the proper form and fed into the machine, then the time to perform the multiplication is as Siegel calculates. And even then the result must be printed out, returned to the interested party, and interpreted.

The example is trivial but the distinction it makes is not. Many attempts to apply computers to problems have failed—and these are expensive failures—because the distinction was not made and fully understood between the time it takes to prepare a computer to do a job, and the time it takes the computer to do it. Just as it is only partially true that Glenn Gould, the pianist, takes four minutes eleven seconds to play the Sinfonia from Bach's Partita No. 2 in C Minor, so too, it is only partially true that computers are as fast as jet planes. For instance, a computer program to schedule a typical secondary school may take three years or more to write, test, and perfect, and even then, between getting the data in proper form for submission to the program and interpreting the results prior to resubmission with new constraints, it often takes an administrator and his computer the entire summer to get the job done. Indeed, computer programs used by banks to keep track of deposits as they are made, calculate interest, check on overdrawn accounts, and send out monthly mortgage statements are sufficiently complex to require, in some cases, the equivalent of twenty years' work before they function properly, and these are not the most sophisticated programs being written.

Similarly, to say computers are accurate is to say too much if this means they have a built-in concern for getting the correct answer. Computers are just as capable of producing the wrong answer as the right one, and they do not know the difference. Computers operate under the control of computer programs and, thus, the person writing the program must decide and specify what procedure will be followed to obtain an answer. When the procedure is wrong the answer is wrong.

How then can people claim computers are accurate? In the first place it is possible to perform calculations with much greater precision than by hand, carrying along each step of the way many more decimal places, for example, than we would have the tolerance for manually. Second, computers are not capricious. A person can be sure that any legitimate operation he calls for will be performed where and when he wishes: computers do not mistake addition for subtraction the way people often do when balancing their checkbooks. Finally, computers are predictable,

[3]Paul Siegel, *Understanding Digital Computers*, Wiley, New York, 1961, p. 1.

performing a set of procedures the same way each time, varying only within limits set by the program. Given the same conditions each time they will obtain the same results.

As with its speed and its accuracy, we must exercise care in what we say about the computer's capacity to store information. We know for instance a small to moderate-size computer has room inside to store 18,700 telephone numbers, far more than a human being can recall from memory, and when augmented by external devices for storing information there is theoretically no limit to the amount of data that can be stored. But implicit in storing is retrieving. It does no good to store something if you cannot get at it or even if it takes too long to locate and retrieve it, and this is where the difficulty rests. Deciding what information is to be retrieved, by what method, and under what circumstances are some of the many problems associated with the retrieval of data from large information files. Then there is the problem of storing data so as to facilitate retrieval, and related to this, the task of adding and deleting items from the file to keep it current. This is just a small set of the major difficulties associated with storing large quantities of data which specialists in information retrieval consider formidable. Just as sinking ships is easier than locating them at the bottom of the ocean and dredging them up, so too is it easier to store data in a computer than it is to retrieve them.

Thus as we become even a little more careful with the words we use, our sense of what computers are begins to change. While the common belief may be correct when it asserts that computers are fast, accurate, and able to store large amounts of data, such belief—based as it is on an uncritical use of language—does not go far enough to provide a full sense of what computers are.

Yet our effort to be careful with the language of common belief about computers prepares only some of the way for our eventual construction of a strong notion of computers and their role in education. Next we must turn up some of the roots of this common belief, seeing thereby what we need to avoid in our own attempts to think clearly about computers.

As we shall see, there lies beneath common belief about computers a tangle of inaccurate definitions and distorted histories. Because these definitions and these histories are credible and because they support each other so well, it will not be difficult to see how the prevalent misunderstandings about computers stem from them. Even as we separate here these definitions and histories—looking into each as a partial source of confusion—their joint effect will be evident.

The Usual Definitions

Among the various modes of defining recognized by philosophers, *naming* and *describing* stand out as the principal modes. Both modes have been used to define computers, and typically, these definitions dissolve into half-truths which provide much of the shaky foundation upon which common belief about computers is based.

The Name

For instance, consider the computer's name. The machine we usually refer to when we use the word "computer" goes by the full name "electronic digital computer" and the typical view of computers derives, in part, from a too literal interpretation of this name. First of all computers need not be *electronic*; they could just as easily be mechanical as, in fact, the first ones were. Computers, in this sense, are like clocks. When we speak of electric clocks, we do not mean to suggest that a clock must be electric in order to work properly, and thus we are not amazed to learn that some clocks will work when wound by hand. Similarly it is a mistake to believe that computers must be electronic in order to function properly. Electricity and computers go hand in hand, of course, and this accounts for the great speeds we have come to expect. It is a great advantage for a computer to be fast, and it is probably true that a slow computer would not interest us very much, but even its speed is not one of the essential characteristics that make a device a computer.

Moreover, computers need not be *digital.* Digital computers, as the name implies, represent quantities as numbers much the way we do in arithmetic. There is another kind of computer, however, that represents quantities not symbolically, but by analogy. Representing things by analogy is not new: thermometers, maps, grandfather clocks, and slide rules each represent quantities not directly but by translating them into other forms. On maps, inches equal miles, and on thermometers, the height of a column of mercury stands for a particular temperature. In analogue computers the number seven, for example, would be represented not by any discrete symbol—as is the case in digital machines—but perhaps by the amount of voltage a signal carries, in this case a 7-volt signal. Addition in an analogue computer is accomplished through an adder which is designed to produce at one end a signal equal to the sum of those introduced at the other end so that a 4-volt and a 3-volt signal introduced at the appropriate point in the circuitry will result in a 7-volt signal. Most computers are digital, but this does not mean that the quality of being digital is significant in determining whether or not a device is a computer.

Often the word "digital" creates an additional problem, one which is particularly serious. Most people draw the reasonable conclusion from the presence of this word in its name that a computer deals with numbers only. But they are wrong in this conclusion. The word "digital" refers to the *way information is represented* and not to the nature of the information itself: the numeral 21 may represent the number twenty-one, or it may represent something else, for instance the first letter of the alphabet. In this way the string 232163 might represent the number 232,163 or the word "cat." This string might also represent moves in a checker game, signs of the zodiac, or the first six notes of a song.

Finally the word "computer" itself, carrying as it does such strong connotations of numerical calculation, has lent support to the notion that computers are nothing more than arithmetic machines. But computers are not at all restricted to performing arithmetic. Indeed, computers can execute any well-defined procedure that involves the processing of symbols, numeric or otherwise. Of course, adding machines, calculators, arithmetic machines in general are part of the computer's lineage—a fact which we shall see the historians making too much of—but to restrict the computer to arithmetic is to make it pay for the sins of its ancestors.

But while we gain insight into common misunderstanding about computers and thus learn what to avoid ourselves, clarifying the meanings of all the words people use when they speak of computers is, in the end, as effective as treating the symptoms of a psychosomatic illness. All you remove are the outward signs of a deeper problem, leaving untouched the source of present and future troubles. We see this with nominal definitions and we see this as well with the usual descriptive definition.

The Description

The usual descriptive definition of a computer begins with the statement that it is a very fast adding machine. Like desk calculators, it says, computers deal with numbers, adding, subtracting, multiplying, or dividing them and producing—quickly and accurately—results for the eye to see. The adding machine provides a convenient metaphor: most people have used one or seen one at their grocer's, and as an example of a machine that does calculations, it makes the computer much less awesome. But the adding machine is an unfortunate choice because people are led to believe that that is as far as it goes, concluding that a computer is an arithmetic machine and nothing more. A computer, however, is more than this, it is a symbol processing device. Computers deal with numbers, of course, but they deal with other symbols as well, including letters of the alphabet. While we often think of computers as calculators, they are in fact capable of performing any well-defined procedure that involves processing, manipulating, transforming, or other handling of symbols. Calculating forms only one set of such procedures.

By restricting its reference to adding machines, the ordinary definition causes confusion among people who recognize that computers are revolutionizing the way we deal with information. It does not make sense to them that an adding machine, even a large, very fast one, should have affected us the way computers have. But having no firm ground on which to argue, some people accept the definition wholeheartedly, concluding that computers are menial clerks doing by rote all they are told to do. Others discard the definition in favor of what they have heard computers do. They fearfully conceive of a computer as a "giant brain" deciding for itself what to do and when to do it. Still others—probably most people—think of the computer in both ways at the same time, and thus confusion becomes contradiction.

Whether taken singly or together, therefore, the two prevailing forms of definition of a computer—the literal interpretation of its name and the oversimplified description of its capacity—provide an inadequate notion of a computer. Nor are these the only sources of misunderstanding and misapplication of computers. An additional source of difficulty, in some respects the worst offender of all, is the misconceived history of the development of computers.

Typical Histories

The *Times* Literary Supplement of Friday, November 6, 1959, contains an essay entitled "Imaginative Historians" in which it is said that American historians are always taking sides about the past in ways dictated by their commitments in the present. "They have taken sides over Hamilton and Jefferson, over the character and intentions of the framers of the Constitution, over judicial review, over racial questions, and, of course, over the Civil War and Reconstruction."[4] Presumably this tendency to take sides stems from the view that history can be used to understand the present, encouraged perhaps by Thucydides' contention that sooner or later the events of the past will be repeated. Often, however, this intention results in a sort of historical journalism where, far from speaking for itself, history becomes editorial, directed at contemporary situations, and thus serving the historian's commitment to the present. Holding this view, the *Times* essay was appropriately subtitled "Telling the News about the Past," and while the author does not mention computers in his analysis, it is true that many writers of the history of computers approach their subject laden with similar commitment.

Some historians of the computer are committed to a definition and, as we have just seen, such definitions often resolve to the inappropriate view of the computer as a very fast adding machine. These histories, to a large extent, depend upon the fact that the word "compute" and the word "count" are related, having their origin in the same Latin word, and conclude from this that a discussion of devices that count constitutes a proper history of computers. But etymology makes dubious history. The word "cybernetics," for example, which refers to the comparative study of control and communication in machines and animals is derived from the Greek word "kybernetes" meaning helmsman. While the connection is clear, it does not follow at all, of course, that the history of ships or of

[4]The *Times,* "Imaginative Historians," London, November 6, 1959, p. xxxix.

helmsmen is an important or even legitimate part of cybernetics. Depending upon a definition, however, many histories of the computer become concatenations of calculating devices beginning usually with the abacus and continuing on with descriptions of such seventeenth and eighteenth century calculating devices as the slide rule, Napier's bones, the flyball governor, Pascal's calculator, and Leibniz's stepped wheel—a machine which capitalized on the fact that one can do multiplication by the method of repeated addition. Eventually, indeed inevitably, we are led to the adding machine, and history becomes a rationalization for present misconceptions about computers.

Other historians of the computer are committed to a mission. To them the computer's history is a vehicle for removing the mysteries and thus the fears which often surround modern man's vision of the computer and its potential. They wish to assure the reader that computers, or at least the essential ideas underlying their operation, have existed for hundreds even thousands of years. Computers, these historians proclaim, are not new things. These histories begin with conjectures about cavemen, arguing that when he scratched the figures of bison on the walls of caves, prehistoric man was beginning the long but somehow sure road that leads eventually to present day computers. Strokes in sand, fingers used for counting, the early Egyptian abacus, even hourglasses and Babylonian maps carved on small clay tablets are brought into these histories, and it is not difficult for the reader to conclude that if they had had the technology, the Greeks might have produced a full-scale computer one hundred years before the death of Christ.

In his popular book entitled *Stonehenge Decoded*, for example, Gerald Hawkins—who tells of how he used a computer to help him prove the theory that Stonehenge, the ancient Druid temple, was in fact built to be a computer—begins his history with the assertion "For about as many years as he has been Homo sapiens, perhaps for *exactly* as many ages, man has used things as tools to help him count."[5] Harold Borko in his history tells of an ancient Greek computer discovered by divers off the Isle of Antikythera. "In a ship that had apparently been wrecked during the first century B.C., they found a gadget with a complicated set of dials, gears, wheels, and enscribed plates."[6] Even B. V. Bowden in his excellent book entitled *Faster Than Thought*, refers to Gerbert who, before he became Pope Silvester II in the tenth century, "was reputed to have made a bronze head which would answer yes or no to any question propounded to it,"[7] and to Blaise Pascal who was only nineteen years old when in 1642 he built the first digital calculating machine as a present for his father.[8] All these things may be legitimate parts of a history of computers,

[5]Gerald Hawkins, *Stonehenge Decoded*, Doubleday, New York, 1965, p. 98.
[6]Harold Borko (ed.), *Computer Applications in the Behavioral Sciences*, Prentice Hall, Englewood Cliffs, N.J., 1962, p. 24.
[7]See Roland Allen, "Gerbert, Pope Silvester II," *The English Historical Review*, vol. **VII**, 1892, pp. 625–668.
[8]B. V. Bowden (ed.), *Faster Than Thought*, Pitman, New York, 1953, pp. 5–6.

but not as they are usually included by those writers who are committed either to a definition or to a mission. Even if it was true somehow that the computer's lineage is comprised of such ancient and medieval devices, it is a simple-minded history indeed that treats the endless enumeration of ancestors as valid historical analysis.

A Century Ago

An interesting example of the folly of hastily linking events to form a history is revealed in the story of Charles Babbage.

Charles Babbage was born in Devonshire, England, in 1792. At the age of twenty or so this Cambridge-educated mathematician became intrigued with the idea that a machine might be used to calculate tables. Navigational tables, logarithm tables, and the like were being compiled by hand and whatever the care, it was not very likely that a particular figure would be correct. To the captain of a ship, of course, this inaccuracy was of great concern and Babbage's interest, therefore, was not a purely theoretical one. In fact, from the day in 1812 that the idea first came to him until his death fifty-nine years later, Babbage spent all his time and inheritance in pursuit of this interest.

Throughout his lifetime Babbage and his colleagues thought about many different machines, including one capable of playing such games as ticktacktoe and chess. But by far the greatest portion of his life was spent attempting to construct two calculating machines, the first of which he called the Difference Engine.

The Difference Engine begun by Babbage in 1820 and one version of which he completed in June 1822 is a machine designed to perform certain calculations using a procedure called "the method of differences." To understand the method of differences imagine that you had to compute various values of y in the equation $y = x^2 + 2x$. Using the differences procedure, the first step is to compute by hand the first few values of y: When $x = 0$, y, of course, equals 0; when $x = 1$, $y = 3$, and so on. Table 1.1 lists the values of y for those values of x between 0 and 5.

x	y
0	0
1	3
2	8
3	15
4	24
5	35

Table 1.1 Some values of $y = x^2 + 2x$.

x	y	D-1	D-2
0	0		
		3	2
1	3		
		5	
2	8		2
		7	
3	15		2
		9	
4	24		2
		11	
5	35		

Table 1.2 An example of the method of differences.

The next step in the method of differences is to take the difference between each value of y in the table and the value that follows it. These are the figures listed in column D-1 (for first difference) in Table 1.2. If we then take the difference between each entry in column D-1 and the entry that follows it, we can create the figures for column D-2. Notice that all the values in column D-2 are equal; in this case they are all two's. This table is all we need to go on to compute successive values of y for new values of x: we need only reverse the process. For example, we know that all successive entries in column D-2 will be two's, which means that the difference between each entry in column D-1 will be a difference of two. Thus, the next number in column D-1 will be 13. But this in turn means that the next value of y will be thirteen greater than the last value; that is, the next value of y will be 48, and this is the proper value of y for $x = 6$. Continuing this process we can go on indefinitely evaluating the function $x^2 + 2x$. This method of differences works for other functions as well, of course, and it was one of Babbage's great contributions to design a machine to perform calculations by this method. Notice, however, that while it is not a trivial task to construct a Difference Engine, much of the ingenuity of such a machine *rests in the procedure itself.* Once a procedure is described in terms of acts which are machinelike, it becomes quite credible that a machine should perform such acts.

The Analytical Machine

One of the many problems Babbage faced in the development of his computing machines was that of finding a mechanical method for providing these machines with the numbers on which they were to operate. It may seem odd that for the solution to this problem Babbage looked to a weaver and his loom, but in fact this was quite reasonable since twenty years before Babbage had started work on his Difference Engine a Frenchman named Joseph Marie Jacquard devised a loom which operated under the control of a system of punched cards, and it was this principle of using punched cards to transmit information to a machine that Babbage adopted.

In the Jacquard loom a given card with holes punched in it would either allow a needle to pass through a hole or, in the case where there was no hole in a particular position on the card, inhibit the dropping of the needle. In this way a system of cards served to control the sequence of colors of the yarn, permitting thereby a variety of patterns to be woven into the fabric, in fact, any pattern which could be described by a set of punched cards. Twenty-four thousand such punched cards, for example, were used to weave a portrait of Jacquard himself. Babbage, who had this portrait of Jacquard hanging on the wall of his drawingroom, was impressed by a visitor who recognized it for what it was. "Babbage was much impressed by the fact that [his visitor] was immediately able to appreciate the fact that the technique which had been used to weave it might be taken over and used in a computing machine."[9]

The idea demonstrated by Jacquard of using punched cards to transmit information to a machine was of as much interest in 1880 to Dr. Herman Hollerith as it was in 1820 to Charles Babbage. Hollerith, a statistician for the United States government, was faced with the task of tabulating the figures of the 1890 census at a time when such tabulating would take more than ten years if done by hand. Before one census was complete, it would be time for the next one. Faced with this prospect, Hollerith conceived the idea of representing the census data as holes on punched cards and of building machines that would sort these cards according to the holes they contained and that would tabulate and otherwise analyze the data. Hollerith's punched card processing machines, as do their present day counterparts, operate in general on the principle that a hole in a card permits a brush to make contact with an electrified surface, thus completing some circuit or other whereas the absence of such a hole serves to block this contact. Therefore numbers when represented as particular configurations of holes on a punched card could be entered into a calculating machine.

Babbage's interest in the Jacquard loom, however, went beyond this relatively simple idea of using holes in cards to represent numbers. While working on the perfection of his Difference Engine, it occurred to Babbage that it would be possible to build a second machine, considerably more complex and more capable, that would perform any algebraic procedure whatever that could be described to it. Between this machine—which he called the Analytical Engine—and the Jacquard loom, Babbage noticed what he called a "nearly perfect analogy." Babbage drew an analogy between the Jacquard loom and the Analytical Engine in the following way: if there is a set of cards in a loom describing a particular pattern, those cards can be used to weave that pattern into any

[9]Ibid., p. 23.

number of fabrics and, of course, these fabrics need not be of the same color; that is, while the pattern which a set of cards describes remains the same, the colors of the yarn may vary from time to time. Similarly, Babbage conceived that his Analytical Engine would be stocked with what he called "operation cards," punched cards that would describe the algebraic operations to be performed. Other cards, which he called "variable cards," would then be used—much like different colored yarn—to describe the particular values which were to be processed. Inserting these values into the formula the machine would then compute and print the results. Whatever the value of the constants inserted in the formula, the pattern of calculations defined by a set of operation cards will be repeated and thus as Babbage argued, "The Analytical Engine will possess a library of its own. Every set of cards once made will at any future time reproduce the calculations for which it was first arranged. The numerical value of its constants may then be inserted."[10]

An Historical Moral

It seems entirely fitting that Charles Babbage and Jules Verne should have been contemporaries. Like Verne, Babbage's visions were well ahead of his time, so much so, in fact that the Analytical Engine was never built. From 1833 when he conceived his plan for an Analytical Engine until 1871 when he died Babbage lived with the fact that he would have to first advance the art of toolmaking and of the construction of gears and wheels if he was ever to get a working version of his machine, and although he contributed most of his fortune and thirty-eight years of his life to this pursuit, he failed. Babbage's sketches so outdistanced the technology of his time that as descriptions of an Analytical Engine they contained as little verisimilitude as Jules Verne's depiction of the *Nautilus*.

Now, the fact that Babbage never completed his Analytical Engine is not at all as important as the fact that his work during the first half of the nineteenth century embodied almost all of the concepts underlying present day computers. Being ahead of his time may have meant that his efforts to build his calculating engine would fail, but it meant as well that his dreams would become a legacy to men of the future. Yet, this legacy was never claimed and this is the point of the story about Charles Babbage.

Historians do not hesitate to link the work of Babbage to the eventual development of the computer. Borko goes so far as to say that the sophistication of technology coupled with the increased demands of business and government, clearly established the twentieth century as the "time to *renew* the vision of Babbage."[11] But as comforting as it may be to

[10]Charles Babbage, *Passages from the Life of a Philosopher*, Longmans, London, 1864, p. 119.
[11]Borko, op. cit., p. 41, italics supplied.

believe that someone thought about computers in 1830, the fact remains that in 1939 when Howard Aiken—then at Harvard University—began work on the design and construction of a machine that was to become the first digital computer ever built, *he did so without ever having heard of Charles Babbage.* Aiken, who finally discovered Babbage shortly before his work to develop a computer was completed, has said that he was startled to find that he and Babbage had been preoccupied by the same problems.[12] Thus whatever homage we pay to Babbage's dreams, the computer belongs to this generation, and the past is inadequate to give us a definition of a computer, or to remove whatever magic we have ascribed to it.

Because we know about evolution we can assert that snakes, alligators, turtles, and tuataras belong to the same family, having as their common relative some prehistoric creature that lived and died during the Age of the Reptiles. But in a discussion of computers, to confuse this kind of natural history with what Thomas Hobbes called "civil history"—"The history of voluntary actions of men in commonwealths"—is to treat the computer as a natural phenomenon. Even arguing that the ideas underlying the development of the computer evolved over time, the way animals or languages do, is saying too much. Histories of the lives and hopes and thoughts of men like Charles Babbage can give us insight into computers and they can even give us a context within which to begin our effort to define computers, but they cannot give us the definition itself.

[12]Jeremy Bernstein, *The Analytical Engine*, Random House, New York, 1963, pp. 51–52.

CHAPTER TWO: the incomplete machine

With the exploration of the previous chapter behind us, we can now assert that the common sense about computers—however reasonable and comforting—is grounded mostly in the half-truths of misconceived beliefs, inaccurate definitions, and distorted histories. By revealing something of these half-truths, the chapter has shown us there are enough grains of truth in our beliefs so that at best we will be right for the wrong reasons. But as we have seen as well, it is more likely the prevailing definitions and histories, by depicting the computer as a fast adding machine with an ancient and easily understood lineage, will persuade us to rely too heavily upon our common sense. Thus for our effort to locate a definition of a computer strong enough to stand scrutiny and meaningful enough to provide us insight into the proper use of computers, the previous chapter has not only cleared away some of the haze, but better still it has shown us where not to look. In this chapter, therefore, we will turn away from common sense, and look elsewhere for our definition.

Computing Machines

It is the irony of most disciplines that their outer reaches deal with their beginnings. Numbers, for example, are the basic elements of mathematics with which every student learns to deal, and yet, mathematical scholars have spent considerable time clarifying and trying better to understand the concept of number and the role it plays in their field. The physicist ponders the nature of matter, his basic element; the analytic philosopher examines in the greatest detail the meanings and connotations of words which make up his philosophical propositions; and schoolchildren faced with noun phrases, dependent clauses, and complex sentences might draw some comfort from the fact that mathematical linguists spend their days in struggles with grammar. Similarly, the machine is the subject of studies by scholars who are attempting to develop what they call "a theory of automata." While these men represent diverse fields of interest—engineering, medicine, philosophy of science, communications—they all have in common their attempts to formulate careful statements about the way machines behave, and it is to these automata studies we must look, even with beginners' eyes, in order to find a suitable definition of a computer.

In the most general sense, an automaton is any device that has certain parts which can be called *inputs*, and other parts which can be called *outputs*, such that what happens at the outputs is in some way related to what happens at the inputs. To be an automaton a machine must accept some input and provide some output. But this is what all machines do. With cigarette machines we put fifty cents in a slot, pull a lever, and out comes a package of cigarettes. With furnaces we shovel in coal and get out heat. So in fact all machines—cigarette machines, furnaces, thermometers, automobile gasoline gauges, pinball machines—fit this definition. To the automata theorist, however, not all machines are worth studying. First, he centers his attention on machines that process or otherwise deal with information. Second, he limits his interest further by requiring that the information machines be complicated, thus ruling out adding machines, tote boards, and other simple calculating devices. Finally, the automata theorist ignores questions of the construction or of the physical characteristics of machines. He does not care what machines look like because his interest is confined to the way machines behave.

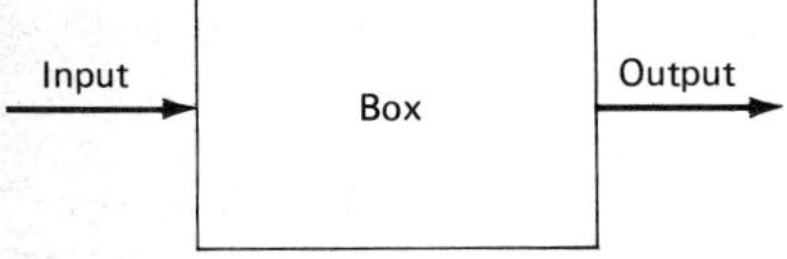

Figure 2-1 Schema of an automaton.

A computer is an automaton, of course, and it may be represented, therefore, as in Figure 2-1, which must seem bare indeed, and hardly a satisfactory definition of anything let alone a computer. But this is where we must begin.

Turing Machines

Why this diagram is a meaningful place to begin a definition of a computer can be seen by looking first at another machine, one which is called a Turing machine. Turing machines have played a central role in the development of automata theory, and a brief consideration of how they work will give us some important insights. We can then return to our consideration of what computers are, armed with all we need to turn the notion depicted in Figure 2-1 into a sturdy and much more satisfying definition of a computer.

Turing machines are named after the late Alan M. Turing, an English logician and mathematician. In 1937 (nine years before the first electronic computer was built) Turing wrote a paper, which has become a classic in automata studies, in which he describes how Turing machines work.[1] To picture what a Turing machine is like, imagine a machine supplied with a tape running through it much the way a ticker tape machine has. This tape is divided into squares and each square can have a symbol on it. There is no particular restriction on what these symbols can be. At any moment there is just one square being scanned (looked at) by the machine.

Now, a Turing machine is able to perform three operations only. It can read a symbol off a square, print a symbol on a square, and move one square to either the right or the left. During each cycle of operation a Turing machine will read a symbol, change it to some other symbol, and then move right or left. The operations of a given cycle might be represented as

1 0 R

which means "if you read the symbol '1' from the square you are scanning, change it to '0' and move one square to the right." If instead we write

1 1 R

that would mean "if you read the symbol '1' from the square you are scanning, change it to a '1' (that is, replace it by itself which, of course, amounts to the same thing as leaving it alone) and then move one square to the right."

If we had a string of 1s printed on a tape and wished to change all the 1s to 0s, then all we would need to do is build a Turing machine which followed the rule 1 0 R. For every "1" the machine read it would print a "0" in its place and move on to the next square, repeating the process.

But, if we wanted to change every *other* "1" in this string to "0" leaving the rest unchanged, then an interesting problem would arise. First, of course, we would need a different Turing machine which followed both rules 1 1 R and 1 0 R since sometimes 1s are to be changed to 0s and other times they are to be left unchanged. But, in addition, the

[1]Alan M. Turing, "On Computable Numbers, with an Application to the *Entscheidungsproblem*," *Proceedings of the London Mathematics Society*, 42, 1937, pp. 230–265.

machine would have to be told when to change the "1" and when to leave it alone. That is, we would have to tell it which of the two rules to follow at any given time.

One way to solve this problem is to give names to our rules—call them "rule A" and "rule B"—and to tell the machine the name of the rule it is to follow first. We then add to this the stipulation that each rule will contain at the end the name of the rule the machine is to follow next. Thus,

A 1 1 R B

would mean "A is that condition in which whenever you read a '1' you change it to a '1', move one square to the right, and then go on to rule B." Similarly, rule B might be expressed B 1 0 R A. Table 2.1 shows what it would look like to put these two conditions together.[2]

Condition	Scanned symbol	Change in scanned symbol	Direction of move	New condition
A	1	1	R	B
B	1	0	R	A

Table 2-1 A simplified set of rules for a Turing machine.

Consider now our string of 1s and what a Turing machine which behaved as Table 2.1 stipulates would do to this tape. Assume the starting condition is condition A with the machine scanning the left most square thus,

1	1	1	1	1	1	1	1	1	1

A

It would replace the "1" with a "1", move right one square, and go into condition B ready to read the next symbol.

1	1	1	1	1	1	1	1	1	1

B

But, in condition B the machine will change the "1" to "0", move right one square and go into condition A. The condition at the start of the third cycle, then, would be

[2] The number of Turing machines that can be built is infinite, each one performing some different task. For each such Turing machine there is a separate table of rules such as Table 2.1.

1	0	1	1	1	1	1	1	1	1
		A							

after which

1	0	1	1	1	1	1	1	1	1
			B						

and then

1	0	1	0	1	1	1	1	1	1
				A					

and so on until the machine was stopped.

What we have been referring to thus far as a rule or a condition is usually termed an *internal state.* At any moment a Turing machine may be in one and only one of a number of possible internal states, each one consisting of a particular configuration of read, print, and move operations. A given internal state of a Turing machine can be described by the quintupel: state, scanned symbol, change in symbol, move, new state. As we have seen, what a Turing machine will do depends not only upon the symbol it scans, but as well upon the state it is in at the time.

Now, changing 1s to 0s in a string is not very interesting, and while it serves as a good example of how Turing machines work, we do not get from this example any sense of the power and the significance of such a machine. After all, a Turing machine's repertory seems limited indeed and hardly noteworthy. As modern men who fly planes, watch television, talk on the telephone, and put together our children's toys, we have come in contact with too much technology to be impressed by such a simple gadget as a Turing machine. If we take a problem a little more complicated than the previous one, however, the elegance and the significance of Turing machines will become a bit more obvious. Obvious enough, in fact, so that we can then return to our attempt to define computers, relieved of the burdens placed upon us by the usual definition.

Consider the following string:

X	0	9	0	5	7	2	8	7	3	6	0	5	1	9	5	4	0	X

Suppose the problem here is to change every instance of | 5 | 7 | 2 | to | 5 | 2 | 7 |. Table 2.2 presents a possible procedure for accomplishing this task. The machine starts out in state Z with the reading head positioned at the first square. (The Xs mark the beginning and end of the string.) It moves one space to the right and goes into state A which says: if you read a "5" then print a "5," move one space to the right, and go into state B; if you read an "X," then stop (the end of the tape has been

State	Scanned symbol	Change in scanned symbol	Direction of move	New state
Z	α	α	R	A
A	5	5	R	B
A	X	—	HALT	
A	α	α	R	A
B	X	—	HALT	
B	7	7	R	C
B	α	α	R	A
C	2	7	L	D
C	X	—	HALT	
C	α	α	R	A
D	7	2	R	A

Table 2-2 A simplified table of rules for a Turing machine.

reached); if you read any other symbol—that is what the α stands for—then print that symbol, move one space to the right, and go into state A (which, of course, is the state the machine is in already). Now, when a "5" is read in state A the machine goes into state B to check for a "7" on the following square. If the "7" is found, the machine goes into state C to check for a "2," which when found is changed to a "7." Then, by moving left and replacing the "7" with a "2" the change is completed and the machine continues its scan.

This example as it stands is as trivial as the previous one, but it suggests how the atomic acts of reading, printing, and moving, when coupled with the notion of state, provide the basis for a fairly powerful way to execute procedures. We become more impressed with this power when we replace the numerals in the string, and correspondingly in the table, with letters of the alphabet. Suppose, for example, we replace the 5s by the letter "C," 2s by the letter "E," 7s by the letter "I," 0s by blanks, and so forth. The original string might become:

X		A		C	I	E	L	I	N	G		C	R	A	C	K		X

Notice that the word, "cieling" is misspelled. But notice further that the procedure described in Table 2.2 would correct that misspelling. When we change the numerals to letters of the alphabet in the string and in the table, we see that the Turing machine we have defined would be executing the familiar rule, "I before E except after C."

The Universal Machine

A Turing machine is not a simple gadget after all. The atomic acts which make up its capability are deceptively limited. They are not so much simple acts as they are basic, fundamental acts and thus when properly strung together, these acts can make up the steps of very complicated procedures. But this ability goes well beyond anything we have found here. Indeed, Alan Turing has shown—and others since his early death have further clarified—that *for any precisely defined computation procedure whatever,* a Turing machine can be constructed to execute that procedure.

This remarkable fact about Turing machines becomes especially important to our effort to understand what computers are when we recognize that the word "computation" is not used here to mean that a procedure must be numerical to be executable by a Turing machine. The word is used to distinguish between *information processing* tasks of all varieties and such procedures as playing the saxophone, painting a doghouse, attacking an island in the South Pacific, and running for Congress. If you can define precisely a way of doing something that involves processing information, then it is possible to build a Turing machine that is able to carry out that procedure.

In spite of this amazing fact there is nothing special about the physical characteristics of Turing machines. If anything, they are technologically primitive devices and their unusual power does not come from any special gears or complicated circuits or cleverly designed relays. Their components, in fact, are irrelevant. Only their behavior is important, and as we have seen, Turing machines exhibit rudimentary behavior. What, for our purposes, is most significant about a Turing machine is not what it is, but instead the relationship it has to the procedure it executes.

A Turing machine is the embodiment of the procedure it executes. Knowing what a particular Turing machine does—how it works—we know what procedure it is executing. But this, essentially, is true of all machines, we just are not in the habit of speaking about machines in this way. The thing that counts about a machine is the way it behaves, and this behavior is prescribed by the procedure it executes. Thus once we state a procedure explicitly, we are not really surprised that a machine can be found to execute it. All automation, far from being magical, is nothing more than the physical expression of well-formed procedures.

This is true because when we say that a machine is the embodiment of the procedure it executes, we are saying, in effect, that a statement of a procedure describes the machine needed to carry out that procedure. We see this with the examples used earlier to show how Turing machines work. But any computational task that can be described at all, can be described in terms of atomic acts and, as we have seen, a table that describes a procedure in atomic acts is sufficient to depict the essential features of the required machine. Thus, if we wanted to build a Turing machine to carry out the procedure described in Table 2.2, we would not need to give an engineer anything more than the table itself because the table depicts unambiguously the desired machine's behavior.

Now suppose we had, say, ten procedures we wanted executed. We would then have ten such tables, each one describing a particular Turing machine that differs from the others in the symbols it is able to deal with and the states it is able to be in. Were we to give these ten tables to an engineer, his first impulse would be to build the ten machines we needed. After a while, however, perhaps as he grew weary of constructing these machines, he might propose instead to build a single machine which would begin by reading a description-table of the specific Turing machine needed and which would then imitate that machine. That is, a single Turing machine that could behave like any other Turing machine. This, of course, is a natural extension of the notion of Turing machines. Because a table stating a procedure in terms of atomic acts is sufficient to describe the desired machine's behavior, a machine that could read such a table would have available to it all the information required to behave like the machine depicted in that table.

This new, general purpose device would still be a Turing machine, but it would no longer be dedicated to a single procedure. It would be what automata theorists call a Universal Turing machine. With this idea of a Universal Turing machine we can return to our effort to define a computer and to understand how it is different from adding machines, desk calculators, giant brains, and all the other things people have called it.

A computer is a Universal Turing machine.

Therefore Figure 2-1, which describes any automaton, and thus a computer, as a device into which something is put and out of which something comes, is not a trivial description once you add the fact that *part of the input to a computer is a description of the machine it is to imitate.* This description is called a *computer program* and is usually thought of as a set of instructions for what the machine is to do. But a computer program is more like a blueprint which the computer uses to build itself into the particular machine needed to execute the particular procedure described by the program. It is as though the computer were armed with pliers and screwdriver, rebuilding itself to conform step-by-step to the elements of our procedure. Having done this, the computer becomes the machine our program described, and it will then function as that machine, reading in data and printing out results.

A computer without a program will do nothing, whether or not it is plugged in, because computers are not like other machines. In a sense the computer is not a machine at all in its own right, and yet, it can become many machines, in fact, any one which is fully described to it. For example, one may build an address printing machine, or he may write a program which will turn a computer into an address printing machine. In either case the results will be the same with the exception that even though both machines will be operationally equivalent, they will differ from each other in one crucial respect: tomorrow the computer will become a different machine.

Whereas the power of most machines is in what they do, the power of the computer rests in what it can become. Computers are not like ordinary machines in that computers do not *do* things, and thus the irony of the claim "we all know what computers do." The essential idea of a computer is that it is an incomplete machine ready to be completed in an infinite number of ways, each way producing a different machine.

Computing Procedures

We get a computer to become different machines by building different procedures, much the way we did with Turing machines. Not just any procedure will do, of course, nor are the tasks that can be accomplished unrestricted. The tasks must be *computable,* and the procedures must be *computational procedures.* To explore the meaning of these two terms and to indicate their significance for our understanding of computers, we begin at the most general level with problems and solutions.

We all know what it means to have a problem and to seek a solution. In some cases—religious matters, for example—going from a problem to a solution may be a matter of expressing conviction, while other problems call for the exercise of preference. What I will have for supper tonight is of this second type. Sometimes the solution is a physical act which is either reflexive, as in jumping out of the way of an automobile, or deliberate, as in running out of a burning house. Once in a while, of course, we are faced with some problem for which there is no solution; but among all the problems we are familiar with, the most common ones are those involving the processing of information.

These information processing tasks make up a considerable part of the lives of modern men. Commuters do crossword puzzles on their way to work, businessmen figure profit and loss, electronic technicians compute the internal resistances of batteries, school administrators assign students to classes, and even though such information processing tasks are complicated, it is almost always possible to state the rules that take you from problem to solution. Because this kind of task deals with information, and because there is for each a set of rules for solving it, we say these tasks are *computable.* Computable tasks are the ones we refer to when we speak about computation.

A computation is any manipulation, according to a finite set of rules, of one string of symbols to obtain some other string of symbols. Problems in arithmetic, trigonometry, and algebra are obvious examples of this, but there are others. For instance, the trumpet player who transposes the song "Spring Is Here" from the key of A flat to the key of B flat is following a computational procedure. Similarly, on December 6, 1941, the Army Intelligence specialists under Brigadier General Sherman Miles followed a computational procedure when they decrypted the top-secret message sent by Tokyo to its Washington embassy. Whatever the application, computation is involved if the task requires the processing of information and if there is a set of rules which specifies how we go from the input string of symbols to the output string of symbols.

But not all rules define a computation. Some rules are too vague or too general and others leave things up to someone's judgment. For a set of rules to constitute a computational procedure it must "tell us, from moment to moment, precisely how to behave."[3]

A little later on we will have to reexamine and qualify this assertion about rules in light of some misgivings Marvin Minsky has expressed, but even this reexamination will not change the basic fact that a computational procedure must leave nothing to judgment or chance. This, obviously, is the reason we can speak about computing machines without immediately contradicting ourselves by attributing the human capabilities of choosing or deciding or creating or judging to such machines.

Iteration

Now just because the rules that go to make up a computational procedure must be exact and precisely stated, it does not follow that such rules always lead to exact results. The procedures we are most familiar with are the ones that produce exact results, but there are many clearly-stated, well-formulated, computational procedures that give approximations for results. Consider, for example, the problem of taking the square root of a number. In high school we learned a fairly complicated method for taking the square root. Usually, if we followed all the steps and managed not to make some calculation error, the results this method produced were exact—we could multiply our result by itself and get exactly the number we started with. A well-known alternate procedure for taking the square root of a number is one which sometimes produces an exact result but most often yields a close approximation to it. It involves guessing the right answer and then using that guess in an equation. Once we solve this equation we start the procedure over again, but this time using the value of the equation as our guess. We repeat this process over and over until we get a result which for all practical purposes is the same as the one we got the time before. This kind of procedure is usually called *iteration,* and

[3]Marvin Minsky, *Computation: Finite and Infinite Machines,* Prentice-Hall, Englewood Cliffs, N.J., 1967, p. 106.

while iteration is a cumbersome and tedious way to do computation by hand, it is often the best way to do things on a computer.

Here is an example.[4] The equation used in the square root iteration method is

$$z = \frac{1}{2}\left(y + \frac{x}{y}\right)$$

where x is the number whose square root we wish to calculate and where the y's are successive approximations to that square root. If we were to write down the steps of this computational procedure so that someone else could follow it without needing to understand the method or why it works, or even how it works, then it might look something like this:

1. Read the number whose square root is desired and call it x.

2. Divide x by 2 and call the result y. (This is one way to estimate the solution.)

3. Calculate $\frac{1}{2}\left(y + \frac{x}{y}\right)$

4. Subtract z from y and call the result w. (This compares the present estimate with the one before to see how close they are.)

5. If w is equal to or less than .001, go to step 8, otherwise go to step 6.

6. Replace the present value of y with the present value of z.

7. Go to step 3.

8. Print present value of z.

9. Stop.

Suppose we wish to find the square root of 16 using this method. We would guess the answer to be around 8, and the first time we use the equation it will look like this:

$$z = \frac{1}{2}\left(8 + \frac{16}{8}\right) = 5$$

[4]The notation used here follows that of Bert F. Green, Jr., in *Digital Computers in Research*, McGraw-Hill, New York, 1963, p. 149.

Now 5 becomes our estimate of the answer, and we get

$$z = \frac{1}{2}\left(5 + \frac{16}{5}\right) = 4.1$$

and then

$$z = \frac{1}{2}\left(4.1 + \frac{16}{4.1}\right) = 4.0012$$

and so on. Sooner or later the answer we get for z will be so close to the one we got the time before, that there will be little accuracy gained by repeating the process any more. For instance, if we go one step further in our example, z becomes 4.00000017 which is a difference of about .001 from our previous answer. This is probably close enough, and in our example, the result would be printed and the procedure stopped.

This square root technique is one of the simplest examples of an approximation procedure,[5] but it serves, nonetheless, to demonstrate that even though a computational procedure must be detailed and exactly stated, the result it provides need not always be exact.

But there is more to this issue of what we will end up with if we follow the rules of some computational procedure. Whether the procedure is direct or iterative, we will sometimes obtain an exact result, other times an approximation. There is a third alternative, however: sometimes we will get no answer at all. One reason we might get no answer, of course, is that the computational procedure is not complete enough to handle all the possibilities. In our example, if we wish the square root of a negative number the procedure will not work. By adding a few rules we could get the procedure to work for negative numbers, but as it stands now the process would go on indefinitely, never coming close enough to stop. A second reason why no solution may result from the execution of a computational procedure is that there is no solution to the problem. A procedure that may be used to find the value of x in equations of the form $ax = b$ (for example $2x = 6$) will not work for the condition $0x = 6$, and there is nothing we can do to the procedure to obtain a solution.[6] The best we can do is realize there is no solution and stop executing the procedure.

Two Alternatives

Now what we have been calling a computational procedure goes by two different names, depending upon how it handles the situation where it is unable to provide a solution.

If there exists a solution to some problem, and if a given procedure

[5]For a good introduction to some other approximation procedures see Green, op. cit., Chapt. 8.

[6]This example is taken from Robert R. Korfhage, *Logic and Algorithms: with Applications to the Computer and Information Sciences*, Wiley, New York, 1966, p. 88. Chapter 5 of this book gives an excellent and readable account of the issues involved in defining a computational procedure.

allows us to arrive at this solution sooner or later—this means after the performance of a finite number of steps—then that procedure is called a *semi-algorithm.*[7] An important fact about semi-algorithms is that they do not know when they are unable to arrive at the solution. When no solution exists, a semi-algorithm will either stop for the wrong reasons or more likely, search endlessly for a nonexistent solution.

The second kind of procedure is called an *algorithm*, and it differs from a semi-algorithm only in that an algorithm provides a way to determine whether or not there is a solution and to stop when none exists. Consider, for example, the procedure we mentioned before which when given the values of a and b will solve equations of the form $ax = b$. Such a procedure would be an algorithm if it first checked the value of a, stopping when a equaled zero. Without such a step, of course, this method would be semi-algorithmic.

Naturally algorithms are usually thought to be more useful than semi-algorithms, but they both have the quality of guaranteeing a solution when one exists. This guarantee stems from the fact that such procedures are essentially "brute force" procedures, following each step religiously, doggedly to the end. Because computers are fast, algorithms are important kinds of procedures to computer programmers. It does not matter how much tedium and drudgery are involved because computers do not get bored or distracted, and although the computer may execute the same steps over and over again, or make lengthy searches, or even stop and start over again, still it usually will produce the answer in a reasonable amount of time. Whether the algorithm is designed to compute a correlation coefficient, parse a sentence, sort a long list of high school students by year of graduation, locate a vacant seat on the next flight to San Francisco, or figure the balance in a savings account, computers are fast enough, in general, to go through all the required steps and complete the procedure in much less time than we are used to.

A Third Alternative

Brute force or not, therefore, the algorithm, combined with the computer's speed, has not only changed the way we tend to describe our solutions to problems, but together they have allowed us to tackle problems we knew in the past to be too complicated or too mammoth to be worth the trouble. It is a surprise, even a disappointment, to many people, therefore, to discover that for some problems even though we can state completely the algorithms for solving them—and thus describe the computer program needed to produce the solutions—it makes no sense at all to have a computer execute such algorithms. For some problems it does not make sense to fashion an algorithmic solution and program a

[7]After Korfhage, op. cit., p. 89.

computer to perform the steps of that algorithm because no matter what computer you use no one will ever live long enough to find out what the answer is.

Playing chess is this kind of problem. At any given point in a game of chess there is likely to be so many moves possible—each one followed by so many moves of the opponent—that the task of figuring for each possible move all responses, and for each of these responses all counter-moves, and for these each counterresponse, and so on to the end of play would take more time than any of us has available. There are just too many possibilities. Claude Shannon, the man who first suggested some techniques for getting a machine to play chess, has calculated that there are something like 10^{120} possibilities for moves in a game of chess. To see what this means, let us pretend that Shannon is wrong in his estimate and that there are far fewer than 10^{120} possible sequences. Suppose there are only 10^{20} possibilities. Now, there are 31,536,000 seconds in a year, and if we assume that a computer could explore one million possibilities every second then in one year the computer would explore 31,536,000,000,000 possibilities. We all know this is a very large and impressive number of operations to perform even in a year. Yet at this rate it would take the computer more than one million years to be finished with our 10^{20} possible sequences.

But we know children win and lose at chess every day, and masters play several games at once, rarely losing, and always finishing in time to play other matches in other towns. Obviously, then, human beings do not solve chess problems algorithmically: they do not figure in their minds all the consequences of all the possible sequences of play, choosing those moves that guarantee victory. Instead they somehow select a few likely alternatives, exploring their consequences several moves ahead, and on the basis of this exploration, they select the "best" move. Thus the search and decision procedure is considerably shortened.

Clearly this approach is not confined to chess-playing. Proving theorems in geometry, formulating logical propositions, bidding and playing out a hand in bridge, even composing a song are just a few other activities in which such a process is useful—indeed mandatory. This process, this alternate to the algorithmic approach to problem solving is called *heuristics*, and even though such a process is not as definite as an algorithm and does not offer the same guarantee, a heuristic procedure is not without form.

A heuristic is a rule of thumb. We are all familiar with rules of thumb, and we know that while they are not exact, and do not always work, still they can be extremely useful guides in solving problems. Some rules of thumb are useful in defining goals. In chess, for instance, one such heuristic is that it is desirable to control the center board and, thus, at some appropriate point in a game this rule might help a player determine those moves that are likely alternatives, removing from consideration moves that are not involved in center board control. Other heuristics would then become useful as he evaluated each likely alternative. One such rule is that it is bad practice to place your queen in jeopardy—a rule, incidentally, which is often violated in the more elegant and exciting games of chess. Suppose, now, that a player had two possible moves either one of which would be consistent with the goal of center board control. If one of these would expose the queen to danger while the second would not, then because of one of our heuristics the second move would be preferred.

Things get more complicated, of course, as other heuristics are added and it becomes necessary to consider priorities among them, and certainly the business of getting a computer to execute heuristic procedures is much more involved than suggested here. The point to remember, however, is that while the sequences of a heuristic procedure may be probablistic rather than certain, and while there is no guarantee, as there is with algorithms, that an optimal solution will be obtained, it is true nonetheless that the steps of a heuristic procedure can be so specified and exactly stated that no understanding is needed to follow these steps. Thus a heuristic procedure when properly formulated is another type of computation.

The Relationship Between Machines and Their Procedures

The two previous sections of this chapter, while dealing primarily with computing machines in the first instance and with computing procedures in the second instance, both deal as well with the issue of how machines and the procedures they execute relate to each other. In the first section, for instance, we reached the point where we were able to assert that automation is nothing more than the physical expression of well-formed procedure. We could say this because we saw from our look at Turing machines that a statement of procedure describes the machine needed to carry out that procedure. Turning to computers we saw that the computer program serves at once as an explicit statement of a procedure and as a blueprint of the machine needed to carry it out.

In the second section, this topic of the relationship between machine and procedure is more implicit. Yet algorithms and heuristics so clearly possess the attribute of describing the requisite machine behavior that there can be no doubt that computational procedures carry all the logical burden of mechanizing an information processing task. Because our later consideration of the role of computers in education depends so heavily upon the relationship between machines and the procedures they execute, we will next deal explicitly with this relationship.

Flow Chart

So far in our general consideration of computational procedures and how they may be described, we have stuck mostly to English as the language with which to state the rules involved. One look at the Internal Revenue Service Form 1040, however, will suggest that English is not always the clearest and most explicit medium when it comes to expressing the steps of a computational procedure. Consider this brief excerpt from page 1 of the form:

> If you do not itemize deductions, and line 9 is less than $5,000.00, find your tax from the tables in instructions. Do not use lines 11a, b, c, or d. Enter tax on line 12. If you itemize deductions, and line 9 is $5,000.00 or more, enter on line 11a the larger of either ten percent of line 9 or $200.00 ($100.00 if you are married and are filing a separate return), plus $100.00 for each exemption claimed on line 4 above. Deductions here are limited to $1,000.00 ($500 if married and filing separately). Subtract line 11a from line 9. Multiply total number of exemptions on line 4, above, by $600.00. Subtract line 11c from . . .

We need go no further to get the point.

One way to deal with a difficult passage like this one is to take it apart sentence by sentence, getting straight at each point the steps we are to follow in this computational procedure. But still we have to read the whole passage being clear about everything even though only a portion of the instructions applies in any given case. An alternate and commonly preferred way to describe such a procedure entails drawing a picture of it. This picture is called a *flow chart* and has the advantage not only of clearing things up a little, but also of allowing us to follow just those aspects of the procedure that pertain to our particular situation. Figure 2-2 is a flow chart for our income tax example.

Notice some of the figures in the flow chart are rectangles, some are diamond-shaped, and the start and stop points are circles. This is a convention, and there is no special significance to it except that using different shapes helps a little to visualize the procedure: the diamonds stand for those steps of the procedure that call for a decision, the rectangles are used for all the other steps.

Now the first thing we see from the flow chart is that there are really six different paths through the procedure. The path one follows depends upon certain facts about his situation, such as whether or not he itemizes deductions. Notice that all the decision points—the diamonds—are expressed as questions whose answers are either "yes" or "no" and our answers determine our direction through the procedure. The trouble with the English language version of the procedure is that it does not indicate clearly that there are six paths and so we have to read and pay attention to the whole paragraph. We have to read everything and keep it all in mind until the end. Then we have to sort it out, following only those steps that pertain to us, discarding the rest. With the flow chart we pick our path as

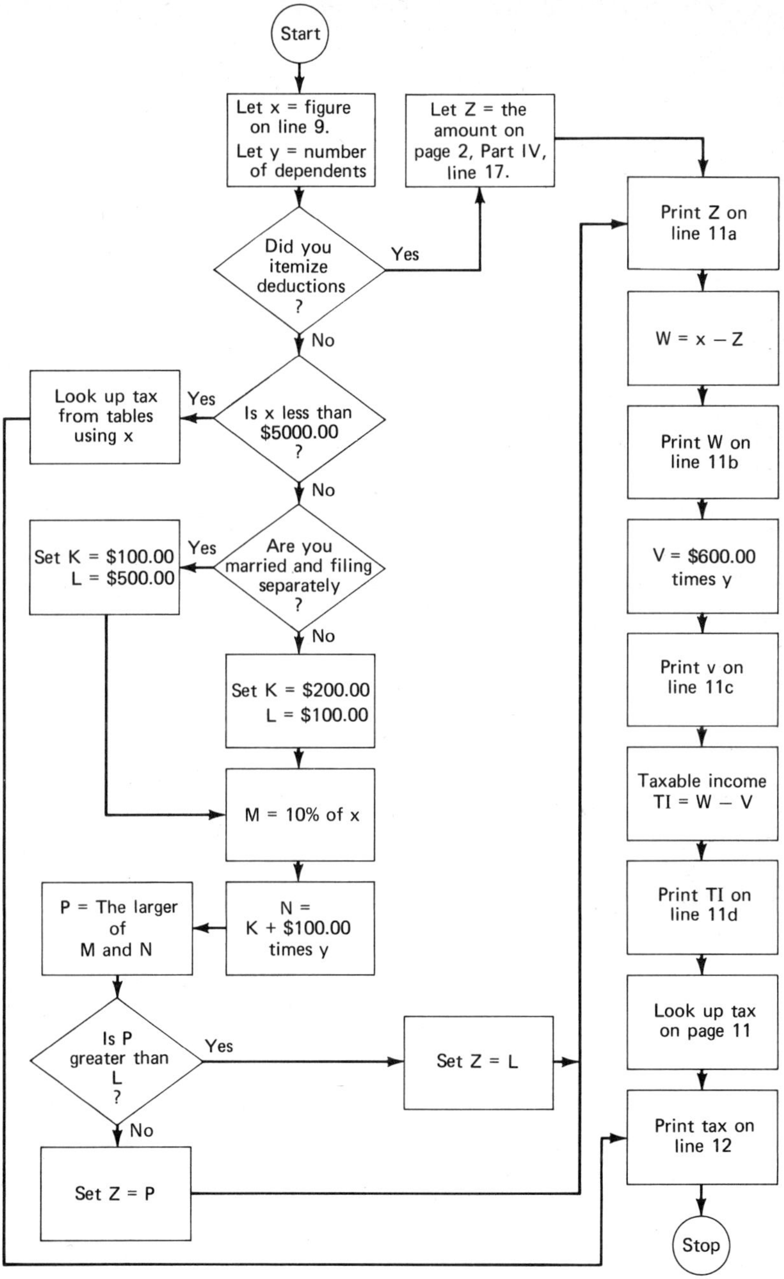

Figure 2-2 A Flow chart of the income tax problem.

we go, never needing to pay attention to the others. We may look at some other paths out of curiosity, of course, but even then we take them one at a time.

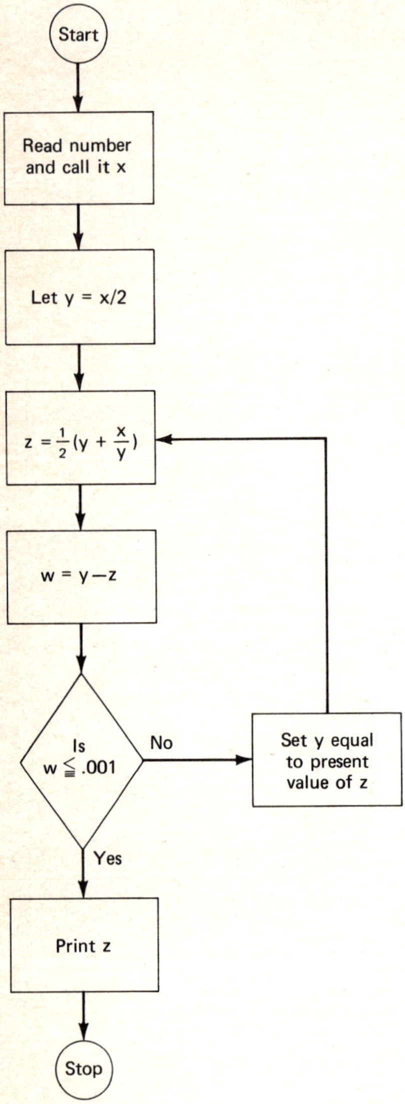

Figure 2-3 Flow chart of the square root procedure.

Certainly, even if we stuck to English as a means of expressing this procedure, we could do a better job than the Internal Revenue Service. We could, for example, adopt the technique we used earlier in the square root example, listing the procedure step by step and skirting steps when they do not apply. But as explicit as our statement of the square root procedure is, probably most people would find a flow chart of it (such as in Figure 2-3) clearer and easier to follow.

Think of what this means. We are saying that even though a statement of a procedure may be explicit, it can still be unclear. This is true because whether or not a statement is explicit depends upon the statement itself, but whether or not it is clear depends upon the person reading it. In our income tax example, everything we need to know is contained in the paragraph; nothing is left out and nothing is to be inferred or deduced. Yet for some of us the paragraph remains unclear. This is a new ingredient which we must add to our idea of computational procedures.

Minsky's Point

We have been saying up to now that a set of rules is a computational procedure when it is explicit, detailed, and exhaustive, and we have suggested that the guarantees such procedures offer depend upon how carefully the rules are stated. But as Marvin Minsky has pointed out, even if the rules tell us from minute to minute how to behave, the matter is not really settled. The argument that an explicit set of rules is a computational procedure breaks down, he asserts, because "*interpretation* of the rules is left to depend on some person or agent."[8] Now that we think about it, it is obvious that Minsky's objection is a good one. Clearly, a person's ability to follow a rule does not depend on the rule alone. Equally important are his intelligence, his background, his experience, in short his ability to interpret the rule. Thus, a procedure can guarantee a solution only if we know something about the person who is to follow that procedure.

A set of rules will be a computational procedure, then, if it is accompanied by a description of the mechanism—human or otherwise—that is to follow the rules. This will settle things. But it is an unfortunate way to resolve the issue because, obviously, it would be a great deal of trouble to have to do all this over again for each individual procedure. Another way out must be found.

The way out of this situation has been provided by Turing. When we expressed a procedure in terms of the atomic acts Turing machines are capable of executing, we were at the same time describing the particular Turing machine needed to carry out that procedure. Thus a Turing table—such as those we looked at earlier in this chapter—does double duty, thereby meeting Minsky's requirement.

The key to this solution is the notion that a procedure be expressed *in terms of* the basic acts of which a set of machines is capable. What Turing has done is to create a language with which to systematically and unambiguously describe the behavior of a class of machines. Thus it should surprise no one that a procedure stated in this language will contain, by implication, the details of the mechanism that is to interpret this statement. Turing then gets around the problem of needing a separate

[8]Minsky, op. cit., p. 106.

machine for each procedure by inventing the idea of a single, universal interpretation machine. This new mechanism is universal not because it can do anything any other machine can do but because it can understand descriptions of other machines and then, by way of imitation, can become these other machines. The theoretical Universal Turing machine—and the general-purpose computer, its real-life counterpart—is able to do this because it treats a computational procedure first as a blueprint and then, once it becomes the machine depicted by the procedure, as a set of rules to be followed.

Because all possible information processing machines are represented in this way by a single universal machine, the net effect is to have established a relationship between procedure and machine such that the procedure implies the machine and such that the machine's behavior renders the procedure deducible.*

*At this point, those readers uninitiated in computers may find it useful to read the Appendix before going on to Part II.

II: some implications for education

Prithee, look back, prithee, look back,
There's blood on the track.
The shoe is too small;
At home the true bride is waiting thy call.

Cinderella

This whole thing suffers from hymenoptera in the nard.

Julian Longstreet

CHAPTER THREE: thinking procedure

At the base of a well-built understanding of what a computer is there must lie the realization that a computer is not an ordinary machine. In a sense a computer is not completely a machine at all, but rather a device that can *become* a machine. A computer is an incomplete machine that can be made into any machine we can describe to it. As we have seen, however, with the computers we do not literally and directly build machines the way engineers or machinists do. Instead, we build indirectly by constructing procedures. We begin with procedure. The machinery comes later. The machine is the consequence of procedure—not the determinant—and therefore procedure comes first logically and chronologically. Because a machine stems from the procedure it is to execute, unless we are concerned about hardware, the only reasonable way to speak about a machine's behavior is to speak about its procedure.

This is why our effort throughout the previous chapter to carefully define a computer depended so much upon the relationship between procedures and the machines that execute them. And we will rely even more heavily than we did before upon this relationship as we now turn in Part II to a consideration of some implications for education of what a computer is.

The first implication we may draw from what a computer is is so connected to all we have said in Chapter Two about the relationship between procedure and machine that it is now obvious: *automating means thinking procedure.* That is, if we wish to automate some process, we must view that process, and eventually come to characterize it, in procedural terms. This is the essential act of automating. But there should be nothing surprising about this implication since we have already seen that automation is nothing more than the physical expression of well-formed procedure. It follows, therefore, that we will be able to automate a process if and only if that process turns out to be procedural.

But that a process must be procedural is not the only requirement imposed on us as we attempt to automate it. A concurrent requirement—another obvious one—is that our *expression* of that process must take the form of a computational procedure. Therefore, of course, before we can come to automate a process we must know what the process is. We must know the components of the process in such a way and to such a level of detail that no ambiguities and no unanswered questions remain. Otherwise our expression of the process will be faulty.

Naturally these requirements—that for us to automate a process, it must be procedural and we must understand it fully—hold for everyone wishing to apply computers in his work. But in the profession of education where debates over whether teaching is an art or a science continue to rage and where even the best teacher does not know completely what it is that makes him a good teacher, these requirements are especially significant. Because we in education will start out not fully understanding many of the educational practices we wish to automate, the act of automating becomes for us an opportunity to come to grips systematically with our lack of knowledge about the components of our craft.

Of course it is reasonable that educators view the promise of the computer to be that of facilitating the conduct of education. But in the end, whether or not we come to automate some or all of educational practice is secondary. The more crucial aspect of the computer's promise for education rests in the opportunity—and the responsibility—it provides us to analyze and to better understand the very processes we automate. Thus we may now restate in terms of education the first implication we have drawn from our definition of a computer. For us the assertion that automation means thinking procedure becomes, *thinking about the computer's role in education does not mean thinking about computers; it means thinking about education.*

As we begin to use computers in education, therefore, our attention must focus directly and fully on the procedures of education. But while this implication is the first to follow from the way we have come to define the computer, heeding it is neither easy nor without considerable risks. What some of these risks are and to what extent, in general, these risks are being dealt with or ignored by the educational technologist are the principal concerns of this chapter.

Fitting The Present

An examination of the current uses of computers in schools would suggest very strongly that the educational technologist has understood and accepted the notion that automation in education means thinking about educational procedure. For example, such an examination would uncover many instances of computer use where in each case it would be clear that the educational technologist had hit upon this application by beginning with a question of the form "of all the current educational practices, which ones are sufficiently procedural to be candidates for computerization?" Of course this is a reasonable question to begin with, and we would see this question behind many applications of computers. For instance we would see it operating in the area of administrative data processing where computers are used to print teachers' salary checks, to make up school schedules, to produce grade reports, class lists, inventory reports, and honor rolls, to keep records of when pupils are absent, and to execute other well-established procedures. Other examples include the automated scoring and analysis of standardized achievement tests, the storage and display of facts on colleges and vocational schools, and the production of library catalogs and acquisition lists.

Drill and Practice

This approach of automating those educational practices that are ready-made for automation accounts in fact for most of the uses of computers in schools. We will look a little deeper into this approach, therefore, to identify some of the risks it entails and to see whether or not these risks are being avoided. Because those who speak of the computer's promise for education speak most fervently about its promise for instruction, we will look there for our subject. Specifically, we will explore the use of computers to provide students with drill and practice in the basic skills.

Computer-based drill and practice systems belong to the broader category of automated instruction most often referred to as computer-assisted instruction or just CAI. Most generally, CAI consists in using the computer in place of the teacher to present units of instruction. That the educational technologist has considerable interest and faith in this application is evidenced by the abundant literature on the various aspects of CAI, offering definitions, details of projects, experiments, field tests, and predictions regarding the role of the computer in instruction.[1]

The first aspect of CAI to be substantially developed and tested is that which involves the use of the computer for drill and practice in basic

[1]See especially, Richard Atkinson and H. A. Wilson, (eds.), *Computer-assisted Instruction: A Book of Readings*, Academic Press, New York, 1969; W. H. Holtzman, (ed.), *Computer assisted Instruction, Testing, and Guidance*, Harper & Row, New York, 1970; Martin Greenberger, (ed.), *Computers, Communications, and the Public Interest*, Johns Hopkins, Baltimore, 1971; Don D. Bushnell, Dwight W. Allen, and Sara S. Mitter, *The Computer in American Education*, Wiley, New York, 1967; John E. Coulson, (ed.), *Programmed Learning and Computer-based Instruction*, Wiley, New York, 1962; Ralph Gerard, (ed.), *Computers and Education*, McGraw-Hill, New York, 1967; Wallace Feurzeig, *Educational Potential of Computer Technology*, Final Report, No. 1672, Bolt, Beranek, & Newman, Cambridge, Mass., 1968; and Anthony Oettinger, with Sema Marks, *Run, Computer, Run: The Mythology of Educational Innovation*, Harvard, Cambridge, Mass., 1969; Erik McWilliams, "Large Scale CAI-The NSF Project," *Proceedings of the ACM Annual Conference*, August 1972.

skills. In drill and practice systems, the student sits at a typewriterlike communications terminal (see Appendix) connected to a computer and, under the computer's direction, he practices some procedures or memorizes some facts. Arithmetic practice, spelling drill, and foreign language vocabulary memorization are the common examples of subject areas for which drill and practice systems have been developed. Because the automation of drill and practice in these areas is, conceptually, so straightforward, this aspect of CAI has been most "perfected" in the sense that where it is used in schools it is not considered experimental.

The computer-based drill and practice system in elementary school arithmetic developed at Stanford University under the direction of Patrick Suppes and Richard Atkinson, for example, has been used for some time in diverse school settings throughout the country and in each case with acclaim. Suppes estimates that as long ago as 1966, a little more than 1,500 students in such states as California, Kentucky, Iowa, Mississippi, Washington, D.C., and New York were using the Stanford drill and practice system on a regular basis.[2] By 1969, this figure increased fourfold, approximately 6,000 students having daily access to the system.

While the drill and practice system is the most extensive component of Stanford's efforts in CAI—in terms of money, time, and energy spent, curricular material developed, and students involved—its function is supplementary. According to Suppes, "the program was designed to drill and review students on concepts previously presented in the classroom by the teacher."[3] In this way, the system is at the disposal of the teacher, who determines "the temporal relationship between the material in the program and the mathematics curriculum in the classroom."[4]

Briefly, the 1967 drill and practice system is designed for grades one through six so that the drill material for each grade is arranged in sequential "concept blocks," there being approximately twenty-five such blocks per grade level. The twenty-seven first grade concept blocks, for example, include such things as "counting in sequence," "mixed addition and subtraction in columns," "sums to 4," and "differences to 10 with variables." Each block consists of a pretest, five days worth of drill, a posttest, review drills, and review posttests. In a typical seven day period, a student will go through each of these components, thus thoroughly drilling and reviewing a concept.

For each day of drill or review, there are five levels of difficulty, and a student will be placed at a particular level depending initially upon his pretest performance and subsequently upon his previous day's perform-

[2]Patrick Suppes, *Computer-assisted Instruction at Stanford,* Technical Report No. 174, Stanford University, Stanford, 1971, p. 9.
[3]Patrick Suppes and Mona Morningstar, "Four Programs in Computer-assisted Instruction," in Holtzman, (ed.), op. cit., pp. 233–234.
[4]Ibid., p. 234.

ance. Thus a student's passage through a given concept block will take into account his mastery of the material presented.

Some Advantages

As we can see from even this brief description, much thought and effort went into the development of the Stanford drill and practice system. Moreover because this thought and effort has resulted in an efficient and thorough version of the traditional drill and practice procedure, few schoolmen would deny its value. Indeed were it not for the expense—for computer, teletypewriters, software, and such—computer-based drill and practice systems would have found their way into substantially more schools throughout the country.

Behind the widespread acceptance of automated drill and practice systems is the argument proposed as early as 1962 by J. C. R. Licklider who wrote:

> Although the teaching procedures called "drill" have unpleasant connotations, there is little doubt that accumulation of facts and elementary behavioral capabilities are prerequisite to advances at conceptual and integrative levels. Drill has a fundamental, propaedeutic function. Moreover, the following facts should be considered:
>
> **1.** In present educational systems a large fraction of the total time and effort is devoted to drill.
>
> **2.** It is inefficient to have $n - 1$ children sit idly by while the nth reports that $3 \times 4 = 12$.
>
> **3.** Neither teachers nor pupils enjoy present kinds of drill enough to oppose its automation.
>
> **4.** Automation of drill can be accomplished with relatively small investment in instructional programming and computer programming.[5]

These arguments which concern the practical values of automated drill and practice have been joined by Gail Young's argument involving its psychological advantage.[6] Surely each of us remembers, with some dread, his experience as a student with this form of instruction—the embarrassment, the emotion, the fear of the public display required by classroom drill. It hardly seems "innovative" to perpetuate the concept of drill and practice by automating it. But, as Young argues, the emotional

[5]J. C. R. Licklider, "Preliminary Experiments in Computer-aided Teaching," in Coulson, (ed.), op. cit., p. 218.

[6]Gail S. Young, "Comments on Social, Psychological, and Mathematical Aspects of the Suppes-Morningstar Chapter," in Holtzman, (ed.), op. cit., pp. 266–276.

concomitants to classroom drill are not included in the automated version. Because using the computer via a terminal is "private," and because drills are easily tailored to the student's level, drilling and practicing are no longer social events filled with risk and prone to unwanted scrutiny.

Thus while automated drill and practice do not represent an especially imaginative, creative, or pioneering application of technology to education, nonetheless they can serve a useful purpose: they can begin to counteract one of the ways schools violate the children they teach. These considerations, coupled with the advent of small, inexpensive computers capable of doing as good a job with drill and practice as are the larger machines, suggest strongly that this form of CAI will find its way, increasingly, into the schools.

The Stanford automated drill and practice system is an example of what results from an approach to the use of computers in schools that begins with the question: "Of all the current educational practices, which are sufficiently procedural to be candidates for computerization?" As we have seen, it is a reasonable result of such an approach. Were we to look at the other applications of computers in schools that have resulted from this approach, we would see them to be similarly reasonable. The results are reasonable because the approach itself is reasonable.

A Risk

There is left for us to consider the risks that attend this approach. Again we will make the general points by looking, when necessary, at automated drill and practice systems in specific. Remember, however, the risks apply beyond the instances cited because the risks are inherent in the approach itself and not just a specific application to which the approach may give rise.

The principal risks attending an approach to the use of computers in education which rests on looking for that which is procedural about current educational practice, stem from the thin line that exists between automating a process that is procedural and automating a process *because* it is procedural. When we set out to find "candidates" for computerization, we create for ourselves the danger of crossing that line, thereby adopting a logic much like that of the politician who believes a candidate's ability to get elected determines his ability to hold office.

Perhaps the story of *Cinderella* will provide a fuller analogy. We may say, on one hand, the fact that the slipper fits is *proof* she is Cinderella. But we may say as well that the fitting of the slipper *makes* her Cinderella. That is, because the prince will marry the person whose foot fits the slipper—whoever she may be and whatever she may look like—it is unclear whether the fitting of the slipper is evidence or cause of identity. Similarly if we fall into the trap of behaving as though that process that fits the computer is therefore that process we should automate, then what starts out to be thinking procedure will become rationalizing procedure.

The rationalization of procedure takes several forms and each of these forms constitutes a risk we must guard against. The first of these risks is that of automating a procedure that is not worth doing at all, even by hand. We must avoid assuming, just because something is part of current educational practice, that it is a worthwhile and justifiable process. Thus when Licklider tells us that drill and practice are important because "there is little doubt that accumulation of facts and elementary behavioral capabilities are prerequisite to advances at conceptual and integrative levels," we have got to be careful. Probably he is correct in what he says, but we must not assume that he is. Whatever we expect our feelings in the matter to be, we should not be uncritical. Indeed, automation in education ought to be a mechanism for the critical assessment of the very educational practice we hope to automate.

"How strange it is," Seymour Papert has said, "that computers in education should so often reduce to using bright new gadgets to teach the same old stuff in thinly disguised versions of the same old way."[7] A good deal of Anthony Oettinger's critical look at CAI is concerned with this same point.[8] Similarly Eugene Fubini voices his concern over the uncritical automation of educational practice when he states, "I am opposed to using the new technologies mainly as direct substitutes for old methods."[9] Fubini continues by asserting that we characteristically do this in the first stage. We use a new discovery to do something we already do, but better. "The second stage," he adds, "is when we employ the discovery to do something *new in a new way.*"[10] Thus, however convincing Licklider may be or however systematized Suppes' and Atkinson's work may be, when we automate drill and practice essentially as is, we run the grave risk of "replicating the best of the worst of regular classroom teaching,"[11] thus legitimizing current practice while missing our chance to construct new practice.

Undoubtedly Suppes would agree with this notion, but he would go on to say that he and Atkinson have not succumbed to such dangers. He would rightly indicate that they have approached the "second stage" by substantially revising the form and structure of the Stanford drill and

[7]Seymour Papert and Cynthia Solomon, "Twenty Things to Do with a Computer," M.I.T., Artificial Intelligence Laboratory, Cambridge, Mass., June 1971, mimeo.
[8]Oettinger, op. cit.
[9]Eugene G. Fubini, "Education in Modern Society," in Greenberger, (ed.), op. cit., p. 131.
[10]Ibid., italics added.
[11]James Becker, "What Ever Happened To The Computer?," *Journal of Educational Data Processing*, vol. 8, no. 1, 1971, p. 4.

practice program in arithmetic. As he indicates in one of his reports on the project's work during the 1969-70 academic year:

> The revised program evolved when attention was diverted from a program that could duplicate and expedite classroom procedures for a given grade to a program that could provide the most efficient drill for a given individual from the start of Grade 1 through the end of Grade 6.[12]

The major aspect of the change from the old block system to the new "strand" system rests in the change of focus from classroom to individual child. Thus the underlying questions used to determine content and sequence have changed from "What grade is the child in?" and "What is usually taught at that grade level?" to "What concepts has the child mastered?" and "What should this child learn next?"[13]

This new strand approach developed by the Stanford group grows out of its five years of experience with automated drill and practice. Developed with considerable care, this new system represents substantial change in emphasis, ordering, and student evaluation. Most significant of all, however, it represents, albeit in a beginning way, a movement away from the traditional. Commenting on this point, Suppes states:

> The student, working on several strands simultaneously, begins at the bottom of a strand and moves upward on each strand as a function of his ability to perform correctly on that strand. Since movement along a strand depends on the student, the level of performance on one strand relative to the level of performance on other strands creates a problem set for one student different from the problem set for another student. Thus, unlike in the traditional classroom, each student is solving a different set of problems, and each set of problems contains problem types from each strand appropriate to the ability level of the student involved.[14]

Surely this approach is not revolutionary and perhaps it is not even the beginning movement in the right direction as it seems to be. Whatever it is, however, this approach recognizes and shows a concern for the first risk we run when we attempt to automate the procedures of education.

Another Risk

A second case where thinking procedure becomes rationalizing procedure—a second risk associated with an approach to automation that "looks for candidates"—is one which to see we must reconsider the argument in support of automated drill and practice offered by Gail Young.

Young's support for the automation of drill and practice stems from

[12]Suppes, op. cit., p. 26.
[13]Ibid.
[14]Ibid.

his justifiable concern over the way teachers typically conduct classroom drills.

> The teacher will say something like "work the odd-numbered problems on page 15." She will then walk around the room correcting errors, chiding slowpokes, making quick explanations of errors, and rewarding good work by approval and rebuking bad work by disapproval.[15]

Young disapproves of this and similar drill procedures on several grounds. As Licklider, Young is unhappy about the lack of individualization, seeing classroom drill as inefficient and mostly a waste of the students' time. As well he sees it as a poor use of the teacher's time and talent. In this regard he asserts that the ordinary teacher is not very well prepared to teach mathematics in the first place and that "by separating the teaching of mathematics from the drill and review, one could economically schedule the work of a specialist in the elementary school,"[16] thus compensating for one of the teacher's weaknesses.

By far the strongest element of Young's disapproval, however, concerns the fact that, in classroom drill, the rewards and punishments dispensed by the teacher are social and emotional rewards and punishments dispensed in public. Young, who recognizes that "the survival of our present society requires an emotionally healthy population" and who sees the school as an essential ingredient in the development of emotional health, argues that the automation of drill and practice will lessen the number of occasions on which the student will be emotionally violated by his teacher. Because the computer does not punish it does no violation and to Young, therefore, automated drill and practice has "definite psychological advantages to some children."[17]

While Young is correct in the things he says about the values of the computer in this aspect of instruction, his arguments are potentially dangerous. The danger is that we will use computers to *compensate* for educational problems, thereby never coming to correct these problems. It may be reasonable to see the computer as a way to compensate for a teacher's lack of knowledge about the subjects he teaches, or to compensate for a teacher's inability to individualize instruction, or to compensate for a teacher's insensitivity to the ways he abuses his students. But notice the irony here: our willingness to compensate for such traits in our teachers amounts to our acceptance of the idea that our teachers may possess such traits. As reasonable as it may be to compensate, perhaps it is equally reasonable to wonder why these compensations are needed. How is it, for example, that we have people teaching in our schools who have such capacity to violate, however unwittingly, the students they are

[15]Young, op. cit., p. 269.
[16]Ibid.
[17]Ibid., p. 270.

supposed to teach? And, furthermore, why do we assume that removing one occasion for such violation will make the classroom an emotionally safer place to be? Surely a teacher capable of abusing his students during drill and practice is equally capable of abusing them elsewhere, in the other educational activities he directs.

So we see how the very reasons we uncover for drill and practice being a good candidate for computerization, carry with them the danger that we will feed the basic educational illness we presume to treat. By not using the act of automation as our opportunity to thoroughly examine the process we wish to automate, we run the risk of automating the surface of things, missing the truer problem. Automation is only partly a mechanism for the solution of problems; as well, it is a mechanism for their proper formulation. As we search among current educational procedures for candidates for computerization, therefore, we should not forget that our first concern is with the educational problems these procedures exist to solve.

Refitting the Present

As useful and conceptually straightforward as the automation of drill and practice is, it has served as a source for some examples of the risks which attend an approach to automation which seeks out educational practices sufficiently procedural to be computerization candidates. We have seen, of course, that this approach is a legitimate component of the first implication we have drawn from our definition of a computer, namely that automation means thinking procedure. But we have seen as well that this brand of thinking procedure is risky, especially when we are not thorough enough in either our understanding or our use of the computer. As we turn now to look at a second approach to the use of computers in education which is potentially a legitimate component of thinking procedure, we will see other risks about which we must be careful if we are to use computers properly.

This second approach to thinking procedure is characterized by the educational technologist who asks: "Among those aspects of current educational practice that are not sufficiently procedural as they stand to be computerized, which ones can be reshaped into likely candidates?" To see what results from this approach and to explore some of its risks, we will consider another popular use of computers in instruction. This second instructional application of computers—generally called "author-controlled tutorial" or, simply, tutorial CAI—is what most people have in mind when they speak about computer-assisted instruction. In terms of such things as technical sophistication, progress-to-date, and extent of perfection, tutorial CAI is not as well developed as are automated drill and practice systems. Nonetheless, tutorial CAI has offered the educational technologist certain quick "successes" in the use of computers in instruction which have been enough to convince him that he is making significant progress toward his goal of "teaching by machine."

In tutorial CAI, to teach by machine means to *replace the teacher.* "The point of the tutorial system," Richard Atkinson asserts, "is that one really expects to carry on all the instruction in a given area within the framework of the computer."[18] Commenting on the role of the teacher in all of this, Atkinson continues,

> The teachers need to be familiar with the material that is being presented over the tutorial system, and they must understand the sorts of supplementary activities that they can engage in. But, when I talk about the tutorial system, for example, in the area of initial reading, I assume that a student could learn to read by exposure only to the computer-based curriculum.[19]

Now, work in tutorial CAI to replace the teacher has been constrained by certain technical difficulties, prominent among which is our inability to get computers to hold natural language conversations with students the way teachers do. In the face of this constraint, tutorial systems developers have heeded the advice of I. A. Richards that

> Those subjects that are most free from attitudinal complexities—those in which the bare typewritten, factual sentence is wholly adequate to what is relevant in the utterance—are best suited to present-day computer technique. The mathematics, the factual sciences, and languages (if confined strictly to the handling of plain sense, factual propositions and to conventional formulae) are the subjects through which the development of computer instruction can best be forwarded.[20]

Richard Atkinson and Patrick Suppes at Stanford University, Donald Bitzer at the University of Illinois, and Duncan Hansen at the Florida State University are just a few of the people providing tutorial CAI of this type for their students on a regular basis. Subjects covered by such efforts include trigonometry, statistics, geometry, physics, Russian, beginning reading, and logic.[21]

Tutorial CAI

At the most general level of description, tutorial CAI entails the presentation of instructional material to a student seated at a video or typewriter display terminal such as those pictured in the Appendix. So as to be

[18]Richard Atkinson, "CAI-Learning Aspects," in R. Gerard, (ed.), *Computers and Education*, McGraw-Hill, New York, 1967, pp. 17–18.

[19]Ibid., p. 18. See also P. Suppes, "On Using Computers to Individualize Instruction," in Bushnell, Allen, and Mitter, (eds.), op. cit., p. 16.

[20]I. A. Richards, "The Creative Aim in Instruction," in Bushnell, Allen, and Mitter, (eds.), op. cit., p. xxiv.

[21]For a general description of two very large CAI projects supported by the National Science Foundation see Erik McWilliams, op. cit. See also Kenneth Stetten, "TICCIT: A Delivery System Designed for Mass Utilization," M71-56, The Mitre Corporation, Washington, D.C., October 1971.

different from a book or a lecture, however, the intention is that the instructional material be presented in such a way that the student will participate overtly by responding to the material, and the student's passage through the material will be tailored to his strengths and weaknesses thus providing individualized instruction. While the student may not "converse" with the computer, the aim of tutorial CAI is that he and the machine will "interact" with each other.

To accomplish these intentions, the early developer of tutorial CAI adopted the techniques of programmed instruction. As in programmed instruction, the subject to be taught to the student via tutorial CAI is broken down into its smallest elements. These elements are then organized in a logical fashion and presented to the student bit by bit in units called *frames.* A frame, according to the theory of programmed instruction, consists of three parts: a stimulus, a response, a reinforcement. For example:

STIMULUS:	The "father" of programmed instruction is____________.
RESPONSE:	B. F. Skinner of Harvard
REINFORCEMENT:	Very Good

Because of the mode of presentation associated with programmed instruction, it is natural that, from the beginning, educational technologists should have seized upon it as the principal mode of tutorial CAI.

Of course, not all efforts at tutorial CAI rely heavily on programmed instruction. The Stanford program in elementary mathematical logic, for instance, is constructed such that instead of learning about logic, the student *does* logic and, therefore, the material need not be as structured as in the typical tutorial system. Other programs adopt just the barest form of programmed instruction, ignoring most of its theory. These programs reduce to lectures, interspersed with multiple choice questions or forced response "YES" or "NO" questions. Karl Zinn points out two examples of this approach when he says, "Much of the work done at Penn State and Florida State can be characterized as individualized versions of lecture, text, or examination material."[22]

Tutorial Systems Without Machines

Whatever the mode of presentation, however, builders of computer-based tutorial systems all accept from programmed instruction the philosophy that the instructional materials must be carefully and systematically

[22]Karl Zinn, "A Basic Reference Shelf on Interactive Use of Computers for Instruction," University of Michigan, September 1968, p. 4, Mimeographed.

developed in terms of clearly-stated educational goals and objectives. Many suggestions, strategies, and models have been proposed, outlining the various steps involved in such careful development of instructional materials for CAI. One of the most thoughtful models is that described by C. Victor Bunderson.[23] Bunderson's "Prescriptive Model for Designing CAI Programs" consists of six stages, comprising a systematic and complicated set of tasks for instructional materials development. Included among Bunderson's tasks are such things as specifying the societal and institutional needs to be addressed by the CAI program, justifying CAI as the most appropriate mode of presentation, deriving a complete set of objectives expressed in terms of desired student behavior, analyzing learner traits, devising flow charts describing the various paths through the materials, constructing curriculum-embedded tests, producing program materials, and evaluating and revising material.[24] These and all the other steps recommended by Bunderson "can require 200, 300, or more hours of work on the part of a team of authors, instructional designers, programmers, and media specialists to produce a sequence that would take an average student only one hour to complete."[25]

Certainly Bunderson and the others like him leave no doubt that to them properly using a computer in education depends upon being sure you know what you are doing *educationally.* Yet while we must recognize the central role the computer played in encouraging Bunderson's careful and systematic approach to the development of educational procedure, we need not assume that such an approach must be confined to computer-based systems. There is no reason why we should not approach teacher-based, classroom instruction with the same care and thoughtfulness. Perhaps this point is the most difficult one we will have to learn about computers: while the computer, properly conceived, becomes a mechanism with which we can come to grips with certain educational problems, *it does not follow that the solutions to these problems must entail the use of the computer.* In this respect, the computer becomes a lens with which to sharpen our view about problems and their solutions, and as important as it may be to us as a physical entity, the computer's final value rests in the notion of computational procedures—the formulation of problems and solutions—we derive from it. That is why it was so important that we define a computer in terms of procedure rather than in terms of its physical components and capacities. Technology is only superficially concerned with machines. So while the effort to develop tutorial CAI has led some educational technologists to focus their concern upon the use of machines in instruction, it has led others toward

[23]C. Victor Bunderson, "The Computer and Instructional Design," in Holtzman, (ed.), op. cit., pp. 45–73.
[24]Ibid., pp. 50–51.
[25]Ibid.

a broader view of educational technology—one which does not depend upon machines. This broader view of educational technology has been expressed by David Engler who said, "Educational technology is a *process* by means of which we apply our knowledge of learning, teaching, communication and other disciplines to the practical problems of instruction."[26] To Engler the term educational technology is a tautology in that "if we define technology as the application of knowledge to practical purposes, then education is and has always been a technology."[27] This same broad view of technology is offered by Robert Stake who asserts,

> The complete technology of instruction is the complete collection of our orderly attempts to instruct. It is more than those methods that rely on books, projectors, linear programs, and computers. It includes all methods of strengthening the student's ability to cope with life.[28]

Thus for some technologists, tutorial CAI has become a base from which to refashion their notion of the relationship between procedure and the instructional process itself.

Naturally, tutorial CAI continues to represent an approach to automation which attempts to reshape certain educational practices in order to make them sufficiently procedural to be turned over to a machine. But to most educational technologists, the belief in the orderly and systematic development of educational goals and related instructional procedures which stems from tutorial CAI—by way of its adoption of the philosophy of programmed instruction—has wider application. Indeed such an approach, they assert, applies to the conduct of instruction in general, whether or not machines are involved. We see then that through its view of instruction as procedure, tutorial CAI offers two prospects. First is the prospect of automating certain aspects of instruction; second is the prospect that even where we continue to use human beings as teachers, the instructional process will be made systematic and orderly.

But these two prospects of tutorial CAI are matched by two dangers of at least equal magnitude, and these dangers constitute the major risks we run by attempting to realize the seeming promise offered by tutorial CAI. Both of these risks stem from the fact that an approach to automation which seeks to reshape educational practice so that it will qualify as a candidate for computerization contains within it the possibility that we will distort our concept of education in the process. As we

[26]David Engler, "Development, Sharing and Utilization of Technologically-Based Instructional Materials: Some Guidelines," in Edgar L. Morphet and David L. Jesser, (eds.), *Designing Education for the Future*, no. 6, Citation Press, New York, 1969, p. 296.

[27]Ibid.

[28]Robert Stake, "Technologically-Based Instruction and Materials," in Morphet and Jesser, (eds.), op. cit., p. 302.

look into these two risks, we will see the principal forms such distortion takes.

Distortion by Limitation

The first risk associated with tutorial CAI and similar approaches to automation thrives on an attitude such as that expressed by Suppes when he predicted "computers will be used not because everyone is happy with them, but because there is no other feasible way to handle the severe problems of growing numbers of new students and rising costs."[29] Seemingly in his justified anxiety over current, pressing educational problems, the educational technologist is willing to make certain concessions just so that automation will be possible. The task then becomes that of somehow getting educational practice to fit the perceived demands of the computer. The danger in this, of course, is that in our anxiety to come up with a feasible solution to our problems we may lose sight of the price we pay with our concessions. Or worse, we may willingly incur the cost, believing it to be a small enough price to pay for the prize of an orderly and systematic instructional process. Just as Cinderella's stepsisters thought nothing of cutting off a big toe or a heel in order to fit into the slipper, and thus gain the prince, so too we may willingly discard one or another component of the instructional process so that what remains will fit the constraints of our technological devices.

In this way the process of automation gets turned around and, because of either their strengths or their weaknesses, machines come to dictate practice. Clearly, such catering to the machine amounts to the belief that technology is made up of devices that exist before the fact of their relevance and are, therefore, external to the educational system which is to make use of them. Thus, it becomes the task of the educator contemplating the usefulness of educational technology to determine how he can make his house receptive to the change technology somehow demands.[30]

We see this approach, for instance, in the educational technologist's eager acceptance of programmed instruction as the mode of presentation in tutorial CAI. Of course, programmed instruction is ready made for this role. Its orderly presentation of facts, its systematic passage through a subject bit by bit, its step by step accounting of student progress all make programmed instruction a natural ally of CAI. That programmed instruction and thus tutorial CAI so heavily emphasize the learning of facts, the control and conditioning of the student, and the definition of learning in terms of observable and specifiable behavior may seem a small price to

[29]Suppes, "Education in Modern Society," in Greenberger, (ed.), op. cit., p. 137.
[30]Allan B. Ellis, "New Myths and Old Realities: A Discussion," *Harvard Educational Review*, vol. 38, no. 4, Fall 1968, p. 725.

pay for the resultant efficiency and enhanced achievement. Nor may it seem unbearable that "much of the material now available for use with computers looks very much like computerized versions of programmed texts, slides or audio tape."[31] That is, we may be willing to adopt current brands of CAI even though it could all be done just as well with pencil and paper.

But consider the distortion we risk. Surely there is more to education than efficiency and achievement, and surely these additional functions come easily to mind. Emmanuel Mesthene summarizes them for us when he writes, "Education also has the functions of socializing individuals, of shaping their values, of preparing for citizenship, of conserving traditions, and of imparting some sense of awe before the wonders of the universe."[32] Addressing himself to the habit of the educational technologist to ignore all but the achievement aspects of education, Mesthene continues:

> The application of technology to the improvement only of the instrumental function of education may thus become an obstacle to a society that is trying to redress the balance between the goals characteristic of the heydey of achievement and economic productivity and the greater pluralism in our values and our culture that we are now beginning to seek.[33]

If that happens, he concludes, we could find that we have contributed to technical richness at the cost of moral poverty.

Mesthene is not alone in his effort to caution us against an approach to automation which depends upon the distortion of our sense of the goals of education. For example, Charles Silberman offers the strong warning that "the approach to instructional technology that most researchers are following is likely to compound what is most wrong with American education—its failure to develop sensitive, autonomous, thinking, human individuals."[34] Then there is the caution of Seymour Harris who reminds us that

> Even at the level of formal education we must never forget that *the school is primarily a social system* [thus] the need for social rather than for merely mechanical inventions must constantly be stressed, for *it would be disastrous to have the machines dominate the development of the social system of learning.*[35]

Ironically the presence of the computer in society reinforces these calls for concern about the moral, humane, and social components of

[31]Zinn, op. cit., p. 3.
[32]Mesthene, "Computers and the Purposes of Education," in Holtzman, (ed.), op. cit., p. 391.
[33]Ibid.
[34]Charles Silberman, *Crisis in the Classroom*, Random House, New York, 1970, p. 196.
[35]Seymour Harris, "The Economics of Technological Advances in Education," in Morphet and Jesser, op. cit., p. 372.

education. That is because the school is an institution of society, its goals come sooner or later to be affected by the trends, the concerns, and the prevailing forces in society. The school is a conserving institution. This is not a new idea, of course, and neither is it new to list among the major movements in our culture and thus in our schools during this century the continuing emphasis on science and technology.[36] Whereas "technology" used to stand for the factory machine, the atomic bomb, and the automobile, more and more it has come almost exclusively to refer to the computer. As society is altered by the presence of the computer, education—as preparation for life in society, which is the school's view of it—must reexamine and refashion its educational goals. Notice that this effect will not depend at all on whether or not schools *use* computers or have them on their premises.

Many people have begun to conjecture about the specifics of this effect. Prominent among them is Donald Michael, who opens an article on the subject by stating "cybernation has an impact on the social context, and hence on the goals, of education."[37] Later in this article he offers some specifics:

> Because cybernation will radically change the work-force composition and the purpose of work, education not only must assume the task of altering its goals and its techniques for dealing with work but also it must develop a radically different capability to educate for leisure. To the extent to which cybernation provides more productivity, it provides the opportunity for more leisure.[38]

What schools must do, then, Michael asserts, is "invent leisure roles, and then invent educative means for inculcating them in both the younger and the older people who will compose most of the working population." But, if leisure is to be self-fulfilling, as Michael contends it must, then the schools have to find ways of "inculcating the cultivation of self." According to Michael, this is such a big challenge because the present orientation of schools is so different from this, being "premised on education for work and administered with a beady eye on efficiency."

Michael summarized his position by saying that the challenge for educators who wish to establish and to reach goals for living meaningfully in a "cybernated society" is twofold: (1) that we be able to produce more intellectually and emotionally competent people; (2) that we be able to produce in numbers and in quality, as never before, wise

[36]See, for instance, Merle Curti, "The Last Twenty-five Years," in American Historical Association, Commission on the Social Studies, (ed.), *The Social Ideas of American Educators*, Littlefield, Adams & Co., Patterson, N.J., 1959, p. xxx.
[37]Donald Michael, "Cybernation and Changing Goals in Education," in Bushnell, Allen, and Mitter, op. cit., p. 3.
[38]Ibid., p. 8.

people.[39] Clearly neither of these challenges is being met or even addressed by typical efforts at tutorial CAI. Perhaps in time this will change, but more likely should we continue to cling to tutorial CAI as a feasible solution to certain instructional problems, we will succumb eventually to the temptation to distort our notion of the educational process.

Distortion by Oversimplification

While the first risk we run by attempting to realize the benefits of tutorial CAI involves distortion of the educational process by limiting what we include therein to the "instrumental functions," the second risk involves distortion by oversimplifying what remains. This tendency to oversimplify emanates from many aspects of the approach to automation typified by tutorial CAI, but principally it stems from the goal of replacing the teacher by a machine and the goal of systematizing the instructional process. Because the strategies that have been developed to achieve these goals are complex, involved, and carefully formulated—as we have seen with Bunderson's model, for instance—the use of the word "oversimplify" may seem unjustified. But we do not refer to a simplicity of approach as much as a simplicity of belief. It is a simplicity of belief which assumes the instructional process when reshaped into an efficient, well-formed procedure remains otherwise unchanged in character. It is a simplicity of belief which ignores Marc Belth's warning that there is a difference between education as technology and technology in education.[40]

We run the risk of such oversimplification when we pursue the goal of replacing the teacher by a machine in that, invariably, we come to believe that replacing the teacher means *imitating* the teacher mimicking his behavior at least well enough to make the student feel he is interacting with a human being. Such meagre attempts at imitation as "Good morning Sophia," "Very good Margaret," and "No it was the Jesuits who expelled them in 1492" abound in tutorial CAI. In the so-called "dialogue" CAI—of which there are no examples outside the researcher's laboratory—the situation improves considerably, as these systems hold at least the semblance of conversation with the student. But it is not lack of quality in the conversations that is so troubling; it is the fact that conversation is considered appropriate—that the machine is made, however imperfectly, to imitate the teacher—that is troubling.

Such an approach is a mistake, first in that it amounts to "yoking oxen

[39]Ibid., p. 9. For a fuller account of Michael's position, see also D. Michael, *The Next Generation*, Random House, New York, 1965; and D. Michael, "Some Speculations on the Social Impact of Technology," in Dean Morse and Aaron W. Warner (eds.), *Technological Innovation and Society*, Columbia, New York, 1966.

[40]Marc Belth, *Education As a Discipline: A Study of the Role of Models in Thinking*, Allyn and Bacon, Boston, 1965, p. 259.

before a tractor,"[41] utterly misusing the technology while abusing the very process it attempts to ape. Discussing this absurdity, I. A. Richards asserts, "early attempts will seek to do by computer just what has been done traditionally by select individual teachers . . . Such underestimates and misuses . . . occur whenever new technical resources become available."[42] Perhaps Richards's example will make the point well enough. He describes a language laboratory in Africa set up as a model, via tape, of pronunciation for teachers. On the tape, Richards reports, "were such things as 'Now, Tommy, I don't want to have any more trouble from you!' 'Put your hand up properly!' 'Go and stand in the corner!' and other samples of the outcomes of incompetent teaching."[43]

But more important and more troubling than the mere misuse of technology, however, is the prospect that by taking the imitation game too seriously we endanger our understanding of the teaching process. We become encouraged by the tasks of the imitation problem to forget what Israel Scheffler calls the "intentional nature of teaching." "Teaching is a distinctive goal-oriented activity," Scheffler has said, "rather than a distinctively patterned sequence of behavioral steps executed by the teacher."[44] By concentrating too heavily on behavior, we act as though teaching is procedural even though we do not have enough evidence for such a conclusion. Now, the educational technologist will argue that he only automates those aspects of the teaching process that are procedural, leaving the rest untouched, and he will think that this tautology settles the matter. But, the point is, of course, that we cannot say with complete certainty what the procedural aspects of teaching are. That is why computers are so important to education; with them we have the opportunity to begin to sort such matters out.[45]

Whatever successes the technologist has had with tutorial CAI should not mislead us into believing that the goal of replacing the teacher is a wise one. It may be, but much depends upon whether we learn to use the computer in our effort to settle this issue. Tutorial CAI, like any other application of the computer in education, can serve as a mechanism with which to explore and come to better understand the process being automated. But to do this, we must be careful not to start by accepting, consciously or unwittingly, the very contentions we hope to investigate.

We run the risk of oversimplification, as well, when we pursue the goal of systematizing the instructional process in that we may become

[41]Richards, op. cit., p. xxii.
[42]Ibid.
[43]Ibid.
[44]Israel Scheffler, "Philosophical Models of Teaching," in I. Scheffler, (ed.), *Philosophy and Education,* Allyn and Bacon, Boston, 1966, p. 99. See, also, I. Scheffler, *The Language of Education,* Charles C. Thomas, Springfield, Ill., 1960.
[45]See Allan Ellis and David Tiedeman, "Can a Machine Counsel?" Project Report #17, The ISVD Project, Harvard University, 1968.

convinced by our successes that it is possible to "engineer" instruction. Already we hear people speak of "flow charting" the instructional sequence, or of specifying subject matter elements and relationships, or of "mapping" event structures, and even our brief look at Bunderson's model for the development of CAI routines revealed the "systems approach" upon which it rests. Perhaps these are all innocent activities. Yet clearly they raise the prospect of confusing the difference between technology in education and education as technology. We see this, for instance, in such statements as

> The computer language used to code the material and to control the teaching process as it is performed by a CAI system represents the complete description of the process of interaction between a student and a teaching system. Together with the content that is presented to the student and expected from the student it constitutes and [sic] instructional program.[46]

which come uncomfortably close to obscuring this difference and, as a consequence, the significance of the difference. Thus education becomes engineering.

We see another example of the notion of educational engineering when Engler and Stake propose—as have so many others[47]—a view of educational technology that goes well beyond the use of machines. Certainly such a broad view of educational technology offers us insight into the idea we have been exploring that automation means thinking procedure. But it offers us something else in the bargain which, if accepted, will severely distort our notion of education. What the broad view of educational technology offers us is—to use Stake's term—a science of education. Recognizing that technology is based on principles and rules, Stake concludes that "the discovery of the principles and rules is the goal of the science of education." From there "the practical organization and application of those rules is the goal of the technology instruction."[48]

Now Stake's assertion is not outrageous, nor is it totally inconsistent with our concept of the computer. Still he goes too far. Surely we do not know nearly enough about how people learn, or think, or grow, or how we can best nurture their development to be very confident that a scientific approach to instruction will provide us with anything. The issue here is not with the use of science, it is with the unreasonable expectation that science, joined by technology, will settle the basic problems of education. Mesthene—who reminds us that what's good for

[46] Lawrence Stolurow, "Some Factors in the Design of Systems for Computer-assisted Instruction," in Atkinson and Wilson, op. cit., p. 66.
[47] Commission on Instructional Technology, "To Improve Learning," *A Report To The President and The Congress of The United States*, U. S. G.P.O., Washington, 1970.
[48] Stake, op. cit., p. 302.

educational technologists is not necessarily good for education—calls this excessive use of science, "forcefeeding." "It is more likely to lead to forcing scientific technique beyond its limits, which is no longer science, but scientism."[49]

Because he has accepted education as science, Stake is able to conclude that teaching is totally procedural—a skill which must be practiced but which does not require insight into the process. "It is clear," he comments, "that teacher insight is not a *necessary* precondition for effective teaching." "As I see it," he says, "in the instructional-system schools, all concepts and skills—intellectual, affective, and psychomotor—will be programmed. . . ."[50]

Such a notion of educational engineering may stem from the adoption of scientific technique, but it does not reflect the scientist's sense of ignorance and his dedication to exploration. In this respect, the educational engineer is essentially self-satisfied. This was not always so, however. Early efforts at CAI were based on the principle that to construct computer-based instructional systems without using them for continued research into instructional strategies, materials development, learning styles, and similar investigations would be to miss the point. CAI was a tool for research as well as for instruction.

The early project in CAI—called CLASS—at System Development Corporation, for example, was established to "provide an opportunity to explore the important interactions among instructional-method, student, and subject matter variables."[51] A second major project, conducted at the Coordinated Science Laboratory at the University of Illinois, listed as its "main goal" the development of "an automatic teaching system sufficiently flexible to permit experimental evaluation of a large variety of ideas on automatic instruction."[52] The work at Bolt, Beranek, and Newman, Inc., as the other projects, had a dual purpose. J. C. R. Licklider, speaking of this effort, asserted "our serious purposes, of course, are research and development: research on learning and teaching; development of a practical, economical system."[53] These projects represent the formative period of automated instruction.

An important outgrowth of this period was the interesting realization that the traditional distinctions between research and development are no longer adequate where automation is concerned. When you develop a

[49]Mesthene, op. cit., p. 390.
[50]Stake, op. cit., pp. 303, 305.
[51]John E. Coulson, "A Computer-based Laboratory for Research and Development in Education," in Coulson, (ed.), op. cit., Wiley, New York, 1962, p. 196. This book contains the proceedings of a 1961 conference on the application of computers to instruction, and while it is by now seriously outdated, the book provides a good account of early efforts in this area.
[52]D. L. Bitzer, P. G. Braunfeld, and W. W. Lichtenberger, "PLATO-II: A Multiple-Student, Computer-controlled, Automatic Teaching Device," in Coulson, (ed.), ibid., p. 205.
[53]J. C. R. Licklider, "Preliminary Experiments in Computer-aided Teaching," in Coulson, (ed.), ibid., p. 224.

computer system for application in some area, say instruction, you create at the same time an environment for research into that application. This is one of the ways computers provide the opportunity to examine the very procedures being automated, and in that way, begin more carefully to approach the problem of educational change.

While instances of this view of automation may still be found, for instance, in the work of Richard Atkinson, it is not the prevailing view. More often we encounter the self-satisfaction of the educational engineer. Or perhaps it is self-deception. In any case, it represents a distortion of the educational process.

This distortion is based on an approach to automation that mistakes quantity for quality. It does not understand that James Moody is a musician not because he plays music but because he has the *capacity* to play music. It tells us that if we can just add to our repertory, by that fact alone we will add to our musicianship. Euthyphro made a similar mistake by believing that one becomes pious by performing pious acts, and Chaucer's Knight appears more of a knight because he has fought in three crusades and not just one. It is a variant of this notion to believe that the more we do with computers in education, the greater will become our capacity to computerize education and nowhere is this self-deception greater than it is among the advocates of tutorial CAI. What these advocates fail to see is that thinking up more and more technological examples of teaching by machine will do nothing to enhance the computer's capacity to participate in the instructional process. Thinking about the computer's role in instruction does not mean thinking about computers. It means thinking about instruction.

CHAPTER FOUR: rethinking procedure

Once we stop seeing the computer as a fast adding machine and come to view it, instead, as a mechanism for the representation and the execution of procedures, we recognize the need to direct our attention away from the machine itself and towards the procedures it executes—in our case, the procedures of education. As we have seen throughout the previous chapter, the crucial aspect of the computer's promise for education rests in the opportunity it provides us to analyze and to better understand the very procedures we automate. Our exploration of this aspect of the computer's promise has centered, thus far, on the notion that automation means thinking procedure. In this chapter, we shall focus on a second, though closely related, notion which grows out of our definition of a computer.

The notion this chapter will develop is that if the first implication we draw from our definition of a computer is that automation means thinking procedure, then the second and equally obvious implication is that automation means *rethinking procedure.* That is, the proper automation of a procedure entails the reexamination and, where necessary, the reformulation of that procedure. While we might be less strict and say that the use of the computer provides us the *opportunity* to reexamine and reformulate a procedure, it follows, as we shall see, that ignoring this opportunity constitutes a severe misuse of the computer. Therefore we may treat this opportunity as a requirement. Moreover since our interest is in the use of computers in education, we may restate this requirement as follows: the automation of an educational procedure requires the reassessment of the educational process which that procedure is designed to serve.

Those educational technologists who fail to see this requirement or who refuse to accept it, leave themselves vulnerable to the two dangers that always accompany attempts at automation. As we examine these two dangers and the extent to which rethinking educational practice serves to guard against them effectively, we will see again what we saw in the last chapter, that educational technology as currently practiced does not generally reflect a full sense of the promise of the computer. As before, the examples we use to explore automation as rethinking will not exhaust those areas of education to which the notion is applicable. It will become clear that the principle holds in general.

Old Compromises

The first danger which we guard against when we reassess those educational practices we wish to automate stems from the fact that no aspect of the educational enterprise is devoid of compromise. Whether we look to the area of school administration, or plant facilities, or instructional materials, or classroom teaching, we will find compromise in abundance. Nor is such compromise without prior foundation. In certain of these cases, however, the enhanced capacity for building procedures which the computer offers may render compromise unjustified. To mechanize such procedures without reexamining and renegotiating these compromises would be a mistake since such mindless automation will not only legitimize these compromises, it will perpetuate them. We can find no better way to shield our compromises from reassessment than to automate them.

Many examples can be found of the risk we run of adhering unnecessarily to old compromises. For example, we could look to the automation of grade reporting where we have found new powers to rank students, to compute averages to four decimal places, and to distinguish as never before between a grade of 89 and one of 91. Or we could look to the automation of standardized tests where our capacity for sophisticated analysis pushes us to believe that schools exist to teach just that which is testable. Finally, we could return to CAI, examining, for instance, the extent to which drill and practice systems preserve "the best of the worst" of an earlier generation's compromises. Because it includes some of these possibilities, and because it shows the risk we run so clearly, we will choose as our example the use of educational measurement and statistics in schools.

In education we have gotten into the habit of *measuring* the student. We measure his height, his weight, his IQ, his eyesight, his ability to do algebra or chemistry or Spanish, and in gym class we measure how long it takes him to run the distance from one fence to the other in the school yard. Sometimes we make these measurements because we are interested directly in the student as an individual. We may determine the size of his foot, for instance, just so that we can get him a pair of baseball spikes that fit. Other times, though, we are concerned with the student in relation to other students, and, in such cases, we have in the back of our minds a question something like, "How do his measurements stack up with those of the average student?" and this is where statistics comes in. With respect to this kind of question, statistics is a set of computational procedures used to compare what we observe to chance behavior.

But this is not a comparison of the usual kind. It does not ask, for instance, if one ear of corn is bigger than another or if one student is taller than another. It asks, instead, whether or not the differences we are bound to observe among measured objects is greater than we would expect there to be because of chance. The girls in this year's graduating class might have an average IQ of 100, and the boys an average of 103, and from all we know about arithmetic, we may conclude from this that in general boys have higher IQs than girls. But to the statistician this is not necessarily correct. Statistical theory asserts that the differences we observe between things may be due to chance variations in either the performance of the things measured or the measuring instruments themselves. Unless we take into account, then, performance variation and errors of measurement—and this is what statistics helps us do—we have no way of estimating the importance of those differences we observe. Thus our question becomes, "What is the probability that we would observe a difference this great between graduating boys and girls by chance when in fact there is no difference?"

Now, statistics is concerned with a lot of other things besides the assessment of observed differences. Sometimes we use statistical procedures to locate similarities between variables and other times our interest centers on one variable at a time without regard for its relationship to any others. In the most general sense, statistics covers a broad range indeed, involving the activities of collecting, looking at, and drawing conclusions from data.[1]

It is clearly no surprise therefore that people concerned with education should have become interested in the application of statistics to their problems.

Simple Interest

Traditionally this interest has related to three types of concerns. The first concern to which schoolmen have applied statistics is that of summariz-

[1]F. Mosteller, R. Rourke, and G. Thomas, Jr., *Probability, A First Course*, Addison-Wesley, Reading, Mass., 1961, p. 2.

ing facts about their students. In the simplest case, they measure several characteristics of their students and then look at these "variables" one at a time. They may represent each variable by plotting a bar graph or a frequency polygon, or they may construct a frequency distribution table showing how many students have each of the possible values for that variable. Other summarizing statistics include the mean, standard deviation, range, and the various errors of measurement associated with such summarizing statistics. Sometimes the educator will look at two variables at a time plotting the "joint-distribution" of the variables or, perhaps, making up "contingency tables" which show for each value of Variable A the number of students who have each of the values of Variable B. We need not go into the details of these summarizing procedures since they are all discussed in the first few chapters of any introductory text on statistics. Remember, however, these procedures usually involve one and sometimes two variables at a time.

The second major concern for which statistics has been a useful tool for the educator is the analysis of group differences. Schoolmen are interested to know if one teaching method is better than another or if one group of students does substantially better than another on some test, and thus the statistical assessment of group differences is fairly important to the educational researcher. Lohnes and Cooley go so far as to assert that "most of the interesting and important research that is done [in education] generally involves contrasts, or the making of comparisons."[2] The statistical procedures to make such comparisons—such as the "t-test" and the "analysis of variance"—are most often used to examine the differences among two or more groups on one variable at a time. One analysis might be made to examine the differences between boys and girls on IQ, a second analysis might examine the difference between boys and girls on performance in an experimental reading program. As in the typical case of summarizing student traits, variables are generally treated in isolation from each other.

This habit of treating variables one or two at a time prevails as well in the third area of concern to which schoolmen have applied statistics. This concern centers on locating similarities between two variables or two groups and is typified by a statistic most educators have heard of called the "Pearson correlation coefficient." The basic question here is of the form "What is the relationship between Variable X and Variable Y?" Sometimes we are concerned with the extent of the relationship for its own sake. We may be interested, for instance, in whether or not ability to learn a second language is related to general intelligence. Assuming such a relationship exists, a second concern we might have is the extent to which we can *predict* from a knowledge of his general intelligence, the

[2]Paul R. Lohnes and William W. Cooley, *Introduction to Statistical Procedures: with Computer Exercises,* Wiley, New York, 1968, p. 177.

degree of success a student will have in learning a second language. The statistical procedure for determining the presence or absence of a relationship between two variables is called *correlation analysis*, while the procedure for establishing a basis for predicting one value given a knowledge of another value is called *regression analysis*. In either case, schoolmen usually have dealt with only two variables at any one time. Indeed until recently the habit of examining student characteristics in virtual isolation from each other prevailed throughout all the areas to which educators applied statistical procedures. Yet, however restricted this approach was understood to be, educators managed to put these basic statistical techniques to use, and from them, to gain some insight into the performance of their students.

There is, of course, an irony to the schoolman's acceptance of this restriction. Few people know better than educators that human beings are complex mechanisms and that therefore measuring certain student characteristics and then examining these measurements one or two at a time, is a questionable activity. Even efforts to place the results of these examinations together fall short, because a human being is not merely the sum of his characteristics. He is, more likely, the product of their interaction and, thus, only when they are viewed concomitantly can we hope to gain a full sense of the relative importance of various characteristics. Yet the difficulties of computing statistics by hand are considerable, and educators have had little choice but to accept the compromise and to stick to those procedures they could figure.

Even so, many of these "computable" statistics push our manual skills for figuring to their limits. One example is the correlation coefficient, which in a typical situation will require about an hour's careful work when done by hand. Another case is provided by the more involved analysis of variance which may take weeks to perform, especially when you accept the need to do them several times to check your accuracy. We cannot be too harsh with ourselves, therefore, for accepting and living with this restriction however severe we know it to be.

Now it would seem obvious that the advent of the computer with its ability to execute involved computational procedures would remove the need to accept this restriction and thus would solve the problem. Certainly you would expect, because of the availability of computers, that the more sophisticated statistical techniques that take into account more of the complexity of human beings, could now be applied to educational problems. But strangely, while there is no question that the computer offers this greater sophistication, its availability to people in education has carried with it an unanticipated risk.

Naturally, having accepted the compromise of dealing with variables one and two at a time, schoolmen over the years have become familiar with those statistical techniques relating to this approach. They know the procedures involved, the questions they can expect to answer, and through experience, they have come to sense the extent to which generalizing from their results is appropriate. In contrast, other, more sophisticated statistical procedures—the ones more suited to the complexities of student populations—may remain unfamiliar to the educator and the questions they are designed to answer may be outside the educator's present point of view. The risk in this, obviously, is that the sudden availability of computers will mean to people in education that it is now *easier to do things the old way.* They may continue to be restricted in their analysis of the educational process and redouble their efforts at these analyses since computers will be doing all the computational "dirty work." Far from being a resource for breaking out of the old ways, the computer then becomes a force for legitimizing outmoded compromises.

It is easier, generally, to view the computer as a device for automating our present procedures than it is to see the computer as an opportunity to rethink and reformulate these procedures. As a result, this danger of legitimizing present practice pervades all aspects of the application of computers to education. Furthermore, in some areas it is not as clear as it is with the automation of statistical procedures that the computer provides a new power to ask new questions and not merely a new power to perform old tasks.

But this power to ask new questions carries with it the responsibility to master the substance of the new procedures involved. To gain a sense for the potential dangers in ignoring this responsibility and at the same time to see some of the benefits of reexamining present practice and throwing off unneeded compromises, we will look briefly at the nature of this new statistical question which, because of the computer, we can now learn to ask.

Compound Interests

"An isolated fact," Truman Lee Kelley once wrote, "is an unthinkable phenomenon." He might have added that human beings are not very good, however, at keeping track of all the interrelationships that are likely to exist among a set of many facts. Even those computational procedures statisticians have devised to deal with these interrelationships end up being more trouble than they seem to be worth when they have to be done by hand. This is what has justified the educator's habit of taking the "unthinkable" position that facts about students can be examined meaningfully in isolation from each other. Due to this habit, educators have dealt, traditionally, with what the statistician calls *univariate distributions.* Univariate means "one variable" and, as we have seen, the statistics used to examine univariate distributions are well known to people in education. On some occasions—when he wants to look at two variables at the same time—the schoolman goes a step further and examines the joint distribution of his variables. On these occasions he is dealing with a *bivariate distribution.* The correlation coefficient which depicts the relationship between two variables—aptitude and achievement, for instance—is one such "bivariate statistic."

Unused, indeed unknown to most schoolmen, is a third class of statistical procedure. Even many educational researchers were unfamiliar with this third type of statistic until the presence of the computer made the difficult calculations involved more practicable to do. This third set of statistical procedures goes by the name *multivariate analysis.* As the name suggests, multivariate analysis deals with many variables at the same time, thus allowing us to treat the measurements we make on students no longer as isolated facts but as systems; we can now deal with the variables in combination. Univariate and bivariate problems are, in an important theoretical sense, encompassed by the more general theory of multivariate analysis since they may be viewed as special cases of the multivariate problem in much the same way that a point is thought of as a special case of a circle. Still, as M. G. Kendall has said, the term "multivariate analysis" is used, by general consent, in a much narrower sense. To him the term properly connotes a situation in which for each individual in a sample, we have values for many variables, and wherein these variables are dependent among themselves so that it does not make sense to "split off one or more from the others and consider it by itself."[3]

But how do we deal with many variables in combination? Certainly with multivariate procedures we do not look at them one at a time, but neither do we collapse them. That is, we do not take their product, or their average, or their weighted sum, or the like; this would amount to transforming the set of measurements into a new, single variable, in which case univariate or bivariate procedures would apply. Instead we must represent measurements in such a way that we can depict their interrelationships while keeping each one sufficiently separate from the others so that its unique contribution to the system is preserved. Statisticians accomplish this by treating all the measurements for an individual as a set of *coordinates.* A set of coordinates is a series of numbers that can be used to define a point in space. If we had a two-dimensional space, for example, where one dimension represents "height" and the other dimension stands for "weight," then a person's height and weight could be used as coordinates to locate him as a point in that space. If Cameron is 5 feet tall and weighs 90 pounds, then we can represent these facts about her by "plotting" them as in Figure 4-1. Other people can be similarly represented as points in this same space, and each point would depict both an individual's height and weight.

Having thus plotted the measurements of a group of individuals, we might statistically examine the entire swarm of points to determine the relationship (correlation) between height and weight. Or we might isolate

[3]M. G. Kendall, *A Course in Multivariate Analysis,* Griffin, London, 1957, p. 5.

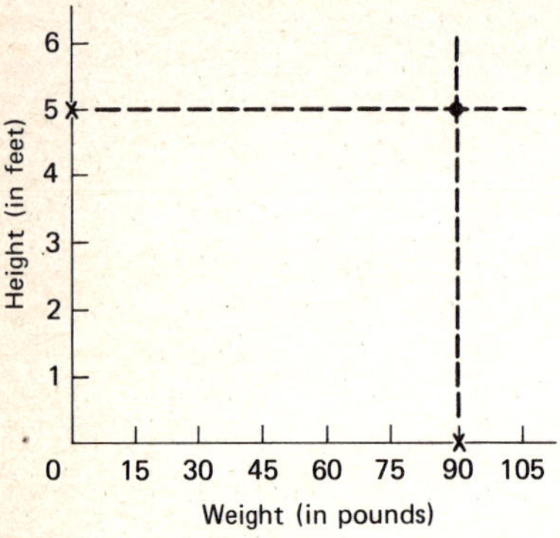

Figure 4-1 Values of two variables as coordinates of a point.

the points belonging to the boys and those belonging to the girls to see if these two clusters occupy different parts of the space. Whatever statistical procedure we select, we have the advantage of treating all our measurements simultaneously instead of in isolation from each other.

In our example we considered two variables and thus plotted them in a two-dimensional space. If we had three variables we would need to work in a three-dimensional space, with four variables, a four-dimensional space is required, and so on. In general, m measurements will define a point in m-dimensional space, and the job of multivariate procedures is to help us analyze swarms of points in such multidimensional space. We refer to this space as the *test space*, and an individual's set of scores is called a *score vector*.

Now even though it helps our understanding to think of a vector of m scores as defining a point in m-dimensional space, it is impossible for us, of course, to visualize more than three dimensions. The multivariate statistician, therefore, does not use geometry to solve his problems. He uses a special kind of algebra called *matrix algebra* which allows him to deal, algebraically, with sets of numbers. In fact the word "matrix" means a set or table of numbers having so many rows and so many columns.[4] An example of a matrix is

$$\begin{matrix} 5 & 90 & 7 \\ 4.9 & 83 & 6 \end{matrix}$$

This matrix has two rows and three columns. Usually, in the matrices used in multivariate analyses, each row is an individual's score vector; each column represents, therefore, a particular variable in the vector, in this case column one is height, column two is weight, and column three stands for grade level. While working with vectors, matrices, test spaces,

[4]For a thorough introduction to matrices and matrix algebra see Paul Horst, *Matrix Algebra for Social Scientists*, Holt, New York, 1963.

and the like quickly gets complicated, still it can be seen from the little we have said about them that with multivariate procedures the educator can ask what is for him a new kind of question. It is a new kind of question because, for the first time, we can ask about more than one or two variables at the same time.

An interesting example of the type of educational question for which multivariate procedures are appropriate and which because of computers the educator can now ask, is provided in the Scientific Careers Study conducted by William Cooley.[5] Cooley was interested in determining what personality factors, if any, were related to the careers that science majors pursued after college. Upon examining their eventual career choices, he discovered that science majors separated into three groups which he called the "research group," the "applied science group," and, for those who dropped out of science, the "nonscience group." One of the several personality tests Cooley had administered to his sample is the so-called "Study of Values Test," and having identified three career groups, he was now interested in seeing if a student's performance on this test was in any way related to his eventual membership in one of the three groups. Since each student who takes the Study of Values Test ends up with six different scores, one for each of the six "value scales," each person could be located as a point in a six-dimensional test space, and some multivariate procedure would therefore be appropriate for the analysis. The multivariate procedure selected by Cooley called *multiple-discriminant analysis* allowed him to investigate the extent to which the three career groups occupied different parts of the test space. Since a person's position (as a point) in the test space depends upon his scores on the value scales—theoretical, economic, aesthetic, social, political, and religious—the question became "What is the relationship between a person's group membership and his six scores on the Study of Values Test?"

Several questions, actually, are involved in a discriminant analysis: "What is the minimum number of dimensions by which we can characterize differences among particular groups?" "How may these dimensions be described?" "How well can we predict group membership?" and the like. The intention here, however, is not to consider multivariate procedures in any detail[6] but to suggest how the educator's scope is increased by these procedures and the questions they permit.

Naturally, multiple-discriminant analysis is not the only multivariate procedure useful to the educator. Another called *canonical correlation analysis* involves the comparison of two test spaces to determine the

[5]See William W. Cooley and Paul R. Lohnes, *Multivariate Procedures for the Behavioral Sciences*, Wiley, New York, 1962, pp. 119–123.

[6]See M. Kendall, op. cit.; and Phillip J. Rulon, David V. Tiedeman, Maurice M. Tatsuoka, and Charles R. Langmuir, *Multivariate Statistics for Personnel Classification*, Wiley, New York, 1967.

maximum relationship existing between them. For each student in some sample, we may have a battery of aptitude test scores and a set of his high school grades, for instance, and we may wish to see what the relationship is between these two sets of variables. *Principal components analysis*, another multivariate procedure, allows one to consider the question, "What is the smallest number of dimensions to which my forty-two (say) measurements can be reduced without losing very much information?" Thanks to these and the other multivariate procedures, we can now ask new, more educationally relevant questions of our data, and because computers are available to execute these procedures, we need not commit ourselves to the endless, error-prone manual calculations such procedures once entailed.

While the sudden availability of multivariate statistical procedures is undoubtedly the most significant contribution of computers to the educational statistician and researcher, they have benefitted in other ways as well. For instance, the computer has allowed a substantial increase in the amount of data one can reasonably expect to include in his analyses. This is a good thing too, because as the researcher increases the number of variables under investigation, as he does when using multivariate procedures, he is required for technical reasons to increase, correspondingly, the number of people in his sample. But, in addition, the ability to deal with large samples has led to such things as Project TALENT. TALENT is an ongoing analysis of the characteristics and development of a carefully drawn sample of 440,000 American school children. The comprehensive set of measurements taken on this large sample (5% of the entire school population) allows researchers to perform many analyses and from them to draw inferences about the full population. As well, the Project TALENT sample can be used as what the researcher calls a "norming group"—a base sample to which other, independently drawn samples can be compared. Still another way the life of the educational statistician has been enhanced through access to computers is in the greater ease with which he can carry on his Monte Carlo studies. A Monte Carlo study is one in which, through the repeated use of randomly generated samples, the statistician can observe the behavior of some statistic. An example of a Monte Carlo study is the one performed by Richard LaBrie.[7] Having developed a new statistical procedure for handling "missing observations"—a situation where some measurements are missing for some people in a sample—he needed to try it out in many different sample cases to see how well it worked. Instead of going out and collecting hundreds of samples of varying characteristics and then following the procedure in each case, LaBrie wrote a computer program to randomly constitute the needed samples and to execute his procedure

[7]Richard LaBrie, "A Procedure for Performing Least-Squares Analysis When Observations Are Missing," unpublished doctoral dissertation, Harvard University, 1969.

on each one. In this way he was able to systematically observe the functioning of his statistic.

But these are not the only benefits the educational researcher has enjoyed as a result of his use of the computer in his work. Indeed, the full range of research activity has been touched and the promise is considerable. Whatever the potential, however, our enthusiasm ought not to be unqualified. The value of the computer to educational research is too well matched by the opportunities it presents for misuse. Indeed, the very capacity that allows us to throw off vestigial compromises, imposes on us the responsibility to learn the limits of our new freedom.

A Mixed Blessing

Regarding statistical analysis in education, for instance, one development which grew out of the substantial use educational researchers have made of the computer is a mixed blessing called the "stat package." Because the source of its virtue is, as well, the source of its potential danger, the "stat package" exemplified some of the complexities involved in deciding how to use computers in education.

"Stat package" stands for *statistical programs package*, a set of ready-made computer programs which perform various statistical procedures. Just about every university computing center makes such a set of statistical programs available to its users, thereby removing the need for each person to write his own computer program. Indeed the person does not even need to know how to program computers because each of the computer programs in the package is "generalized." That is, each program is written in such a way that it can function under varying conditions. The user need only specify the particular conditions that apply in his case and the program he has selected will accommodate to these conditions. A program to perform a correlation analysis, for example, might be able to operate on any number of variables from, say, two to fifty, with any number of subjects. Further, such a program is likely to allow one the option of receiving his results either in printed form or on punched cards, and, probably, he would be able to elect to preserve the intermediate results for use in other programs. Such flexibility is achieved by having the programs begin by reading in a statement of particulars and election of options—these are usually called "input parameters"—and then proceeding with the analysis under the constraint of these parameters. The idea, while powerful, is quite simple: instead of performing some operation five, ten, or thirty times, for example, the program is written to perform that operation n times; when the program is executed, n is specified by the user and treated by the program as an input parameter.

Libraries of statistical programs have grown out of the work in such fields as bio-medical research,[8] the social and behavioral sciences,[9] and, of course, the various physical sciences where statistical techniques are appropriate. In 1964, there was produced the first comprehensive, integrated set of statistical programs designed especially for education. Its developer, Kenneth J. Jones, calls it the *Multivariate Statistical Analyzer* (MSA, for short).[10] Beside the fact that it is specifically geared to educational problems, MSA is unusual in three respects. First, among the thirty or so programs in MSA are all the major multivariate statistical routines an educator is likely to want. Second, the programs are not independent of each other; the output of some programs can be used directly as input to other programs without intervention of the user. If you wish, therefore, you can perform in one session a series of analyses on your data. Finally, Jones has expended considerable effort in the handbook which accompanies MSA to explain the procedures involved not only in the programs but, as well, in the statistical analyses they perform. For many people, as a result, using MSA has been an excellent way to learn some statistics. Clearly, MSA is one of the most valuable tools for an educator interested in using computers in his analysis of data. It is ironic, therefore, that MSA should provide such a fine example of how computers can be misused in education.

Misuse of the computer programs that make up MSA stems mainly from the fact that to use them you do not have to know any statistics. Jones—and this is true of most "stat packages"—makes things easy for the user. One temptation this leads to is to select a statistical procedure because it is available and convenient to use. Far more serious is the situation in which the user selects an appropriate statistic, but is unaware of the underlying assumptions about the data made by that statistic. For instance, the number of variables we may include in a multivariate analysis is limited by the size of our sample. If the ratio of sample size to variables gets too low, the statistic can still be computed but the results are either questionable or meaningless. Violations of other assumptions or conditions produce similar weaknesses. A third blunder stems from the opportunity MSA provides to substantially increase the number of analyses we perform. The statistician discusses his results in terms of probability because he knows the possibility always exists that his results are due to chance. When we increase substantially the number of times we compute some statistic on a given set of data, we increase, as well, the likelihood that we will obtain some results that are due to chance. Suppose we had fifty measurements on each member of a sample and

[8]T. Sterling and S. Pollack, *MEDCOMP. Handbook of Computer Applications in Biology and Medicine. Part I. Statistical Systems*, University of Cincinnati, Cincinnati, 1964; and L. C. Hayward (ed.), *BIMD Computer Programs Manual*, University of California, Los Angeles, 1961.

[9]Arthur S. Couch, *The Data-Text System: A Computer Language for Social Science Research*, Harvard, Cambridge, Mass., 1966.

[10]Kenneth J. Jones, *The Multivariate Statistical Analyzer*, Harvard, Cambridge, Mass., 1964.

were interested in computing all the 1,225 different intercorrelations among these variables—a task no one would attempt without a computer. We would need to be careful not to be overly impressed if, say, twenty of these correlations were statistically "significant" because, depending on the level of accuracy we select, a substantial number of apparently significant correlations may be the result of chance variations in data.

These are just a few of the misuses of statistical procedures permitted—perhaps even encouraged—by the typical stat package. Certainly Jones and other authors of such computer programs are not to be blamed for such misuse and yet uncritical, sloppy use of statistical procedures abounds, and some of this abundance is due to our access to systems such as the MSA. Perhaps the approach of Albert Beaton is the solution.

Beaton's approach rests at the other extreme from that of Jones in terms of its concern for accessibility. Beaton[11] derived six procedures—he calls them "special matrix operators"—which, depending upon how they are combined, perform any statistical technique which "assumes a linear model." These are the commonly used statistics including the multivariate procedures. He then composed, for each of these special matrix operators, a computer subroutine subprogram. A subroutine subprogram is not a complete computer program. It is a self-contained unit which can be called on by a computer program, and thus one can make use of these operators without having to program them himself. But he must write the computer program that "calls" these subroutines. Such a program must also read in the data, print the results, and perform all the other housekeeping that is usually necessary. And, of course, the user must decide the order in which the subroutines must be called. Beaton's system is, like that of Jones, an outstanding accomplishment, particularly since at the base of this computer system is a clean and elegant theoretical structure. But the two burdens Beaton places on the user are not easy to assess. First, of course, the user either must be able to program computers himself or he must have an agent who will do this for him. While this is not unreasonable since the brand of computer programming required is not at all difficult to learn, still there is nothing in the *logic* of using a computer that requires one to be a programmer any more than pumping foot pedals on a player piano requires the knowledge or even the vaguest notion of how piano rolls are made. Coupled with this first burden is the need for the user to know which operators he must use and in which sequence in order to perform the desired statistical procedure; the user must master Beaton's "statistical calculus," and, for most of us, this requires a reeducation. Now, learning enough statistics to properly use Beaton's system is not a bad thing since the more statistical

[11]See, for example, Albert Beaton, *The Use of Statistical Matrix Operators in Statistical Calculus*, Research Bulletin RB-64-51, Princeton, N. J., Educational Testing Service, 1964.

theory we know, the less likely it is that we will improperly use statistical techniques. But, of course, once we have such knowledge we are in a position, as well, to properly use Jones's system. Thus we best resolve the issue of misuse of stat packages by asserting the obvious: if the user is familiar with the procedures he employs, then the chances of misuse are lessened. Thus the discarding of the old ways is best accomplished by mastery of the new ways.

New Successes

The second danger we guard against when we take seriously the need to reexamine and, where necessary, reformulate the educational procedures we wish to automate is very similar to the first danger. This second danger is that, because we achieve noticeable gains, we will come to believe our efforts at automation are worthwhile and in the right direction. We become satisfied, thereby, and run the risk of ignoring the possibilities of reassessing a more basic aspect of the procedure we automate. As with the first danger, we face the prospect of uncritically legitimizing current practice, perpetuating what may be its most indefensible features. To see something of this danger, we will look at some efforts to use the computer in schools as a problem solving tool. Increasingly the computer is joining the chemistry laboratory, the reference library, and the machine shop as a student facility for working out solutions to problems. In this role, the computer comes to be used in schools the way it primarily is used everywhere—as a calculator and data processor. Of all the ways the computer might assist in the instruction process, its use as a problem solving device is the most widespread and, to date, there have been three principal aspects to this use of the computer.

Writing Programs

The first of these aspects consists in having students use a computer facility to write their own computer programs. In its simplest form a student will be given a problem in, say, mathematics; he will figure out not the answer to the problem, but an algorithm for solving it; then he will write a computer program to execute this algorithm; finally he will run the program on the computer and end up with either a working procedure to deal with the problem or a sense of what is wrong with his program or algorithm and how they might be altered to produce the desired results. Naturally, things get more complicated than this and neither the student's use of the computer nor the instructional process surrounding that use can be so neatly summed up. Yet, this chronology points up the basic character of that aspect of computer-based problem solving that involves students writing their own programs.

Usually students write these computer programs in a FORTRAN-like language, that is, a language particularly designed for numerical calculation, although in some places students use COBOL, the business-oriented compiler, and in other places an assembly language is used. Most often, however, the language students use to write these programs is BASIC. BASIC—developed at Dartmouth College under the direction of John Kemeny and Thomas Kurtz—is a fairly powerful language which, nonetheless, is very easy to learn. This fact is important because, being easy to learn—rarely does it take a student more than a day or two to begin to program—BASIC does not get in the way of the student's problem-orientation. That is students do not become so focused on difficulties of using the language that they forget their problem.[12] It is not the intent to make the student a computer programmer.

Two outstanding examples of efforts to use the computer in this aspect of problem solving are the "Dartmouth Secondary School Project" and "Project LOCAL."[13] These two projects, both of which started in 1967, are similar to each other in many respects. One interesting way in which these two projects are similar is that they both operate in a time-sharing mode.[14] That is, students communicate with the computer by way of teletypewriter terminals, writing programs in the "interactive" mode. There are many advantages to this, of course, including the fact that students can compose their programs "on-line" and then execute them immediately to find out whether or not they work and, if not, make corrections and run again. Indeed, for certain errors—errors of syntax mostly—the student does not have to wait even until his program is fully written. As he enters each statement of the program, the computer looks it over to see if it is a "legal" statement, and informs the student when an error has been made.

The alternative to on-line programming is "batch" processing of student programs, and batch processing takes a lot more time: the student writes his program down using pencil and paper; then he punches his program onto data processing cards and carries the deck of cards to the computer center where it becomes part of a batch of programs to be run; finally he returns, some time later, to pick up the output to see how the program ran. There are variants of the batch process, but, usually, batching takes more time. Yet it is not clear that the additional time matters. There is no evidence that indicates it is *educationally* more beneficial to write programs at a terminal than it is to write them at a desk. It is more convenient, of course, to program at a terminal, but the price for

[12]For a description of the BASIC language see, for example, John G. Kemeny and Thomas E. Kurtz, *Basic Programming*, Wiley, New York, 1967; or William F. Sharpe, *BASIC. An Introduction to Computer Programming Using the BASIC Language*, Free Press, New York, 1967.

[13]For a general description of these and other "problem-solving" projects, see Dudley L. Post (ed.), *The Use of Computers in Secondary School Mathematics*, Newburyport, Mass., ENTELEK, 1970.

[14]Actually LOCAL operates mostly in multi-access mode, but this distinction is not important at this point.

this luxury is that fewer students get to use the computer. The number of students that can be programming at terminals at the same time depends, obviously, on the number of terminals located at a school. Typically, this ranges from two to eight terminals per system. In the batch programming mode there is no such limit, although of course, when there are many people wanting to run programs, the delay—the "turn-around" time—may be as much as twenty-four hours.

Now, in the Dartmouth project the participating schools—"dispersed across the five New England states"[15]—all use a *central* computer located at the Dartmouth College Computing Center. For them the terminal is the only reasonable means with which to enter programs into the computer. They do not have a choice to make in the "on-line" versus "batch" issue. But each of the Project LOCAL schools has its own computer on its premises. Strictly from the simple description of problem solving given so far, it seems that LOCAL's decision to use a terminal-based system was made at the expense of those students who, as a result, would be unable to gain easy access to the computer. Given that fewer students can use the LOCAL system as it stands than could otherwise, this conclusion is correct. But the situation is complicated by the fact that there are some substantive benefits that a student gets from a terminal-based system.

Prominent among these benefits is the opportunity to write what we may call "dynamic programs"—programs designed not to solve a particular problem or even a class of problems, but instead to demonstrate some phenomenon or concept by behaving differently under varying inputs.[16] Imagine, for instance a dice-throwing program. It might function by selecting a number at random from 1 to 6 and then selecting another one the same way. This would constitute a "throw" of the dice. Suppose, now, that the program for each throw keeps track of the resulting number, and assume that the output of the program is a count of how many times each number comes up. To run the program we must tell it each time how many throws to make. Unlike the other problem solving programs a student might write, the value of the dynamic program stems only partially from the experience in writing it and mostly from the experience in *using* it once it is written. By using such a program over and over again, each time varying the number of throws it is to make, a student can begin to explore the idea of probabilities and how they distribute in the dice-throwing problem. Other examples of dynamic programs—for coin tossing, curve plotting, sampling, and the like—come easily to mind, and, while it would not be unthinkable to run dynamic programs in batch mode, surely it is clear that running these programs from a terminal is an advantage. Using such reasoning, Project LOCAL has concluded, as have other school districts involved in computer-based problem solving, that a terminal-based system is preferable.

[15]Post, op. cit., p. 181.
[16]Some people call such programs "simulations" or "analytic models" but these terms seem pretentious.

A second way the Dartmouth project and Project LOCAL are similar —and representative of other such efforts—is that, in both of them, use of the computer is confined pretty much to problem solving in mathematics and science. This restriction was reasonable when these projects were getting started since, certainly, the uses of computer-based problem solving in mathematics and science are easy enough to visualize. Besides, the backgrounds of the teachers of these subjects made it more likely that they would be able to handle the technical aspects of computer use, and thus be better able to integrate the computer into their curricula. But time has passed since the beginnings of these projects, and no longer is it reasonable to exclude the other disciplines.

Both projects have done some work in other disciplines, actually, but their efforts have been minimal and largely disappointing. One Dartmouth project participant refers to project work in the humanities and social sciences as "sporadic," although he points up some of the potential when he speaks of the possibilities for "sophisticated simulations."[17] Project LOCAL has given this issue some attention also, asserting that "another important goal of LOCAL is to improve students' understanding of the social implications of the computer."[18] What they mean by this, of course, is to have social studies students discuss things such as, "the relationship between individual privacy and the evaluation of large, nation-wide computerized data banks," or the ways computers will create new jobs, or how the computer will free individuals "to live more creatively through automation."[19] These are all important topics, but they involve talk about the *effects* of computers, they do not involve using the computer.

Surely it is possible to think of legitimate applications of computer-based problem solving in areas other than mathematics, chemistry, physics, and such. It should be just as reasonable for a student in English or social studies or history to be writing computer programs, as it is for anyone else. In social studies, for instance, it seems appropriate to have students begin to explore such things as computational procedures for predicting election outcomes. The point of such an exploration would be not to make social studies "scientific" or to make the student technically oriented to political problems. It would be, rather, to give the student a different perspective on the study of one part of the political process. For example, a student project to write some computer programs to process election data would require a careful look at such notions as voter-type, regional voting patterns, issue-clusters; and cross-pressure patterns.[20] These terms and the notions they denote do not come from the computer

[17]Post, op. cit., p. 187.
[18]Robert Haven, "Some Results to Date: Project LOCAL," in Post (ed.), op. cit., p. 221.
[19]Ibid.
[20]Such variables and their roles in election simulation are discussed in Ithiel deSola Pool, Robert P. Abelson, and Samuel L. Popkin, *Candidates, Issues, and Strategies, A Computer Simulation of the 1960 Presidential Election*, M.I.T., Cambridge, Mass., 1964.

scientist, they come from the political scientist. Similarly, it seems quite reasonable that English students should explore, on the computer, some of the simple algorithms for language data processing, and some of their applications to literary studies.

This brand of problem solving—wherein students write and run their own computer programs—promises to affect the instructional process to an even greater extent than has been realized thus far. Moreover the advent of the small and the mini computers has changed the economics of using computers to such a degree that we can expect the availability of computers in schools to increase sharply. Doubtless, there will be a corresponding increase in the use, not only of the type of computer-based problem solving we have considered so far, but as well of the other aspects of problem solving.

Using Programs

One such "other" aspect of computer-based problem solving resembles the one we have just looked at, except in that it does not entail student programming. Central to this second dimension of the computer as a student facility for working out solutions to problems is the idea of the "canned" program. Instead of writing a program, the student executes a computer program already written. One kind of canned program we have already considered and called a "dynamic program." From that consideration we have seen how a canned program can be used to demonstrate some phenomenon such as a probability distribution. Another example of the use of this sort of program is given by Oettinger who describes a graph plotter that accepts an equation as input and provides as output a graphical representation of that equation. Such a program serves to help the student to "cross Descartes' bridge from algebra to geometry."[21] Such examples of dynamic programs offer what Oettinger calls the glint of promise of computers as instruments to aid student understanding.

Even if the use of canned programs in schools was confined to helping students to gain insights into such concepts and phenomena, there would be little argument against their value. But there is another, growing use for canned programs in schools, one which involves a somewhat different kind of problem solving. Designed neither to teach students about algorithms nor to provide insights into various phenomena, the principal function of this type of canned program is to have the student engage in some particular decision-making process.

One such program is BALPAY, developed by John Williamson as part of a Northwest Regional Educational Laboratory project called Program

[21]Anthony Oettinger, with Sema Marks, *Run, Computer, Run: The Mythology of Educational Innovation*, Harvard University Press, Cambridge, Mass., 1969, p. 203.

REACT.[22] The acronym stands for BALance of PAYments, and the program is, in Williamson's words, "a decision-making game."

> The user plays the role of decision maker for the country. He finds that his country is currently in a very poor balance of payments position: either an unhealthy surplus or a serious deficit position. The objective of the game is for the user to make decisions that will give the country a healthy balance of payments position within a specified number of years.[23]

In using the program, the student decides how much to change such things as taxes on investments abroad, tariff rate, and the prime interest rate. He then discovers how well his decisions have corrected the situation. Based on this result, and new information he may be fed, "there has been a revolution in Peru and restrictions on your imports have been imposed," the student makes another set of decisions, and so on, for some specified number of years.

Similar programs for decision making, often called games, have been developed elsewhere. For example, the Board of Cooperative Educational Services in New York has produced such programs as the Sumerian Game, "designed to teach sixth graders some basic principles of economics" and the Sierra Leone Development Project, "to simulate the economic problems of a newly emerging nation."[24]

Another variant of the canned program is the use of programs *by the teacher* for classroom demonstrations. Haven describes this use by explaining that

> . . . it is often difficult in math instruction to promote a good understanding of the concepts of series convergence or divergence and approaching a limit. However, if a computer terminal is available in the classroom, the teacher can create a simple program which will place in easily understood terms, the operation of the principles involved.[25]

When Oettinger speaks of this use of canned programs he uses the phrase "animated blackboard," suggesting clearly the extent to which this application alone has the potential to affect the instructional process.[26] Add to this all the other dimensions of computer-based problem solving that we have considered up to now and the potential role of the computer in instruction appears to be a considerable one, and, if we apply the usual

[22]See Program REACT, *Social Studies: Application Units*, Teacher Training Course, Computer Utility for Education, SOC S/300, Northwest Regional Educational Laboratory, undated.
[23]Ibid.
[24]Richard L. Wing, "Two Computer-based Economic Games for Sixth Graders," in Sarane S. Boocock and E. O. Schild (eds.), *Simulation Games in Learning*, Sage Publications, Beverly Hills, Calif., 1968, pp. 156–157. See also, Sema Marks Rosenbaum, *Computer Simulation for High School Students*, New York, Westinghouse Learning Corporation, 1970.
[25]Haven, op. cit., p. 219.
[26]Oettinger, op. cit., p. 214.

logic, an indispensible one. Yet with all the power and sophistication and promise represented by these problem solving uses of computers, none of them approaches in significance the third aspect of computer-based problem solving.

Breaking an Unfortunate Distinction

How this third approach is special and different from the first two is central to our understanding of the danger we face of having our successes with computers convince us that we do well. Even though these be legitimate, worthwhile successes, they may still build a shield against the reexamination and change of educational practice.

This third approach to computer-based problem solving, unlike the other two, is characterized by the notion that you should not be able to tell the difference between a student's work in a discipline and his work on the computer: in mathematics, for example, the act of programming problem solutions on a computer should constitute *doing* mathematics. Neither does the student learn a concept in the classroom and then go to the computer to apply it, as is typically the case with our first brand of problem solving, nor does he gain insight into some phenomenon from a canned program and then go to the classroom to discuss it. The computer is the classroom—or, more properly, the laboratory—where the student engages in "an experimental approach toward solving problems.[27]

One effort that can be said to entail this dimension of computer-based problem solving is called the LOGO Project. Indeed, it is this effort that brings this dimension to light and, in so doing, offers us a glimpse at the true potential of the computer in education. The LOGO Project involves "research and teaching directed toward the development of a new mathematics curriculum whose presentation depends *fundamentally* on the use of computers and programming."[28] Besides fully integrating the computer and the instructional process, this orientation makes the computer a principal component in the effort to rethink and reformulate that instructional process.

An hypothesis of the LOGO project is that a computer programming language can serve as a language with which to talk about mathematics education in several ways.[29] Some of these contributions offered by "a suitable programming language" are the encouragement of rigorous thinking, the provision of insight into such notions as "variable" and "function," and the fostering of "self-consciousness and literacy about

[27]W. Feurzeig, S. Papert, M. Bloom, R. Grant, and C. Solomon, *Programming-Languages as a Conceptual Framework for Teaching Mathematics*, Bolt, Beranek, & Newman, Cambridge, Mass., Report, No. 2165, vols. 1, 2, 3, p. 10.

[28]Ibid., p. 1.

[29]Ibid., p. 7. Copies of this report on the first phase of the LOGO project, which is required reading for anyone who seeks an understanding of the computer's role in instruction, can be obtained through the ERIC system.

the *process of solving problems.*" With such ends in mind the project began to plan for the task of teaching programming to students but in such a way that far from being just an ancillary topic of the curriculum it became "the foundation for an integrated course in mathematics."

Naturally, the first problem to be faced was that of deciding which computer programming language to use. Many exist, of course, and it is not an easy thing to distinguish among them in terms of their suitability as problem solving languages. To assist them in considering the suitability of the various languages that might be used, the LOGO project directors composed a statement specifying the characteristics that a language must have to be appropriate. These characteristics are:

1. It should be accessible to young children and others who have not acquired the elements of mathematical thinking. The only prerequisites for using it should be an acquaintance with the counting numbers and the ability to read at about *second-grade* level.

2. It should be transparently direct, natural-seeming, and easy to use for expressing procedures for simple tasks like many non-numerical problems already familiar to children.

These two requirements alone are sufficient to rule out every programming language under consideration as being too technical and as assuming too much mathematics background on the part of the user. Yet there were still two other requirements that the desired language would have to meet.

3. It should be organized to facilitate the extension and generalization of simple mathematical algorithms to more advanced and powerful ones.

And finally,

4. The structure of the language should embody mathematically important concepts and foster the development of a constructive point of view about mathematical work.[30]

It did not take Seymour Papert, Daniel Bobrow, Wallace Feurzeig, and the other LOGO Project staff members long to realize they would have to create their own programming language if these four requirements were to be met. They call it LOGO and with this new programming language they were able to begin their exploration of means for using LOGO "as the foundation and framework for a mathematics curriculum."

[30]Ibid., pp. 13–14. These criteria and the results of the various LOGO development efforts are described in *Programming-Languages as Conceptual Framework for Teaching Mathematics*, Report no. 2165, vols. 1, 2, 3, Bolt, Beranek & Newman, Inc., Cambridge, Mass., June 1971.

Thus far, in its work with average elementary school and junior high school students, the LOGO Project has been able to teach mathematics *by teaching LOGO.* Probably it is more accurate to say that these students learn mathematical "things" by building LOGO "things." This stems, in part, from the fact that such mathematical concepts as function, equation, variable, formula, and the like have "*conceptually* very clear analogs in LOGO." To do one is to do the other. In this way, the LOGO project has begun to turn the computer into a mathematics laboratory, and to develop sets of mathematical "experiments" which allow the student to "set in motion a sequence of mathematical events or a mathematical process, and then [to] see its effects unfold.[31]

As we compare the other two approaches to computer-based problem solving with this third approach, we see how one-dimensional they are. Indeed, these other applications seem to become excellent examples of how computers can be used, unwittingly, to legitimize present practice. They are legitimizing forces, not because these first two approaches are uncreative or trivial, for certainly they are not, but because they are not *fundamentally* different in orientation from what is already going on in schools. In clever, imaginative, and interesting ways these uses of the computer assist in the instructional process, but they do just about nothing to encourage anyone to reexamine and reformulate any of the basic tenets of this process. On the contrary, they tend to make us proud and satisfied with what we are doing. They tend to convince us that the promise of the computer in education is simple. The LOGO project begins to reveal how this promise is complex.

[31]Ibid., p. 11. See also Seymour Papert and Cynthia Solomon, "Twenty Things to Do with a Computer," M.I.T., Cambridge, Mass., June 1971, mimeo; and Seymour Papert, "On Making a Theorem for a Child," *Proceedings of the ACM Annual Conference,* August 1972.

CHAPTER FIVE: participating in automation

The advent of the computer has led to the creation of many new jobs and job titles. As early as 1965 the *Computer Dictionary and Handbook* could list forty-five such new jobs ranging in importance from work processing scheduler, lead systems analyst, and senior programmer, to data examination clerk, data converting operator, and tabulating record control-trainee.[1] These job titles mean little to the layman, although they confirm his suspicions that the world of computers has innumerable mysterious facets, each one requiring its own highly trained specialist. When we add to this the bits of computer jargon that make their way to us from time to time—such terms as "contingency interrupt," "real-time control system," "relative addressing" and "scratchpad memory"—no doubts remain concerning the endless complexities associated with the use of computers. Clearly computers are not for amateurs.

Still we must be careful with such a distinction between expert and amateur because the matter is not so simple. Certainly if we believe, as common sense supposes, that using a computer in education means developing involved mathematical formulae, or generating webs of flow charts, system design specifications, and program parameters, constraints and operating instructions, then without question the educator would be the amateur. Even the current brand of educational technologist would be on shaky ground, being able to converse with the expert, perhaps, but

[1]Charles J. Sippl, *Computer Dictionary and Handbook*, Sams, Indianapolis, 1966, p. 448.

being no expert himself. But if we believe, as this book proposes, that the most important way to conceive of the computer is in terms of the procedures it executes then the tables are turned. Down the end of the logical road which begins with the definition of a computer as an incomplete machine is the notion that if computers are to be used fruitfully in education then the educator must be an active participant in this use. That is, because automation in education means thinking and rethinking educational practice there can be no expert in this endeavor other than the educator. Everyone else is the amateur.

But surely there is too much to learn to expect the schoolman to carry alone the burden of automation in education. Even if he knew the details of computing, no teacher, administrator, or guidance counselor could find the time to properly take on this extra task. Thus it is not unreasonable that a new job within education—the educational technologist—should have emerged to provide a bridge between the technical expert and the education expert. In practice, however, this has amounted to the turning over of the crucial issues of education to a single group, and as prior chapters have suggested, the educational technologist is not especially disposed to rigorous thought about the educational process.

While the need for the educator to participate directly in the process of automation in education is an easily drawn logical implication which flows from our definition of a computer, the participation itself is not easily accomplished. To see something of how difficult it is we will look in this chapter at an experimental project whose goal was to foster the active participation of schoolmen in the automation of educational practice. This project, which lasted eight years, confined its attempts to achieve this goal to the automation of administrative practice. The failures and successes it experienced, and the lessons it learned, however, are generally applicable and not restricted to this area of computer application.

This project, called the New England Education Data Systems—NEEDS for short—had the ostensible goal of using computers to help teachers and school administrators perform the clerical tasks associated with running a school. Compiling school statistics, scheduling classes and assigning students, producing report cards, scoring and norming tests, creating and updating pupil cumulative records, and maintaining teacher personnel files are just a few of these distracting tasks.

Applying computers to this aspect of the education enterprise is usually called *educational data processing* and abbreviated EDP. Now EDP with its concentration on the mundane educational chores, and its lack of any direct concern with educating children cannot be considered one of the glamorous applications of computers to education. Yet for many educators, EDP has become a crucial element in their professional lives. Indeed, on the day the project ended, NEEDS listed seventy-seven

New England school systems among its membership. These systems—ranging from Mexico, Maine to Darien, Connecticut—looked to NEEDS for a substantial variety of data processing services including scheduling of their 106 secondary schools and producing grade reports for the more than 120,000 students who attend these schools. And, NEEDS was not the only project engaged in educational data processing. Other centers, mostly commercial, in such diverse locations as Palo Alto, Houston, Chicago, St. Louis, Memphis, and Montreal have been doing EDP for some time. Because it was the first regional data processing facility in the country, NEEDS had served as a model for some of these other centers, and thus had participated both directly and indirectly in the development of what has become a commonplace application of computers in education.

That someday EDP should become commonplace was just what the founders of NEEDS hoped for. Instead of guarding its developments and keeping them proprietary, therefore, NEEDS placed all its products in the public domain, encouraging their use or adaptation and fostering—often creating—competition for itself. Behind its continued efforts to get EDP as an idea to prosper was a seeming dedication to "go out of business"—not by failing, of course, but by succeeding and thereby becoming superfluous. In pursuit of this goal, ironically, NEEDS became the largest, best known regional EDP center, possessing the latest in computer hardware and software sophistication along with a staff as large as that of some of the schools it serviced. The choice that eventually would face NEEDS, therefore, was either to continue maintaining this large organization or to turn to new things and leave the job of carrying on to other groups.

In the story of how NEEDS was conceived and of how it developed, grew, and eventually came to be faced with this choice, much can be seen of the problems, issues, and frustrations associated with any attempt to get the educator's direct participation in the process of automation.

The Beginnings of the Experiment

In late winter, 1961, two men visited the Orange, Massachusetts, regional high school to help evaluate the school's use of simple unit record equipment to perform certain clerical tasks. Using such equipment—keypunches, sorters, collators, accounting machines, and the like—was not new in education. By this time many school systems, some as far away as Palo Alto, California, and Jackson, Michigan, others as close as Boston, Newton, Worcester, and Danvers, Massachusetts, had already installed their own punched card machines. Other enterprising systems had made independent arrangements with local insurance companies, supermarkets, banks, or other businesses to "borrow" their machines on off hours for school data processing. Orange was obtaining its use of data processing equipment through a project sponsored by the Ford Foundation called Industry Aids to Education, and the purpose of the two-man visit was to consult with the school personnel on their use of this equipment. No one knew then, and few people remember today, that as a result of their visit these two consultants would formulate the bases for a school data processing cooperative that would grow to become the New England Education Data Systems.

Neither of these men was a stranger to the use of machines in education, of course, and to some extent their respective backgrounds and experiences prefigured their eventual collaboration to move educational data processing out of the realm of the rudimentary unit record machines and into the world of computers. Donald P. Mitchell, for instance, who at that time was starting his second year as the Executive Secretary of the New England School Development Council (NESDEC), a regional school study council with 160 member schools, had already organized three major NESDEC conferences to acquaint school administrators with the potential applications of data processing machines to administrative problems. Mitchell's interest centered on the school schedule which he recognized as the primary expression of a school's instructional policy. As a high school principal he had to build master schedules, and he knew all the problems and the compromises involved when they must be done by hand. He knew, as well, that this task of creating the schedule of classes under which a school operates takes one quarter of a principal's time and costs the system three months of his pay. Later, as a Harvard University lecturer in educational administration, Mitchell had considered with his students the extent to which the constraints imposed by the mechanics of scheduling a school became *educational* constraints on the ways teachers could function. Finally, as Director of Kargman, Mitchell, and Sargent, Incorporated, educational consultants, he had worked directly with many schoolmen to help them solve these and other related administrative problems. It was quite natural, therefore, that Mitchell should have been one of the first educational administrators to become interested in using computers to process school data and that now, as the chief administrator of NESDEC, he should encourage its members to begin to explore a role for computers in their schools.

Bolstering Mitchell in his belief that computers could indeed play a role in education was his companion on the trip to Orange, David V. Tiedeman, then professor of education at Harvard University, who had been teaching a graduate course in "Machine Procedures in Educational Measurement and Research" as early as 1946. About ten years later, with computers becoming increasingly available to university researchers, Tiedeman had worked extensively with computer programs to figure various statistics, especially those to compute and test the applicability of multivariate procedures to educational problems. Still another ten years later, in 1966, Tiedeman was to remain in the front of computer applications to education by participating in an extensive four-year project to develop a computer-based information system for career guidance. But at the time of his visit to Orange, Tiedeman's main concern with machine use in education was in the problem of "product." His experience as a user of other people's programs had taught him well that the results produced by computer programs are always credible, even when they are incorrect. The computational procedures may be wrong in a number of ways and yet rarely is it possible to notice this from the results. He was concerned, therefore, that schools using machines for data processing—especially computers—be certain that their computational procedures were appropriate and properly formulated and that the results were accurate. This feeling was extended by Tiedeman to include the idea that however mundane educational data processing tasks may be, schools depend upon them; they must be done correctly and on time, and the more glamorous applications of machines, while of obvious importance, must not intrude to the point that EDP becomes haphazard.

Mitchell's interest in extending the school's use of machines beyond mere record keeping, and Tiedeman's concern that such an extension avoid the pitfalls of poorly conceived or hastily executed plans were thus the two ingredients these men brought to the discussions that followed their visit to Orange. They were pleased, naturally, that machines, even of the rudimentary punched card variety, were beginning to play a role in the production of school reports and records, but equally they were disturbed that the schools were "going it alone." It seemed silly for schools not to make this step toward automation cooperatively. With independent, isolated work in this area the best to be hoped for was duplication of effort while, more likely, the result would be meager, untransferable developments. Automating the creation of a school schedule, for instance, would not be accomplished by schools alone, because as the most difficult computational problem in education, it would require extensive technical know-how and experience with computers. Whether or not this and similar administrative problems could be solved with computers was not certain; but clearly if a serious effort was to be made, it would entail some concentration of resources. Furthermore, such an effort would render, as a by-product, a set of well-tested and thus reliable procedures which schools could count on. To Tiedeman, therefore, a cooperative endeavor to automate certain educational procedures would be a significant step toward easing his concern for "product."

A First Brand of Participation

Based on the ideas developed by Mitchell and Tiedeman, NESDEC formally established early in 1961 a project in school data processing.

During its first two years the project remained small, concentrating on creating computer programs and testing them in the Newton and Weston public schools—the project's two member school districts. By the time the second year ended, the library of computer programs was becoming substantial and, through NESDEC's effort at disseminating information about its project, other school systems were beginning to express interest in joining the venture. It was at this point that the project began to seriously include participation and service among its concerns.

When seven more school systems became members of the project at the start of its third year, it was no longer possible to be casual about the provision of EDP services. The time had come to create a formal smoothly operating service division so that the schools' first experiences with computers would not be stained by the delays, the errors, and the misunderstandings that would plague an inefficient operation. If services were to be performed, they would be performed in earnest. This was the point toward which the project had been heading, of course, even from the time Mitchell and Tiedeman met to discuss its creation. They recognized that without the presence of a center to make EDP service available to schools, the incorporation of valuable computer techniques into school practice would undoubtedly follow the usual course, requiring somewhere between twelve and twenty years to show signs of any widespread use. But they realized also that they must be careful about this because service is a potentially dangerous commodity and any effort to establish a service center would have to keep these dangers in mind.

Why EDP services are potentially dangerous is suggested by I. A. Richards who states that most of us will see in computers the relief from those bothersome tasks that unnecessarily take up so much of our time, thus freeing us for the "tasks of ultimate choice."[2] But, he warns, we deceive ourselves in this because we run the risk of giving up the very thing we need if we are to deal properly with these tasks of ultimate choice. "Almost all of us," he asserts, "are products of the assistance we can accept. Equally, we are potential victims of those who, for whatever motives, would like to run things for us."[3]

Now, the statesmanship of educational data processing—to borrow another term from Richards—demanded that the NESDEC project start out by "running things" for schools. The mysteries that surrounded computers, the schoolman's lack of knowledge about them and their promise, even the economics involved, all made it clear that the project must take the initiative to provide EDP services to the schools. But however successful it became at it, this must not become the end the Project sought, but rather the first step toward becoming an effective force to encourage from *within* the schools the systematic development of

[2]In Bushnell, Allen and Mitter, op. cit., 1967, pp. xvii–xxvii.
[3]Ibid., p. xviii.

improved practice. Otherwise, the more it grew in its ability to serve the schools by automating various administrative and clerical procedures, the more it would tend unintentionally to legitimize these procedures. As unlikely as it may have been that schoolmen would reevaluate their procedures when they performed them manually, it would happen that applying computers to schools would tend to decrease—indeed all but remove—the likelihood that such procedures would come under scrutiny and reassessment. Thus, while data processing in education held the promise of encouraging schoolmen to come, increasingly, to reconsider and reevaluate the very procedures being automated, the fact was that the NESDEC project, were it not careful, would begin to bolster resistance to such reexamination.

Should the mere automation of present practice become an end in itself, the schoolmen would forfeit their equity because they never would come to fully grasp the role computers can play not in their schools but *in the way they think about their schools.* What they would receive amounts to outside help for which they must pay the price of ignorance and thus of continued dependence.[4] What Richards tells us in his essay, and what Mitchell realized as he set out to define the structure of service in the project is that "like all power sources, the computer is not going to lessen our responsibilities but to increase them."[5] Only when the schoolman shares this responsibility therefore will he no longer be dependent. To insure the responsibilities would be shared among the members, the project would have to be a cooperative, and a way would have to be found to give the schools both control of what happened and insight into the processes involved in applying computers to educational problems.

But if control and participation were to be the benefits of membership, the organization and the operating procedures of the project would have to be overhauled to insure these benefits. If things were left to chance, the natural course of events would turn the project into a service bureau and none of the goals would be reached. So, on July 1, 1963, the project was formally separated from NESDEC and completely reorganized; even its name, which had been the NESDEC-Newton Educational Data Processing Project, was changed to NEEDS. The related ideas of control and of participation were merged and the basic principle governing NEEDS's activities was school control through school participation.

At the most detailed, day-to-day level of school participation in NEEDS was the coordinator. One professional staff member from each of the school systems comprising the NEEDS membership was charged by his superintendent with the responsibility to oversee and coordinate data

[4]See Ellis, "Regional Data Processing for Schools," in Richard Wolf (ed.), *Uses and Values of the Computer in Education*, International Review of Education, vol. **XIV**, no. 2, 1968, pp. 226–232.
[5]Richards, op. cit.

processing for that system. Working with NEEDS personnel, the coordinator decided, usually with counsel from other members of his school system's staff, all matters of form, substance, and change relating to service. When, for example, a computer run produced a list of student schedule conflicts, the coordinator examined the "output" and determined what changes were to be made to accommodate these students. While he might work closely with NEEDS personnel it was he and not they who decided things. You might say, the coordinator was himself a NEEDS staff member, although he functioned more like an ambassador in his embassy who, while situated within the boundaries of a foreign country, is yet on his own soil.

School participation existed at other levels as well. Several superintendents of schools, for example, sat on the NEEDS Board of Directors and thus had a strong voice in determining policy. These superintendents shared this responsibility with university professors, commissioners of education, and other leaders of education in New England, all of whom comprised the directorate of NEEDS.

Between the detailed involvement of the school coordinator and the school's representation on the NEEDS Board of Directors, there existed another aspect of school participation in the form of the NEEDS coordinating committees. There were three such coordinating committees at NEEDS representing each of its major interests: schools, universities, and state departments of education. One function of the school coordinating committee—whose membership varied from principals and other administrators to guidance personnel and teachers—was to evaluate existing operations and to consider possibilities to enhance them. A second of its functions was to devise meaningful ways to extend computer applications to other areas of the school. The coordinating committee, thereby, linked the school's involvement at the policy level and at the level of day-to-day operations.

This extensive participation of school personnel was not the only way the goal of enhancing the schoolman's view of computers affected NEEDS's operations. Naturally, to participate wisely he must know what he is doing and to this end, NEEDS spent considerable effort in in-service training. Formal institutes for coordinators began with a comprehensive introduction to computers, covering such topics as the NEEDS operating system, use of unit-record equipment, computer programming, and the role of the computer in education. Such institutes, which were given regularly, were augmented by private consultation with individual coordinators where issues relevant to his school system were discussed.

NEEDS did not direct such educational activities at coordinators alone. Chief school officials, guidance personnel, principals and their assistants, central office staff, and teachers all have enrolled in specially formulated institutes conducted at NEEDS. For administrators the topics were more general, designed to give them an overall view of automation in education, while for guidance counselors and teachers the topics were directed toward their particular interests: automating cumulative records, test scoring and analysis, grade reporting, and the like.

These educational activities extended beyond NEEDS's premises to such institutions as Harvard University and Boston University where several NEEDS staff members held academic appointments. These individuals taught formal courses in education data processing and in educational research which were attended not only by university students, but by many NEEDS members as well. In this way, NEEDS provided instruction in a wide range of topics relating to the uses of computers in education, and, thus, went out of its way to keep no secrets and to conjure no mysteries.

These two features—the participation and the education of school personnel—established that NEEDS was not proprietary and therefore not self-perpetuating as are service bureaus. Of course, a service bureau may well serve the data processing needs of a school; but NEEDS, while accomplishing as much, made no effort to spare schools the troubles and the burdens of responsibility. The education of school personnel and their extensive participation were steps toward the point where schools would possess the know-how to begin to do the job themselves. Indeed, as it was, a school becoming a member of NEEDS was agreeing, in effect, to provide data processing services to itself.

The internal organization of the project was changed substantially when it became NEEDS in hopes of supporting this notion of school involvement. The operating structure was divided into four areas called data processing services, operations research and development, in-service training, and basic research and formal instruction. Through careful coordination of the efforts of these divisions, NEEDS intended not only to provide EDP services to member schools, but also to use such service as the context for the reexamination of educational procedures and practices.

The data processing services division of NEEDS supplied the ongoing services to schools and supervised all the related dissemination functions. In this division were the technicians who operated the machines, ran the computer programs and maintained close contact with the school coordinator. The operations research and development division, where all experimental work on future EDP programs was performed, supported this role by developing new systems which, when documented and tested, were turned over to the service division. Similarly the in-service training division supported the operation by teaching the school coordinators to utilize the facilities of NEEDS. It conducted the technical sessions and summer institutes to instruct schoolmen in the methods and techniques of EDP. Finally, the division for basic research and formal instruction was to develop a systematic program for educational research on problems confronting schools, with particular emphasis on the role computers might play in their solution.

With its philosophy of school participation, with a program of activities geared to protect the schoolman's equity in the venture, and with an operating structure designed to create within the context of service a mechanism to foster the meaningful growth of computer applications to education, NEEDS was indeed ready to pursue the goals Mitchell and Tiedeman had set for it two and a half years before. But who would pay for this? Surely the $25,000 grant from Harvard for its third year—plus the $15,000 granted by the Fund for the Advancement of Education to identify the major educational problems of NEEDS membership—would not go very far towards realizing such an organization. Even the membership charge for services—$300 a year plus $2.50 per pupil serviced—would not provide nearly enough funds to support service, instruction, development, and research. In order for membership fees to support the full organization, the ten school systems participating in NEEDS would have to be joined by ninety more. But before these additional systems could be accommodated, NEEDS would have to be functioning full strength. Thus the logic of the philosophy developed by NEEDS made it seem unlikely that it would ever achieve its goals.

The alternative of providing service on a piecemeal basis, treating members as customers and abandoning temporarily the idea of their participation might work to get the organization started, but it was still unthinkable: if ignorance and the consequent servitude of schoolmen are undesirable at all, they are so because they cannot be tolerated even in the short run. The logic of participation as a device against the evils of service and for the encouragement of new thought about old procedures dictated that service at NEEDS must go hand in hand with other things and must never be allowed to stand alone as the organization's sole product. NEEDS, then, would have to function from the start as though it were fully developed. It would have to go directly, somehow, from what it was to become a self-supporting regional center for educational data processing, skipping the stages and years of growth in between. For this a source of major financial support would have to be found.

The Experiment Grows

On January 3, 1964, the Winchester *Star*, a Massachusetts weekly newspaper, printed the following news item:[6]

> WINCHESTER SCHOOLS BENEFACTOR OF
> FORD FOUNDATION GRANT
>
> As one of the ten participating schools in the New England Education Data Systems project, the Winchester school system will be a participant and benefactor of the $490,000 grant just made by the Ford Foundation to the NEEDS program.

[6]Quoted by permission.

Announcement of the three-year grant was made in Boston and New York at the end of last week. This is one of the largest grants ever to be given for a cooperative educational purpose for the New England region, and in announcing the grant, Edward J. Meade, Jr., program associate of the Education Division of Ford Foundation, said of the project, "Such a demonstration presents a model of regional cooperation in education that might be duplicable in many regions of the nation. Perhaps most important, the project establishes ways for more and better information to be derived and analyzed more effectively without a waste of manpower, as is the case presently, thus enabling educators to plan better and to develop improvements in instructional and educational opportunities in schools."

Winchester has been a participant in the three-year old New England Education Data Systems program since last June. At present its association in this is with the Harvard Graduate School of Education, the founding Newton school system, and the systems in Arlington, Manchester, Stoughton, Westford, Weston, Branford, Connecticut, and Middletown, Rhode Island.

According to Norton E. Demsey, Jr., director of guidance and coordinator of data processing in the schools, local use of the N.E.E.D.S. project will benefit from the Ford grant in that the grant will bring expansion of the program, advancement of computer techniques (N.E.E.D.S. expects to acquire its own 1401 computer) and further opportunity for research use of automation in assessment and improvement of the program here.

"The gift from the Ford Foundation will not mean a cut in the Winchester share of the cost of the program," said Mr. Demsey. "The roughly $2.50 a year for each student for the scheduling, marking records and attendance will, however, in all likelihood, not have to be raised," he said, "and the money will allow the development of a more localized system so that eventually we may be able to do much more of our work right here in town."

The official announcement about the grant goes on to say:

"The NEEDS Project began three years ago on a modest basis with the goal of utilizing computer hardware and developing "software" (computer programs) to advance the technology of scheduling secondary schools. Through the cooperation of the Newton Public Schools, an initial grant of $10,000 from SUPRAD, and the technical background of the present Director of Research and Development, G. Ernest Anderson, coordinator of data processing in Newton, a level of sophistication has been achieved which permits the assigning of students to classes in a high school with 1,500 students and 200 courses in two minutes.

"The NEEDS computer programs for pupil assignment are now in actual use in systems as far away as California. The Project, now in its third year, has continued to receive the support of the Newton school system and two successive grants of $25,000 from SUPRAD.

"The administration of the NEEDS project stated the goal of the project to be an expansion of school system membership at 50 per cent each six months until it has over 100 systems by July, 1966. In addition the organization will plan to serve many requirements of state departments and colleges and universities in the region. It is expected that NEEDS will be self-supporting by 1967 at which time the total commitments in the region are expected to approximate 1 1/4 million dollars annually."

The problem facing NEEDS's development had been solved, and thanks to the Ford Foundation, it could now get on with the considerable business of bringing EDP to New England schools. The plans formulated during its early period could now be implemented, and with so many school systems wanting to join NEEDS, and the opportunity it now had to demonstrate the values of EDP, the task of becoming self-supporting by the 1966-67 academic year, would not be difficult. Having existed formally for just six months, NEEDS was a full-scale regional center.

NEEDS rented an IBM 1401 computer and made arrangements with the Harvard Computing Center to use one of its IBM 7094 computers. These were the two machines for which the NEEDS systems would be written. By the spring of 1964, NEEDS had moved to new quarters, installed its computer, staffed its four divisions, and begun to redefine and reshape its EDP operating systems. By the time the Ford grant was to end in 1966, the NEEDS membership was to grow from ten to fifty-two school systems, and EDP services were to be considerably expanded, even though no meaningful work was to be done outside the area of pupil personnel services.

During this period, services rendered by NEEDS to its members fell, for the most part, under five pupil personnel service systems: file creation and maintenance, scheduling support, mark reporting, attendance accounting, and test scoring and analysis. Most of the computer programs operating under these five service areas were developed during the first two years of the Ford Foundation grant, and all of them were "operational" by winter 1965. The scheduling support area alone had gone from five programs used to schedule Newton and Weston high schools in 1962, to some twenty-six tested and functioning computer routines. Such an increase in programs might lead us to assume a corresponding increase in the amount of service performed, but this assumption would be unjustified. The interesting lesson NEEDS was to learn during these "Ford years" is that having gone from an experimental mode of operation to one of service, additional programs were required just to get the same jobs done. Programs to check the input for errors, to sort and collate files for use by various routines, to create student identification numbers, to update records, and to check and verify computer output are merely a few of the programs needed to support ongoing EDP services. Such support programs are indispensable in a service operation, yet they do not enhance the service in the sense that they expand its scope or increase the options available. They serve to ensure accuracy and dependability and, clearly, no service operation can function without this surety. Yet we cannot point to them as evidence of the development of either new applications or new services. We may regard these support programs as necessary-evil software, and in so doing, make the distinction between front line and rear guard routines, but unfortunately, this distinction has nothing to do with the amount of effort required for software development. It takes time to properly produce a computer program whether it be to create a master schedule or merely to check new card files for illegal Hollerith punches.

When NEEDS learned this lesson it realized its development plans would have to be changed. Because NEEDS would have to scrupulously guard against each of the many errors that would otherwise plague its operation, it became clear that, for the time being at least, its development activity would need to be confined to the general area of pupil personnel services, thus allowing a full effort to be made in the production of the needed support programs. The other areas in which NEEDS originally planned to work—"computer-based programmed instruction, simulation studies, automated financial accounting systems, hardware design and specification, and computational aids to the teaching of mathematics"—would have to wait for another time. But even within this area of pupil personnel services, NEEDS's expectations about development were to change. Perhaps the most significant of these changes concerned the development of computer programs that would create the schools' master schedules. There would be no time, given other commitments, for NEEDS to produce such a "master schedule builder" and the best it could do was to make use of whatever automatic schedule builders it could find that had been developed elsewhere.

Fortunately, by the time NEEDS began to realize the extent to which its service orientation would dictate the form of its development activities in this area, two sophisticated automatic schedule builders had already been created: the Stanford School Scheduling System (S-4) and the Generalized Academic Simulation Programs (GASP). NEEDS had been aware of these two systems as they were developing, of course, but since it had harbored the notion of creating its own system NEEDS had given little thought to how these systems might be fitted into its operation. Now realizing that it must adopt at least one of these systems if it was to bring automatic schedule building to its members, NEEDS began a careful study of both S-4 and GASP. From this study, which included a comparison of the results of submitting the same school data through each system, NEEDS discerned a number of similarities and differences between them. Each system, given lists of class meeting times, teachers, and rooms, created a usable master schedule to which students could then be assigned. Each was expertly programmed so that technical inefficiencies were minimal, and each system would substantially increase the schoolman's ability to organize his school schedule in educationally meaningful ways. These two systems differed, however, in the audience to which they were directed, S-4 being developed specifically for use in secondary schools and GASP being originally created to do nothing more than build the schedule of final exams at M.I.T. Even so, it turned out that NEEDS was to find GASP the more appropriate system to recommend to its member schools.

To begin with, the creator of GASP, Robert Holz, and his two associates, Richard Willard and Robert Hewes, had their laboratory a little more than a mile away from NEEDS's Cambridge headquarters. A joint venture with these men would be more convenient than with Robert Oakford, Robert Bush, and Dwight Allen—the creators of S-4—3,000 miles away at Stanford University. Second, a couple of New England high schools—Wayland and Cohasset—had used GASP and, thereby, had some first-hand experience with which to counsel NEEDS in its exploration of this new area of EDP.[7]

A third reason NEEDS preferred GASP over S-4 was the practical one that since S-4 required what was then an unusual configuration of hardware NEEDS would have to do extensive reprogramming to get the system to work on the computer it had available. But, of course, it was the lack of development and programming time that led NEEDS to explore these other systems in the first place, so the fact that GASP could be used without major reworking was an important factor in its appeal. Finally, S-4 was designed to create a revolution in educational organization fostering the so-called "flexible-modular schedule," whereas the developers of GASP while building a system capable of creating such a schedule were just as happy to see their system used to generate a more "conventional" schedule. To NEEDS, this meant schools could move toward new ideas of classroom scheduling without either rushing into them or needing to accept a particular brand of innovation such as that being fostered by the Stanford group.

For all these reasons, then, NEEDS adopted GASP, and with the help and advice of Holz, Hewes, and Willard began to offer its membership a new service called, "Automatic School Scheduling." Related to the provision of this service was the need to complete the documentation of GASP. To ensure that the schoolmen participated in the use of GASP in their schools—instead of being just customers—NEEDS would have to prepare manuals and forms which would make clear the procedures involved. A second task, stemming from the wish to make GASP as compatible as possible with NEEDS's systems, was the conversion of GASP output to a form usable as input to the NEEDS student assignment program. That way once a schedule was built by GASP, the NEEDS systems and procedures could take over completing the service. Thus in January 1965 when it formally adopted GASP as a service to its members, NEEDS set out as well to accomplish these two tasks of documentation and integration.

A Second Brand of Participation

While NEEDS had come, at this point in time, to temporarily restrict the scope of its development activities, it did not become a docile organiza-

[7]This application of GASP was due to the staff at the Educational Facilities Laboratories—the foundation supporting its development—who first saw the possibilities of extending GASP to the secondary school level.

tion thereby. On the contrary, with GASP, with the extensive development of computer programs within the five areas of pupil personnel services, and with the formulation of procedures to handle the service demands of its membership—grown now to include thirty-two school systems—NEEDS was a busy, inchoate place in which only its plans for the future could compete, in ambition, with what it had become. And these were not the only things happening at NEEDS as it started the final year of the Ford Foundation grant. For instance, NEEDS continued its program of in-service training and, for a time, there was no better place in New England for the schoolman to go to learn about the various aspects of applying computers in education. Moreover as the number of people attending these sessions increased, and as NEEDS expanded the topics and themes considered, an interesting thing occurred: these training sessions became two-way streets, and NEEDS came to recognize in them opportunities not only to reveal the truths of automation but as well to learn of those problems facing schools that seemed to administrators, teachers, and guidance counselors to be the most pressing. If, through such communication with the practicing educator, NEEDS could discuss these problems, then it could begin to address them from the vantage point of its experience and know-how with automation. To this end NEEDS, in its training program, began to ask the participants to identify and talk about what they saw as the crucial issues.

Quickly, NEEDS discovered a pattern in the issues schoolmen identified to be crucial. Emerging as their principal concerns were questions such as, "Who are the underachievers in my school system?," "What is the relationship between teacher effectiveness and years of experience?," "What effects does the mobility of the pupil population have on the instructional program as reflected in, say, standardized test results?," and "What pre-school experiences best prepare a child for school experience, especially with regard to reading, and motivation to learning?" Such questions, NEEDS began to see, were troublesome not because they were unanswerable nor because the procedures for answering them were difficult to specify. It became clear that the trouble with such questions was that while schoolmen knew, in theory, how to deal with them, the data needed to answer them were virtually inaccessible.

Now by "virtually inaccessible" the participants did not mean that the appropriate data did not exist, but rather that the effort required to retrieve them or to rearrange them manually would be so great that, for all practical purposes, the data were best treated as nonexistent. For the most part, therefore, the questions schoolmen were pointing to as the central ones seemed to resolve to the single question, "How can we collect, store, and effectively analyze the large amounts of data relevant to our assessment of the education enterprise?" Seeking an acceptable answer to this question was to become the first task undertaken by the research division of NEEDS.

NEEDS's interest in addressing the problems associated with collecting, storing, and analyzing large quantities of educational data, while generated by the schools' demands, was further nurtured by the realization that both colleges of education and state departments of education were asking the same questions and were just as stymied as the schools by the virtual inaccessibility of data. Thus by tackling this problem NEEDS felt it would be considering as well the wider issue of what commonalities existed among schools, universities, and state departments of education. NEEDS hoped to take a step toward "fostering cooperation among them as each attempts to pursue one or another facet of the education of children."

Data Banks

Contributing further to NEEDS's interest in looking into this issue of data storage and analysis was a practical problem it had created for itself. While the product of NEEDS's activities was service, the by-product was data—when NEEDS printed student report cards, for instance, there was left behind on computer tape such data as course names and numbers, meeting times, rooms, teachers' names, students' grades, credits, previous credits, and attendance figures—and although it seemed a shame to throw them away, it was not clear how they should be used. But it was clear that in addressing the overall problem of data accessibility in education, NEEDS would be determining, also, what it should do with the data it was unwittingly creating by providing EDP services. For all these reasons, therefore, the research division of NEEDS established, in the summer 1964, the NEEDS-Harvard Data Bank Project.

The full name of this project was "Planning and Utilization of a Regional Data Bank for Educational Research Purposes," and the plan of the project was to convene a series of conferences of educators to elicit from them notions of what such a data bank should contain, what form it should take, and what kinds of analyses one should expect to make on the data.[8] The first of these conferences brought to NEEDS the outstanding educational researchers in the country. These men—educational psychologists, educational measurement specialists, educational sociologists, curriculum research specialists, data processing and computer experts, and researchers in the field of educational administration—spent three days at NEEDS during mid-winter 1964 focused on the issues underlying the creation and use of data banks. The eight most central questions among those considered were:

1. Is the concept of an educational data bank useful at all? Should educational data banks be established, or should efforts to develop them be abandoned?

[8]This project was supported by the Cooperative Research Program of the United States Office of Education (contract #OE-5-10-097), and a full account of its conduct and findings is contained in John B. Carroll and Allan B. Ellis, "Planning and Utilization of a Regional Data Bank for Educational Research Purposes," Harvard University, Cambridge, Mass., 1965.

2. Ideally, what should a data bank contain? Indeed, can any firm specifications be made for data banks in view of the fact that school conditions and the needs of educational researchers may change continually?

3. In what form should the data be organized? (The concern here was not with technical details of computer storage and data retrieval, since these details are generally specific to the particular software and hardware employed, but with the specifications for data organization.) What particular problems would be encountered in updating information in the data bank?

4. How should the data be collected? What problems may arise in coordinating diverse kinds of data from different school systems or in attempting to obtain at least a modicum of uniformity among school systems in the kinds of data collected and the formats in which they are obtained?

5. What types of research might be attempted by drawing upon the resources of educational data banks? What kinds of research would be especially facilitated by the availability of such resources? What kinds of research answers might be expected, and what would the utility of these answers be?

6. How can educators draw upon the data accumulated in data banks? What administrative arrangements might be involved in the use of data banks, particularly where data banks are also used for ongoing administrative procedures in school systems? How can possible conflicts of the interests of administrators and researchers be avoided?

7. To what extent can education data banks contain data truly representative of the total educational endeavor in their respective regions?

8. How can a data center foster increased communication among universities, state departments of education, and local school systems?

These same questions were examined from a different viewpoint the following spring when NEEDS held a second conference on educational data banks, this one among the New England State Commissioners of Education and their Associate Commissioners for research and statistics. Finally in July 1965, NEEDS convened a conference of school superintendents to examine these questions. Perhaps the most interesting aspect of these meetings was not the resulting set of recommendations concerning data banks but instead the fact that NEEDS, which only a few years before had managed to help schedule just one high school on an experimental basis, had become a meeting ground for the most prominent educators concerned in one way or another with the use of computers in education. Indeed, the idea Mitchell had had in 1961 that EDP could be not just an end in itself, but a means to consider the broader subject of educational change was beginning to prove itself, and the future of NEEDS could be seen to extend well beyond the mere provision of EDP services.

But the data bank conferences had a more immediate consequence as well, namely the establishment of the NEEDS Data Bank. Based on the recommendations of the conference participants and on a careful look at the data used in its services, NEEDS began to store on magnetic computer tape all its data files.

This data bank, it was expected, would grow in two ways. First, NEEDS would locate or create new files containing such things as school building data, data on innovative programs, compilations of student and teacher characteristics, and facts and figures relating to schools' financial activities. Second, NEEDS would enter into the files each year's new data resulting from its service activities, and, of course, as new services were established additional kinds of data would become part of the NEEDS Data Bank. In these two ways, then, there was built into the operation of the data bank, provision for its systematic expansion, and by the middle of 1966 NEEDS had accumulated 125 computer tape reels' worth of data.

The Metaphor Reconsidered

But as significant as it was to have accumulated 125 computer tape reels' worth of educational data, readily accessible and easily processed by computer, the establishment at NEEDS of a storehouse of data was not the most important product of the year-long Data Bank Study. Indeed, to some extent the creation of this storehouse was in opposition to a second and potentially more profound outgrowth of the study. This second product was a deeper understanding of what one ought to mean by the term data bank and a realization that the common sense notion of data banks completely missed the point of the metaphor upon which the term was based. It was a reconsideration of this metaphor that led NEEDS to its second concept of participation.

The metaphor in question, of course, is the one that likens data banks to money banks. The idea behind it was that money banks—savings banks, trust companies, and so forth—take your money and put it in a vault, and you can have access to the money whenever you like. Now, this idea is all right, and how it led to what NEEDS discovered to be the prevailing conception of a data bank as a storehouse of data is clear to see. But anyone who has ever borrowed the down payment on a car, or paid his telephone bill by check, or used his bank as a reference to get a charge plate at Macy's knows better than to consider a bank and a safe to be the same thing. The trouble with the metaphor then was that it was based on too simple minded a view of what banks do. NEEDS sensed this, and while it was clear that taking metaphors too seriously is always dangerous, NEEDS began to examine more carefully what a money bank is and how it might serve as a model for a data bank.

NEEDS discerned three central facts about banks. First the "contents" of a bank include more than money, and principal among the contents are the people who run the bank. Not the tellers or the typists or the guard at the front door; these people work at the bank, but they are not part of its contents. But the men who advise you how much to deposit in each of the different types of accounts, or who help you decide whether or not it is wise to borrow money, or who invest the bank's money—these men are part of the *resources* of the bank. Second, banks do not process money as much as they process commitment. That is, when two people exchange checks with each other, they are exchanging economic commitment, and they can do this because they accept the role of the bank as the processor of that commitment. Yet in all of this transaction, no one involved need ever see or touch any greenbacks. Obviously money is conceptually part of the process, but it is not money that is processed. The third thing NEEDS learned about banks is that the uptown branch of the East River Savings Bank can lend a customer $5,000 and write him a check for that amount even though they may not have the money in the branch office safe. More generally, it is a matter of no concern to us where the money is stored as long as we have access to it or its buying power when we want it. These three facts about banks caused NEEDS to change drastically its notion of the definition and function of educational data banks. NEEDS came to believe that "it takes more than data to make a data bank, and, in fact, data are the least of the determining factors."[9]

Educational data centers may be considered, for convenience, under three headings—archives, clearinghouses, and consortia. It is a mistake, however, to consider any of these centers data banks merely because they contain data, whatever the quantity.

For the most part, archives are storehouses of data generally associated with a large research project and designed to facilitate research in a particular area by maintaining comprehensive files. Often called "data bases," these archives—which function much like vaults, providing a place for safekeeping—can be thought of entirely in physical terms as places where one goes to obtain data on which to do analysis.

Clearinghouses have as their concern the accumulation of all material relevant to a given research domain and the establishment of mechanisms for disseminating such material. They differ from archives in that they are more gregarious; their main function is dissemination, to which storage is merely a means.

Of the three types of data centers, however, the consortium looks most like a data bank, both in organization and in operation. Although the consortium is concerned with research and dissemination to a large extent, its major role is to foster communication among individuals and their institutions in order to encourage joint research or coordinated research on problems in a given area. It is by incorporating functions of

[9]Allan B. Ellis, "Some Characteristics of Educational Data Banks," in Bushnell, Allen, and Mitter (eds.), op. cit., p. 109. The following account of data banks is excerpted from this source.

the two other forms of data centers, with top priority placed on enhancing interaction among individuals, that the consortium becomes the most complex type of data center, and most nearly a data bank.

In fact, a data bank is a consortium, with the important qualification that it not only incorporates the major functions of archives and clearinghouses, but redefines them. Merely taking on the tasks of storing data and disseminating information is not enough because these operations are essentially one-sided: in the first case, individuals contact the storehouse for data they may need in their research; in the second they periodically receive information which may be of interest to them. In neither instance is there ordinarily any substantial interchange among the parties involved. Within a data bank, however, effort is directed not toward storage but to access and not toward dissemination but to interaction. There is a shift away from the one-way roads of transmitting or receiving toward a two-way road of communication, and traffic should flow heavily in both directions. Where the data are stored—that is, whether or not they are stored in a single location—becomes operationally irrelevant, so long as one has access to them when the need arises and one's chances to be meaningfully informed are increased by greater communication with people working in related areas. The data bank becomes the organizational mechanism that creates and maintains the network of relationships necessary to ensure both access and communication. The data bank is an established environment of cooperation within whose confines are three ingredients: data, access, and communication—and whose major activity is to process the commitment of the individuals who fall within its bounds.

Expanded Notions

These concepts—data, access, and communication—while continuing to carry their usual connotations, take on special meanings within data banks. Data, for example, come to include people—or, more broadly, resources—to which those involved have access. This is a major source of the dynamic quality of educational data banks and is the reason why the concept of a data bank as a storehouse is so totally inadequate. In the case of acess, the added ingredient is a sort of faith. *It is a psychological state of assurance that a person's capability is generally enhanced by his involvement.* Not only does the individual feel confident that the data bank will work effectively, he is confident about the relationships themselves, since he feels he can incorporate into his own functioning the capabilities and talents of other members. A partnership, insofar as it differs from a corporation, comes closest to resembling this dimension of access. When a partnership fails, its creditors can reach into the personal funds of the partners—and what one cannot bear, the other must—to gain satisfaction. This kind of commitment justifies the expectation that when one partner speaks, he speaks for the others, and not merely for himself.

Each man integrates into his own functioning the commitment of the others. This is the kind of commitment that is fostered and "processed" by the data bank.

Finally, the idea of communication is expanded so that the parties involved play active rather than passive roles in the enterprise. Schools, for example, do not, as is often proposed, become the recipients of good research, or innovation, or such; rather, they actively participate at all levels in the generation of such activity. There are no poor relations in an educational data bank, and to the extent that education is enhanced, it is enhanced in concert. The educational data bank is the key element in the process of confrontation, discourse, and participation in which the major educational institutions engage.

To view an educational data bank, therefore, as merely a container of data is to miss the point. The currency is data, to be sure, but they are ineffective as media of exchange without the commitment and the communication such exchange implies. Thus the data bank becomes the organizing notion for the educator's deepest possible participation in the automation of educational practice.

This was a new concept of data banks, one which was more appealing to NEEDS since it seemed to fit so well into the organization that NEEDS was becoming as it grew. But the idea that NEEDS might "establish" an educational data bank was really inappropriate because it suggests that a data bank could be *part of* NEEDS. Yet it did not take much reflection to see that statements about a data bank could pass as statements about NEEDS itself: *all of NEEDS was becoming an educational data bank.*

Realizing this, NEEDS changed the name of its data files from the NEEDS Data Bank to the NEEDS Data Storehouse, and, by this act, broke even further away from being just an EDP service center, coming more and more to resemble the cooperative organization Donald Mitchell had envisaged five and a half years before.

The Final Problem

The three years of Ford Foundation support had brought many deep changes in the character and scope of NEEDS's activities: membership had grown from ten school systems to fifty-two, and the pool of prospective members gave clear evidence the limit had not been approached; the computer program library had come to number in the hundreds; service had been extended to include all five major aspects of pupil personnel accounting; automatic school schedule building, not yet a reality in 1963, had become a service available to any school in New England; the in-service training program had been extended to reach an average of five educators from each of the member school systems; and an educational data storehouse had burgeoned, becoming an integral part of the organization, and offering the schoolman for the first time the promise of relevant analysis of school data. Most important of all, NEEDS had lived through this time, dodging the perils and the traps that wait for anyone who tries to foster participation by the device of mixing development with service.

Moreover, NEEDS had begun to provide services to the state departments of education. NEEDS participated, for instance, in the derivation and statistical justification of a new, more equitable formula for the distribution of state aid to Massachusetts schools. For New Hampshire, NEEDS developed computer programs to allocate state aid to schools and to study changes in distributions over the years. For Rhode Island, it specified the basic procedures for a statewide school enrollment projection system, and as the period of Ford Foundation support closed, NEEDS was beginning to program this system. Besides these cases of assistance to individual state education agencies, NEEDS undertook a two year project with the U.S. Office of Education which involved all six New England state departments of education. This project, called the "NEEDS Title I Assessment Project," entailed working with the state commissioners of education to depict and evaluate the use of federal funds to develop remedial programs in New England schools. During this time, as well, plans were beginning to form for a "region-wide information network" in which the state departments of education were to be the principal elements.

And then there was the university. One NEEDS staff member developed two university level courses in computer applications in education which were then offered at Harvard University's Graduate School of Education. Another NEEDS employee developed and taught a course in data processing at Boston University. In addition, NEEDS performed certain administrative services for Harvard, including analysis of its alumni questionnaire and the creation and updating of its mailing list. Most significant of its activities with universities, however, was a project it began to formulate in the winter of 1965. This project was to create a computer based information system for vocational decisions, and from NEEDS's point of view its major significance was in the fact that the schools, represented by NEEDS, and a university—in this case Harvard—were participating as equal partners in the application of the computer to educational problems. By the spring of 1966, this project had been funded by the U. S. Office of Education for a three year period at a total of two million dollars. Clearly, NEEDS had come of age in terms of both what it had accomplished and what it had created as a future for itself.

NEEDS had started its "Ford years" with many goals to pursue. Some of these goals were altered as experience accumulated at NEEDS, a few were postponed in the face of the unanticipated rigors of development, fewer still were abandoned as NEEDS came to adjust its perception of what was relevant, but during these three years a clear majority of its goals had been attained, and the schoolman's involvement in automation was assured. Just one goal went unmet. But, as things turned out, it was upon the attainment of this one goal that NEEDS's existence depended. So in the spring of 1966, even though its success was unquestionable, and even though its accomplishments gave it prescience enough to expect much more from the future, NEEDS, it seemed, was just a few months away from shutting down.

This goal, which was so crucial to NEEDS's continuance, was that of becoming self-supporting. The support from the Ford Foundation while allowing NEEDS to function as though it was a fully established organization, was predicated on the assumption that within the three year period, dues from the membership would become large enough to carry the operation from there. But this had not happened even though fifty-two schools were each contributing $2.50 a year for each pupil processed at NEEDS. The operation, to be self-sustaining, needed one hundred member systems and the original schedule was to approximately double membership each year until this goal was reached. Thus membership was to have numbered twenty in July 1964 (NEEDS had twenty-one), fifty in July 1965 (NEEDS had thirty-eight), and finally, one hundred in July 1966 (NEEDS had fifty-two). By this reckoning, NEEDS was just one year behind schedule, but it had become obvious that the intent of doubling membership each year was unrealistic. NEEDS should have planned on slower growth.

The NEEDS project director added to this point in March 1966 in a letter to the Ford Foundation in which he explained that "inadequately projected costs and their combined effects upon the fiscal health of the project also indicate a need for more time to grow at a more realistic rate." In another report to the Ford Foundation, NEEDS offered a more detailed analysis of this problem of growth that had placed it in such imminent danger of disbanding. "When the membership was quite small," the report asserted, "doubling the number of school systems involved was not difficult, but as the membership increased, adding 100 percent per year became impractical." The report concluded that an increase of ten to twenty members a year was "more realistic" and it seemed there was sufficient demand to expect such a yearly increase for some time to come.

A New Proposal

This report, which eventually came to be treated by the Ford Foundation as a request for continued support, went on to depict the situation in the following way:

> Not only must new members be "recruited" for the project but each new member school system's personnel must be "trained" and quickly brought up to the level of the older members in order to participate effectively in the

project. NEEDS is unable to supply this kind of training to more than a limited number of districts in any one school year. This then is NEEDS's most pressing current challenge: buying enough time for a reasonable rate of growth toward fiscal independence *and at the same time maintaining the quality of the training and operating systems it is supplying for the member systems.* The earlier budget projections were predicated upon a larger number of school systems for the next school year than NEEDS will be able to handle. Therefore, NEEDS will have difficulty meeting its fiscal requirements without additional external support.

As was noted in the 1963 proposal, NEEDS began as a pioneering organization with little outside experience to draw upon. The cost of many ventures in such areas as experimental scheduling had never been fully documented before. NEEDS had only intelligent guesses to rely upon in the estimation of future costs. Data processing is expensive: this is hardly news. However, the cost estimates developed in 1963 were too low. Space originally projected at $4.00 per square foot per year was not available near adequate parking. NEEDS was fortunate in locating its present facility but even so was forced to increase its budget for space. Paper costs, projected at $.20 per pupil per year, have exceeded $.50 per pupil per year. Beyond the cost of renting NEEDS's own computer facility, funds were budgeted to buy outside time on large computers for such processing as the running of scheduling simulations which could not be performed on NEEDS's relatively low capacity machine. Those costs were projected at less than $1,000 per month. Experience indicates that $3,000 per month would have been a more reasonable figure. Program development costs were also higher than originally estimated. This is in part due to the flexible type of programming NEEDS deliberately develops.

Offering further detail on this issue of "flexible" programming and the effects that such development has upon the way schools formulate their data processing requirements, the report (proposal) went on to say:

It is now clear that local school systems can handle data processing on a cooperative basis through a central facility. However, this requires computer programs of sufficient flexibility to allow variations in the data processing demands made by the various schools without having to design special programs for each school. This is something like building an automobile assembly line designed to handle a wide variety of body styles, trim, color, motors, and the like, on the same line at the same time. These types of systems are expensive to develop and operate but they are essential if schools are to be supplied the tools necessary for innovative activities. This type of programming would not be necessary for a single large school system but NEEDS's programming is geared to many school systems, each one politically independent, each with its own ideas of what a good school should look like and each with its own individual demands that must be met if it is to be allowed the opportunity to experiment and grow. It was found that not only did schools have their own special requirements in the design and content of such systems as report cards, but also new ideas about design and content which stemmed from member coordinators as a result of the training received at NEEDS. As coordinators learned more about the computer's potential they became more adventurous in their requests.

This kind of development, we have discovered, stimulates a need for further developments. That is, the more schoolmen learn how to utilize modern technology, the more technology they demand. The able school administrator demands better techniques for arriving at decisions about future change. The ongoing development so critical to this concept continues even as the word "service" begins to change its meaning. The current "package" that NEEDS has developed to date continues to be modified and changed.

Oddly, NEEDS was in financial trouble, but it was not broke. The Title I Assessment Project coupled with the joint NEEDS-Harvard vocational decisions project would together bring in about one half million dollars during the 1966 fiscal year. But these and the other projects were for the performance of specified tasks and none of the money was to support the "core" activities. As far as the provision of EDP services was concerned, NEEDS required programmatic support—funds earmarked not for specific projects but for underwriting school costs and for financing general software development. Consequently, NEEDS's second proposal to the Ford Foundation pursued two lines of thought: the first to analyze the factors behind NEEDS's failure to become self-supporting; the second to indicate the expanse of development work that lay before it. In the absence of programmatic support NEEDS would have to shut down its service operation, and in one sense this would not be tragic. NEEDS had set out to demonstrate the role computers can play in education, and since, unmistakingly, it had made this demonstration, closing its doors would not be disastrous for NEEDS. But for the schools it would bring chaos, because *the schools had become dependent on NEEDS.* Schoolmen, thanks to NEEDS, had become wiser, more sophisticated, and more knowledgeable about computers, but they were not yet ready—economically or spiritually—to take on the full burden of EDP themselves. Thus it became essential that additional programmatic support be located.

The Ford Foundation was pursuaded by the argument that NEEDS's expansion to self-support must be slowed down to the point where just ten to twenty new members would be added each year. To assist in NEEDS's efforts to attain this position of self-support—and to provide help for the substantial development effort that lay ahead—the Ford Foundation voted to continue its support of NEEDS for another three years. Since NEEDS now had a carefully formulated schedule for realistically adding to its membership over these three years so that self-support was assured, the Ford Foundation funds would be given to NEEDS on a decreasing scale, complementing this growth. The grant—totaling $600,000—was thus apportioned, $285,000 the first year beginning July 1, 1966, $210,000 the second year, and $105,000 the third and final year of this second grant to NEEDS. By this grant—which when added to the first one came to $1,090,000 over six years—the Ford Foundation was giving NEEDS, in effect, the attainment of the one goal that had eluded it, and consequently NEEDS began the summer of 1966 fixed on fresh vistas and new goals.

But NEEDS had not seen the last of this issue of self-support. The immediate problem had been solved, to be sure; but ironically in the solving, NEEDS's courage about the future was damaged; in averting the severe consequences of insolvency, NEEDS had come to see these consequences close-up, and the mark this confrontation left was deep enough to remain in spite of the substantial Ford Foundation grant. NEEDS had obtained all the money and all the time it would need to become self-supporting, but in the process it had gotten something else: for the first time, intruding in NEEDS's hopes of bringing the power of computers to schools was the possibility of failure. Thus while NEEDS began what was to be its last three years with the same ambitions it always had had, subtly its courage about the future was becoming caution about the future, and this caution was to influence every significant decision NEEDS was to make from then on.

A New Organization

The first aspect of NEEDS that this growing caution was to affect was its relationship to NESDEC, its founder. Through the years NESDEC had been the fiscal agent of NEEDS, but otherwise NEEDS was relatively independent: the NEEDS Board of Directors established policy and the Director of NEEDS implemented that policy. But in 1966 when NEEDS was facing its financial crisis, it became shockingly clear that NESDEC, being the fiscal agent, was legally responsible for the debts and the commitments of NEEDS. Thus, had the Ford Foundation been unwilling to support NEEDS at that time, NESDEC would have had to produce the money necessary to liquidate NEEDS. In the face of such far-reaching responsibility, it made good sense when NESDEC began to feel it should have an equally extensive say in the policies and the operation of NEEDS. To accomplish this, NESDEC would have to take a direct interest in its now five year old data processing project.

Accordingly, certain changes were made in the organization of NEEDS to foster the more direct involvement of NESDEC. First, the function of the NEEDS Board of Directors was redefined to be "advising NESDEC on the various technical matters associated with the use of computers in education." No longer would the Board formulate policy or approve proposals of the NEEDS Director concerning future directions; these and related prerogatives were now to fall within NESDEC's province. Second, growing out of this shift in function, the Director of NEEDS would now "report on all matters to the Executive Secretary of

NESDEC" who would function as chief administrator of the NEEDS enterprise and as such, would be the one to recommend policy to the NESDEC Executive Committee. Before long, as the Executive Secretary became increasingly involved in the day-to-day aspects of running NEEDS, he came to take on the duties of the Project Director. Indeed, the position of NEEDS Project Director was eventually dropped, and all the division heads came to report directly to the Executive Secretary. Accompanying this development was the restructuring of both NESDEC and NEEDS into a new organization called NESDEC/NEEDS, in which each of the major activities of NEEDS was incorporated into one or another division of NESDEC. For example, the activities of software development and special projects became part of the NESDEC Research Division, consulting services became part of Field Studies, and training joined NESDEC publications and printing activities in a "dissemination division." What was left of NEEDS formed the heart of a new division called "school services."

Not all the effects of these changes were beneficial. True, the reorganization permitted the increased monitoring of NEEDS's financial condition, a situation central to the systematic growth in membership and thus to attaining self-support. As well, NEEDS was now functioning from within the educational context of NESDEC—consisting by this time of three hundred school systems—suggesting the greater involvement and participation of schoolmen in the application of computers in education and assuring that such application would be approached from an *educational* point of view rather than a technical one. But, for all this, NEEDS had been split up, causing a basic change to its identity. By treating NEEDS's activities of development, service, research, and training as separable into discrete compartments, NESDEC had unwittingly upset the relationship among them: increasingly, each activity came to be pursued independent of others; and service, the most visible activity of the four, quickly became all anyone thought of when he thought of NEEDS. Furthermore, in its eagerness to preserve the educational point of view about data processing, NESDEC hired several educational administrators to direct its EDP activities. As a result, by 1968 EDP at NESDEC/NEEDS was under the direction of a chief administrator and division directors, none of whom had ever worked with computers before.

Now, such consequences of the reorganization of NEEDS were portentous in themselves, but as well they established a new environment within which all the other decisions about NEEDS were to be made. Thus the first result of a justifiable caution about the future promised, before it was through, to encompass much more than the relationship between NESDEC and NEEDS. And this was not the only aspect of NEEDS to be affected by the remnants of the 1966 financial crisis and the subsequent caution it engendered.

A New Membership

Equally touched was NEEDS's concept of membership. When a school system joined NEEDS, it joined the whole project. It paid $2.50 per secondary school pupil and, in return, received all the EDP services it wanted. While there was no reduction for using less than the full range of services, there was no increase in price as new services were added. Also included in the membership fee were the institutes, the training sessions, the consulting, and all the necessary documentation. The intention with this approach, of course, was to foster the notion of NEEDS as a *consortium* of schools, attacking together the problems associated with EDP. It was this concept of membership, too, that distinguished NEEDS from an EDP service bureau, and made reasonable the likening of NEEDS to data banks. But not all good ideas are economical, and sometimes good business practice requires that they be modified or even abandoned. It was not inappropriate, therefore, when NESDEC reviewed the membership policy at NEEDS, to see whether or not it was "economically feasible." Stemming from this review was the decision to increase membership dues. In a statement concerning this increase, NESDEC stated:

> Every reasonable attempt has been made to hold to the original dues structure. However, even with additional external support we now anticipate increasing the dues to members by $.50 per pupil commencing July of 1967, and (unless projected cost estimates prove to be overly conservative) by a similar amount in July of 1968.[10]

Had this been the only change in membership policy, the repercussions would have been minimal, although a number of school systems were forced by the increase to reconsider their membership in NEEDS. They felt this increase resembled taxation in that it was determined not by service performed but by money needed to meet anticipated costs. Eventually, partially in reaction to such feelings among some schoolmen and partially in the hope of increasing income, NESDEC decided to "break up the service packages." That is, each of the services performed by the School Services Division (NEEDS) would have a price attached to it. Any school system could then decide which particular EDP services it wanted, and pay accordingly. An added value of this approach, it was argued, was that the smaller systems in New England could now avail themselves of that portion of NEEDS's services that their smaller budgets would allow, thereby "bringing EDP to the rural districts throughout New England."

Unfortunately, NEEDS was sold before it could be determined that this policy had the anticipated effects. It did not take much time, however, for the unanticipated effects to become manifest. Most school

[10]Correspondence between NESDEC and the Ford Foundation, 1966.

systems signed up for just enough services to bring their total dues to the same level it had been under the old policy. But, given the new pricing, this meant most systems would receive fewer services. Thus the program of EDP in most schools suffered, many becoming fragmented and arbitrary. Along with this the training program at NEEDS changed drastically, becoming limited to just that which a school needed to know to submit data and interpret output. Then there was the inevitable anonymity that accompanies piecemeal service. No longer could anyone claim to be part of a consortium; even the term "member" was out of place and much less accurate than "customer." The schools were now customers and by 1968 the unintentional dismemberment of NEEDS—internal and external—had been accomplished.

Dissemination Reconsidered

Another aspect of NEEDS that was to feel the weight of the concern for self-support was its commitment to dissemination. NEEDS was created to spread EDP throughout New England and, thereby, make it commonplace. To do this, NEEDS would have to give to others—schools, service bureaus, consulting houses, state departments of education, universities, and the like—its potential for developing EDP systems. It was not a matter of just writing computer programs and then placing them in the public domain. It was much more than that: the goal was to place in the public domain, the *capacity* to conceive, develop, and apply EDP programs to schools. "NEEDS will have succeeded," Mitchell used to say, "when it is no longer needed"; and it would be no longer needed, only when others could do the job. It was in this respect that NEEDS was always prepared to "go out of business."

The idea of disseminating its potential worked well at NEEDS. Whereas in 1961 schoolmen had no place to go for the systematic application of EDP in their schools, by 1967 or so those who had not yet acquired their own equipment could choose among many EDP centers, comparing prices, quality of service, and scope of applications. But, as NEEDS became more and more service oriented and as the membership concept dissipated, this idea of dissemination no longer seemed reasonable: the pool of prospective customers was being substantially diminished by the presence of other centers, and, as a result, NEEDS's plan for increasing "membership" was threatened. Concern over this dwindling pool obscured the fact that the schoolmen benefited from having a wide choice of centers. Increasingly, NEEDS was coming to treat those other EDP centers, to which it had in part given rise, as competitors. Consequently, what NEEDS meant by "dissemination" changed: the product of its work was still to be placed in the public domain, but this now meant that, upon request, "any responsible agency engaged in EDP can receive copies of the NEEDS computer programs." Behind this change in the spirit of dissemination was the reworking of NEEDS's attitude towards its survival; NEEDS had become dedicated to achieving perpetuity. Voluntarily giving over itself was no longer a possibility at NEEDS, and going out of business, far from being a goal of the organization, had become a sign of failure.

Development Abandoned

So it was that NEEDS's caution about the future, stemming from its 1966 brush with economic failure, had led unintentionally to the break-up of the components within NEEDS, the breakdown of the concept of membership and all it implied, and the redefinition of "dissemination" and thus of NEEDS's mission. Hit hardest by all of this was development—the area most likely to encourage school participation. Indeed by autumn 1968, in the wake of these changes, development at NEEDS had come to a halt. First, the work of documenting the GASP scheduling system and that of developing programs to make GASP input and output compatible with the other NEEDS systems had been discontinued. As a result, GASP remained a "special service" at NEEDS never becoming truly integrated, and while some schools were to benefit from this special service, NEEDS was never to experience the full promise of GASP. Second, efforts to expand or even to keep up the NEEDS Educational Data Storehouse had been abandoned. The 125 computer tapes comprising the data store went unattended for about two years, and then as "work tapes" became needed for production, these storehouse tapes were erased and "pressed into service." Third, NEEDS's involvement in the NEEDS/Harvard project to create a computer based information system for vocational and career decisions had become minimal. The idea, the plans, the proposal, the orientation, the entire scope of this project had been developed at NEEDS, and in the end NEEDS was to turn over all its substantive responsibilities and interests to Harvard. Indeed, all NEEDS was to contribute to this project was four hours of computer time a day, for which it received $7,000 a month. What promised to be the first thorough application of computers to the mammoth information handling problems facing guidance counselors, became to NEEDS little more than a source of income.

Behind NEEDS's disinvolvement in these three areas of development, of course, was its new and growing dedication to service. Yet, strangely, during the three years of the second Ford Foundation grant, not one new area of EDP service was developed—not one new EDP applications program written, not one new EDP service area mapped. Besides, the Title I Assessment project ended abruptly when the Office of Education decided to "cut back" expenditures, the enrollment projections program NEEDS had begun to develop was dropped, and all relations with New England state departments of education concerning data processing evaporated. As well, NEEDS and the various universities it had worked with drifted apart: as NEEDS focused on the day-to-day, thereby seeing less and less of the future, universities naturally became unclear about its relevance to them and to their work. And, by this time, NEEDS had completely forgotten about the early dream expressed in 1962 to "develop systems in the areas of computer based programmed instruction, simulation studies in education, automated financial accounting, computational aids to the teaching of mathematics, new optical scanning hardware, and educational research on school data." As hectic as NEEDS's last three years seem to have been, development was utterly still.

Foremost among the causes of the torpid state of software development in NEEDS's last years was the estrangement of the service function and the development function. The more NEEDS relied on the provision of routine EDP services as the way to ensure economic self-sufficiency, the more the potential incompatibility between service and development became manifest. This incompatibility stems, in part, from the logic of service which requires that the work be done on time and in the manner promised, whereas development can be neither so fully scheduled nor so well controlled. Moreover, service and development deal with different times, one with the present, the other with the future. Should they be made to compete, the present will win because failing in the present forebodes failing in the future. Besides, present demands are real ones and cannot be postponed or ignored. It does not matter if development is given higher priority, because the very meaning of service as practiced at NEEDS requires that it prevail. If service and development are seen as separable activities, with separate ends, and if service becomes production at all costs, then curtailed development becomes a small price to pay. Mitchell had understood this, of course, and was careful when NEEDS was first created to give development and service a common purpose, thus making them function together. (But Mitchell had left NESDEC in 1965—at the height of NEEDS' development—to become director of the Washington Internships to Education Program.) When he said that automating school practices was a way to get a better look at those practices, he was saying that service—like development—can be a mechanism for change. This approach brought service and development together on behalf of the reconsideration—instead of the legitimization—of existing practice; it acted like an electrolyte allowing development to enhance service the way a copper anode coats a platinum cathode. But this idea belonged to an earlier NEEDS.

Victory and Defeat

NEEDS began the spring of 1969 with just one certainty: it would not be a self-supporting organization when the second Ford Foundation grant period ended that June. By this time the NEEDS membership had grown to seventy-seven school systems but that would not be enough to carry the project. Twenty-three more school systems would have to join NEEDS before economic independence would become a possibility, and these new customers were nowhere in sight. Besides, NEEDS had all it could do just to keep up with the work for the customers it had. As a service center, the NEEDS of 1969 was just a small part of the NEEDS of 1966—devoid of the scope, the ambition, the goals, and even the commitment of the past—and yet it was unable to become a fiscally sound operation.

Once again NEEDS saw the prospect of insolvency. The caution about the future, the economizing, the incorporation of NEEDS into NESDEC, even the breaking up of services into packages, all left NEEDS facing the same financial crisis it thought it had solved three years before. It still needed money to continue. Closing down was still not a reasonable possibility because so many schools remained dependent on NEEDS. Almost everything about the situation seemed the same. There was just one difference: the Ford Foundation would not consider another extension of the grant. Some other solution had to be found.

This excerpt from the minutes of the NESDEC Executive Committee meeting of May 15, 1969 best states what NESDEC decided to do about the situation it faced:

> The Executive Secretary reviewed the recommendations of the Special NESDEC-NEEDS Joint Committee on the future of NEEDS, and the action taken by the NESDEC Executive Committee and NEEDS Board of Directors at their Joint Meeting held on May 2.
>
> First, it is agreed that NESDEC has fulfilled the goals set forth in the two proposals to the Ford Foundation regarding the development of NEEDS and its ability to be self-supporting on July 1, 1969.
>
> However, because of the development of many commercial service bureaus offering computer services to schools during the past few years, it is agreed that NESDEC should not run a computer center in competition with private enterprise.
>
> The Executive Secretary reported that, acting on behalf of NESDEC and NEEDS, he had contacted those companies which have expressed an interest in acquiring NEEDS.
>
> He presented a list of those companies which have submitted proposals to acquire NEEDS.
>
> The criteria upon which NESDEC will make its decision were reviewed. They are in order of priority:
>
> 1. The ability of the company to continue at least the same level of quality, within the present range of costs, to those NESDEC schools currently using NEEDS services.
>
> 2. The commitment of that organization to retain the staff at NEEDS, since

the ability of NEEDS to perform the quality services is directly related to the staff.

3. The financial responsibility of said organization.

After a great deal of deliberation and analysis, with the emphasis on the three criteria in order of priority as stated above, the NESDEC Executive Committee voted unanimously to enter into negotiations with Westinghouse Learning Corporation, with the goal of Westinghouse Learning Corporation acquiring NEEDS no later than July 1, 1969.

It was further voted to empower the four officers of NESDEC, working with the Executive Secretary, to finalize the contract with Westinghouse Learning Corporation on behalf of the NESDEC Corporation.

NESDEC voted a unanimous expression of appreciation to the members of the NEEDS Board, past and current, who have contributed freely of their time to advise NESDEC on the operation of NEEDS, to the Ford Foundation, the Harvard Graduate School of Education, and the Newton schools for their support of the NEEDS Project, and to the NEEDS staff *who have done a remarkable job of making NEEDS a first-rate Computer Service Center.*

NEEDS was to be sold, and there are two things we can say about this. We can say NEEDS had to be sold because it could not much longer go on the way it was going and expect ever to fulfill its early dream of getting schoolmen to participate in automation as partners rather than customers. Or we can say, with equal legitimacy, that finally NEEDS had reached the point where it was worth buying. We know that NEEDS never reached its goal of becoming a New England-wide consortium of schools, universities, and state departments of education, but we know, also, that NEEDS processed data each year on more than 125,000 students covering a wide range of EDP services. It never got to develop applications of computers in CAI or educational simulations or administrative decision making, or the other areas it had set out for itself in the early days, but, still, NEEDS managed to take EDP off its shelf of promise and potential and make educational data processing commonplace in New England. Its membership never became large enough to provide full financial support, and yet no school district in New England that had any EDP service being performed by anyone, including itself, could be said not to have felt the influence and the benefits of NEEDS. Because of NEEDS, more schoolmen learned what computers are, more university professors and their students came to recognize the role of the computer in education, and more computer power became available to schools than ever would have been possible otherwise.

Thus, whether NEEDS was a success or a failure depends upon which parts of its history or its dream we look at, and upon the weights and valances we assign to each part. That is, if we judge "participation" to mean the collective receipt of services for which NEEDS was to be the provider, then NEEDS succeeded. But if we judge "participation" to mean the tendering of commitment for which NEEDS was to be the processor, then NEEDS failed.

But in *An Essay on Criticism*, Alexander Pope advises us against judging by part and not by the whole. It is "the joint force and full result of all" that matters, he says, and we must follow his advice if we expect to properly assess the significance of there having been a NEEDS. Some parts succeeded, some parts failed, but it is a mistake to judge NEEDS as having been one or the other. It is an oversimplification to wonder whether NEEDS was a success or a failure, because it was neither and it was both.

III: building an education machine

But if there were such a machine . . . there would always be two absolutely certain methods of recognizing that it was still not truly a man. The first is that it could never use words or other signs for the purpose of communicating its thoughts to others as we do. . . . The second method of recognition is that, although such machines could do many things as well as, or perhaps even better than, men, they would infallibly fail in certain others, by which we would discover that they did not act by understanding, but only by the disposition of their organs.

René Descartes
Discourse on Method

CHAPTER SIX: the theory

Throughout Part III we will bring together the things we have been considering separately up to now about the proper role of the computer in education. To accomplish this fusion we will describe in detail an ambitious yet thoughtful effort to apply the computer to problems of providing guidance and counseling in schools. Describing the steps and phases of this comprehensive project—called the Information System for Vocational Decisions (ISVD) Project—from its inception through to its termination four years later, will serve two purposes for us. First, it will provide an extensive example of how the computer can be used as a mechanism with which to fashion a point of view about a complex educational problem. Second, it will serve as a case study of the principal steps involved in actually building a computer into an education machine.

Of all the reasons why the ISVD project has been selected as the most appropriate vehicle with which to explore the details of implementing a computer system in education, three reasons stand out as being especially persuasive. First, because the author was one of the several responsible developers who designed and conducted the project, he is thoroughly familiar with its strengths, weaknesses, intentions, successes, and failures. Unfortunately, when computers are involved, it usually takes such intimacy with a project before we can tell whether or not it was worth the considerable effort, money, and time it demanded. Second, ISVD is the *only project in the history of the use of computers in education* to go so far in attempting to combine and implement advanced notions relating to natural language processing, data storage and retrieval, information processing, and the interrelationships among instructional, administrative, and guidance applications: thus the assertion that ISVD was an attempt to construct an education machine. Finally, we look to ISVD because every other major project in the use of computers in guidance and counseling—those of IBM, ETS, Willowbrook, Flint, Pennsylvania State, and the like—have been significantly influenced and altered by the work of this project.[1] Thus ISVD will serve us better than any other project as we attempt to draw together the arguments and the basic principles of computing considered in Parts I and II into sequence within the context of a single effort at automation in education.

The Impetus

When Frank Mullen was in high school he met with his guidance counselor every day. His counselor, Mr. Estrin, was also the track coach, and Frank Mullen was the best high jumper Andrew Jackson High School ever had. He was so good, in fact, that he and Mr. Estrin never needed to talk to each other much about school work or career plans or college entrance examinations or vocational opportunities or any of the other things students and guidance counselors are supposed to talk about. Everyone just knew that Frank would continue his education at some college like Villanova or Manhattan or Georgetown, because they had the best track teams in the East. It was common knowledge—even before Frank won the Indoor National Schoolboy championships in Madison Square Garden—that each of these colleges had put aside one of its four-year athletic scholarships just in case he decided to apply for admission there. Counseling Frank Mullen, all of us knew, would have been a waste of his time.

It was different for Vincent Brown who could have used some counseling. Vincent Brown is an alumnus of Brooklyn Automotive High School, the school he attended because his junior high school guidance counselor told him to. Eventually, under a special ruling by the Admissions Committee, Vincent managed to go on to New York University to study his favorite subject, sociology. But this was unusual because people who go to Brooklyn Automotive do not become sociologists, they become automobile mechanics, and that was the vocation Vincent's counselor felt was best for him. On reflection, Vincent does not blame his counselor for the bad advice because he recognizes that counselors have a

[1]For an account of these and other efforts to apply computers to guidance and counseling, see Donald Super (ed.), *Computer-Assisted Counseling*, Teachers College Press, New York, 1970.

difficult job. "The schools are just crowded and, anyway, working on cars sounded great in the ninth grade. It was nothing personal."[2]

Much about guidance counseling in schools ends up being nothing personal, and one's first impulse is to blame this on the counselor. After all, he is the one students must go to for guidance, and it seems only fair, therefore, to hold him responsible when things go wrong. Yet Vincent's excuse that counselors are kept too busy to give each pupil the attention he needs probably comes equally close to the truth. Indeed, few educators would dispute the fact that just about every school counselor in the country has assigned to him more students than he can possibly handle. Now, the true extent of the counselor's burden is difficult to document because every statistic on the subject needs to be qualified one way or another, and it is not always clear which way is the fairest. For instance at last count,[3] there were in the United States public schools 6,485 elementary school students for *each* elementary school counselor. No counselor can do anything with 6,485 pupils. But not all schools have guidance programs; in fact only about 11 percent of all the grammar school students in this country is offered any approved guidance services and these students are the only ones we should use in the arithmetic to compute the counselor/pupil ratio. It is not fair to include the other 89 percent (23,295,667 children) because they do not even have counselors. Making this correction to the statistic then, it turns out that, on the average, if an elementary school student has a guidance counselor at all, he shares him with 698 other students.

In this matter of counselor/pupil ratios, the secondary school student appears better off in two ways. First only 6,220,125 (36 percent) of them do not have any guidance counselors to talk to about career plans, and the like. Second only 450 high school students will be assigned to any one counselor. But, like the other ratio, this ratio of one counselor to 450 pupils is an average. In Idaho it runs 1:454 while in Hawaii it drops to 1:433. Ohio and Utah have ratios of 1:417 and 1:373 respectively, while in Wisconsin the figure goes as high as 1:555.

In Massachusetts the counselor/pupil ratio is pretty good. In the average high school in Massachusetts, for instance, the principal assigns 353 pupils to each counselor. This figure is not bad compared to the other state averages, and yet a closer look at it uncovers an important fact about the counselor's burden. Given the amount of time schools are in session from September to June, a counselor/pupil ratio of 1:353 means that a counselor can spend with each student *no more than 3-1/2 hours a year.* This is about as much time as a student spends riding the school bus in a

[2] *The New York Times*, New York, May 25, 1968, p. 19.

[3] The figures presented in this section regarding the ratios of counselors to students are taken from Department of Health, Education, and Welfare, "Review of Progress Under Title V-A, National Defense Education Act of 1958, as Amended," Bureau of Elementary and Secondary Education, Office of Education, OE-25054, 1969.

week or watching television on a Saturday morning, and typically, a senior will take more time than this just to fill out one college application. So, Vincent Brown is right, and there is no point in blaming the counselor when things go wrong, or even in wondering if he is competent. It really does not matter whether or not the counselor is any good at his job because there is no time.

Now one may argue that three and a half hours of counseling is better than no counseling at all, and, of course, he would be correct except for the fact that during this time counselors rarely counsel. Instead they dispense facts about the "world of work." They have no choice in this. Students need to be informed that Queens College is on Kissena Boulevard in Flushing, New York, and that you need four units of English and of history and three units of math, science and a foreign language to get in. They need to be told that after basic training the salary of an Army private is $90.60 a month, and it is possible to "volunteer" for the draft, thereby signing up for only two years instead of the three you commit yourself to when you enlist. A girl who hates to work in the kitchen and wants to become an airline stewardess to get away from it all needs to know that a stewardess spends most of her time heating and serving food and doing dishes. The student must have heard such facts and must have thought about them before counseling can begin. That is why most textbooks on guidance refer to the activities of providing students facts about themselves and about the world of work as *pre*-counseling activities. But few students are conversant with facts about themselves or the world of work when they show up for their appointments with their counselors. Thus the best part of their three and a half hours is spent not in counseling exactly, but in pre-counseling, wherein the counselor transmits facts to the student.

Of course, all the facts counselors transmit to students can be found in books and catalogs and pamphlets; that is where the counselor himself gets them. But it would be wrong to conclude from this that sending the student directly to the school library to search out such information would improve matters much. First of all, most collections of career information are too small to be of appreciable value. But, oddly, if a library has enough relevant material on hand to adequately cover the full range of career information, then the collection will be too large for anyone to go through. The Newton (Massachusetts) Career Information Library, for example, lists among its collection approximately 11,000 publications concerning occupations alone, and even though these materials are grouped and cross-referenced, no student—just as no counselor—could be expected to go through them thoroughly.[4] He must be selective. But this means he must know which questions to ask himself in

[4]See Duncan Circle, David Clemens, Arthur Kroll, Dorothea Overholt, *Career Information Service*, Commonwealth of Massachusetts, Bureau of Vocational Education, Department of Education, 1968.

order to locate the data he needs. As well, he must know how to go about answering these questions—where to look, how to look, and when to stop looking. And all of this is just the first step. Then the data must be studied, summarized, contrasted, and finally pieced together to form a picture of some part of the world. For the typical student left to manage on his own, such tasks of data retrieval and processing can quickly become overwhelming. Thus it has come to make better sense for the counselor to decide which facts are important to a student and to give them to him directly. So the few hours they have together are spent just this way and little opportunity exists for the counselor to do the things that can make guidance personal. The press of time and the resultant concern for efficiency have turned much of the guidance program in schools into a mechanical operation.

We will agree, of course, that it is not a good thing for guidance to be so mechanical. We may be reluctant to agree, however, that the greatest promise of making guidance less mechanical rests with the computer. Surely the most basic objection to this assertion comes easily to mind: computers eventually become machines, and it is intuitively obvious that nothing can be more mechanical than that. Thus, introducing computers into the guidance process in any but the most limited way ought to make matters worse than they are. But strangely, just the opposite is true; with the computer we have the potential to make guidance in schools less hurried, less directive, and even less factual, and how this is so is the subject of our present exploration.

More specifically we will explore the parts a computer can play in the guidance process by looking at three major aspects of the ISVD project: its theory, its development, and its workings. In what remains of this chapter, we examine its theory.

The Basic Notions

In June 1966 the United States Office of Education granted funds to Harvard University to conduct a thirty-six-month project called the Information System for Vocational Decisions project (ISVD).[5] Cooperating with Harvard in this project were the New England School Development Council through its NEEDS project and the Newton, Massachusetts public school system. The intention of this project was to create a working model of a computer-based information system that could become an integral part of the career guidance efforts of school systems.

While this intention grew out of a concern for the excessive burdens

[5]Contract number OEG-1-6-061819-2240. The full documentation of this project including all the relevant computer tapes, are on file with the ERIC system, Center for Vocational and Technical Education, The Ohio State University, 1900 Kenny Road, Columbus, Ohio 43210.

guidance counselors are forced to bear, the ISVD project did not address itself directly to these burdens. Doing so would have meant giving in to a temptation that confronts anyone who sets out to apply computers to guidance. "In considering computer applications for guidance," William Cooley has warned, "the temptation is to identify the major data processing tasks which have faced guidance workers in the past and then attempt to speed things up with the aid of a computer."[6] The trouble with this approach, of course, is that it offers little more than the considerable risk of perpetuating—even legitimizing—outmoded practices. We have come across this problem before, in previous chapters, where we saw that the dangers of "legitimizing through automation" are ever present. They exist for guidance data processing as well, and it was precisely these dangers that the ISVD project leaders hoped to avoid. To do this they would proceed from a different starting point. They would resist the temptation to focus on how to use computers to alleviate the specific burdens and bottlenecks so often associated with guidance counseling. That would be like treating merely the symptoms of an illness. Instead they would look beyond guidance practice to guidance theory, specifically a theory of career development, recognizing that the computer offers an excuse for systematically reconsidering this theory. From this reconsideration they then could derive appropriate guidance practice.

Career

The theory upon which ISVD was to be based is due principally to David V. Tiedeman formerly of Harvard University who headed up a group of researchers, psychologists, school guidance counselors, and computer specialists comprising the project staff.[7] This theory begins with a notion about *career.* For most of us when we use the word "career" in ordinary language we mean "what a person does for a living," but for Tiedeman this meaning is incomplete. Far from being just a job or an occupation or a vocation, a career, Tiedeman asserts, is the direction and the purpose implied by a person's whole set of vocational activities. My career includes all my vocational activities—past and future—not just my present one, but it is not defined as these activities. It is defined as *the purpose I impose upon these activities.* Career is the "expression of hope and desire and limitation upon life."[8]

Now the mechanism for devising this expression of hope and desire

[6]William W. Cooley, "Computer Systems for Guidance," in *Computer-based Vocational Guidance Systems,* Alice Scates, (ed.), U.S. Office of Education, Document No. FS5.225:25053, Washington, D.C., 1969, p. 61.

[7]E. Gil Boyer, Russell G. Davis, Richard M. Durstine, Allan B. Ellis, Wallace J. Fletcher, Edward Landy, Robert P. O'Hara, David V. Tiedeman, Michael J. Wilson were the Principal Investigators.

[8]David V. Tiedeman and Robert P. O'Hara, *Career Development: Choice and Adjustment,* College Entrance Examination Board, New York, 1963, p. iv.

and limitation upon life and thus for forming a career, the theory goes on to say, is the activity of deciding. Deciding is central to career because throughout a person's life the continuity of his career is interrupted by decision points. These decision points are points of *discontinuity*—open parts of a person's life when he is moving from something he has experienced to something he may only have anticipated. Examples of typical points of discontinuity include choice of secondary school curriculum; choices about style of family life including size of family, location of household and allotment of time among work, family, and recreation; and choice of entry job.[9] Tiedeman identifies four areas —Education, Vocation, Military Service, and Personal and Family Living—as the principal contexts within which discontinuities arise. As diverse as these contexts are, and as varied as the discontinuities they present may be, they all have in common the fact that resolution is best achieved through the decision-making process. Indeed since it is at the points of discontinuity that one's career is fashioned, we may speak of career as the time extended set of choices occurring during the life of an individual.[10] Thus, to Tiedeman, the decision-making process is central to career because it is the process by which career is built.

What Tiedeman means by decision making is depicted by a paradigm devised by him and O'Hara in 1963.[11] According to this paradigm, the process of decision making is divided first into two aspects called *anticipation* and *accommodation.* The anticipation aspect consists essentially of a person's preoccupation with the pieces—facts, alternatives, options, consequences—out of which a decision is to be fashioned and with the aspirations, hopes, expectations, constraints, and the like which will determine the form of the decision. The accomodation aspect—also called "the aspect of implementation or adjustment"—represents the movement from anticipation to induction; it is the point where imagination meets reality. In the case of both anticipation and accommodation it is possible to speak about "subaspects" or stages.

The first stage of anticipation, called *exploration,* begins with a person's awareness "that a problem does or will exist and that a decision must be reached in order to resolve it in a satisfying manner" (p. 38). In discussing exploration, Tiedeman and O'Hara state:

> In the step of exploration . . . a number of different alternatives or possible goals . . . may be considered. Relevant goals are those which can possibly be

[9]For a more detailed account of discontinuities and the "socially-determined choice contexts in which progress in career takes place" see *Annual Report 1966-1967,* Information System for Vocational Decisions, Harvard University, 1967, pp. 10-12.

[10]See, for example, Donald Super, *The Psychology of Careers,* Harper & Row, New York, 1957; and Anne Roe, *The Psychology of Occupations,* Wiley, New York, 1956, as well as Tiedeman and O'Hara, op. cit.

[11]Tiedeman and O'Hara, op. cit., pp. 38-44.

> attained from the opportunities associated with the problem under consideration. . . . During the exploratory step fields are relatively transitory, highly imaginary (perhaps even fantastic), and not necessarily related one to the other. They may be a relatively unassociated set of possibilities and consequences. . . . In the step of exploration in relation to a problem of career development, a person probably reflects at least upon his aspirations, opportunity both now and in the future, interest, capability, distasteful requirements that still can be tolerated, and societal context for himself and his dependents. These are relevant aspects of the field set by each goal. In short, a person attempts to take the measure of himself in relation to each alternative as he senses it. (pp. 38 & 41)

Of *crystallization*, the second stage of anticipation, they assert:

> In [crystallization] the cost of the several goals can be considered in relation to the return from each. The value of alternatives can then be assessed. Relevant considerations are organized or ordered in this process of valuing. . . . The process of valuing gives rise to values which tend to fix the organization or order of all relevant considerations in relation to each of the goals as crystallization occurs. . . . Crystallization normally represents a stabilization of thought. A setting of thought is achieved which is ordinarily of some durability and hence of some reliance. This set readies the person for investment of self along a line that then becomes more noticeable. The situation becomes defined, so to speak, at least for a time. (p. 41)

The third stage is that of choice and it follows readily on the heels of crystallization. Quoting again from Tiedeman and O'Hara:

> With *choice*, a particular goal, and its relevant field . . . orients the behavioral system of the person of relevance for his problem. . . . This goal may be elected with varying degrees of certainty and its motive power will vary as a result. . . . Furthermore, the degrees of clarity, complexity, and freedom generally available to the person in the solution of this problem and in the pursuit of the indicated decision will also affect the motivating power of the resulting resolution of alternatives. (p. 42)

The fourth and final stage of anticipation is called *clarification*. We might expect that once a choice had been made that aspect of decision making which precedes action would have been finished. But even though the decision is made and held firmly, often doubt about the decision will arise. This is true

> . . . in even a short period of waiting (a week or more, say) for the expected situation to begin to unfold . . . doubt experienced in the waiting period causes the individual further to clarify his anticipated position. An elaboration and perfection of the image of the future . . . ensues. . . . *Clarification* not only perfects the image of self in position, but also dissipates some of the former doubts concerning the decision. (p. 43)

The three stages of accomodation may be briefly described in the following way:

> Induction: . . . A general defense of self and a giving up of an aspect of self to group purpose; . . . the individual's goal and field assimilatively become a part of the region . . . of the social system in which the person is implementing his desired solution of his problem. He learns the premises and structures-in-interaction required for continued identification. This process leads to a further perfection of individual goal and field in the social system. . . .
>
> Reformation: . . . The receptive orientation of induction [gives] . . . way to [an] assertive orientation. . . . The person is well immersed in a relevant group. . . . He has a strong sense of self and actively enjoins the group to do better. . . . Since . . . the person acts both upon the in-group and field. . . in order to bring that group into greater conformance with his modified goal and field. . . and upon the out-group to bring their view of his identification into greater consistency with his, the effect, if any, is the modification of group goal and field. . . .
>
> Integration: Synthesis is, of course, the essence of integration. . . . A differentiation in identification has been achieved. The new-found appreciation of self is integrated with its larger field. This new part of the self-system becomes a working member of the whole self-system. In integration, individual and group both strive to keep the resulting organization of collaborative activity. . . . The individual is satisfied, at least temporarily, when integration occurs. (p. 44)

This model of the decision-making process, and the posited relationship between decision making and career development form the basis of Tiedeman's theory. Yet he considers the notions of career, discontinuity, and decision making to be most important in terms of how they shape the goals that guidance counseling should have for the individual student. The primary goal of guidance counseling in schools, Tiedeman asserts, is to get the individual to take title to his career. He means by this that it is the job of the guidance program to get the student to understand and to believe that his career is his to fashion. A related job is to help the student recognize discontinuities as the points at which this fashioning occurs. Implicit in these two tasks, of course, is the student's need to learn the decision-making process as it pertains to career choice.

Specifically the student needs three things relative to the decision-making process before he will be able to take title to his career effectively. First, and most obviously, he needs a sense of the process of deciding: he has to learn the process, and he needs an environment within which to practice what he has learned and to evaluate how well he is doing. Second, he needs the sense that he is the prime agent in the determination of his choices. This sense—Tiedeman calls it a "sense of agency"—is essential if the student is to be free in his choosing. Finally, the student needs the sense of himself as a decider. That is, he must pay attention to—monitor—himself as he goes through the process of deciding. The purpose for this monitoring is that he comes to "see himself in process" and to glean from this view facts about himself as a decider—his style—and facts about the substance of his decisions. To Tiedeman this constitutes a "working out of self" that is central to the individual's career-making.

A sense of the decision process, a sense of agency, and a sense of self as a decider, then, determine the individual's ability to take title to his career, and therefore, it is toward the fostering of these senses in the student that guidance practice should strive. The purpose of the ISVD project was to take the first steps in this direction.

The Computer and Career Decisions

Like most first steps, the ISVD project was as focused on its beginnings as on its destination: its impetus was a reconsidered guidance theory; its goal was an improved guidance practice. Throughout the project both theory and practice prevailed as areas of work, and when it was completed, the project had specified substantial changes in each. For instance, regarding the assertion that the individual needs to develop a sense of the decision-making process, the project not only explored at length the theoretical derivatives of this assertion, but as well it specified and constructed a model of the environment in which such a sense can be developed. Similarly with the contentions about the student's need for sense of agency and sense of self as decider, ISVD dealt with the spectrum of considerations touching upon each. Those times when ISVD turned its attention from the task of specifying improved guidance practice it did so to focus on the further explication of the guidance theory from which such improved practice was to emanate.

This means that the ISVD project was about guidance and not about computers. If anyone would speak about computers in ISVD he would do so only because he absolutely had no choice. To talk about a computer for its own sake would severely distract the project team from its central purpose—the study of guidance theory and practice. Yet by the time the project ended, the staff had created in archetypal form just about the most powerful and sophisticated computer software system in use in education. Why this should have been, why ISVD ever should have mentioned the word "computer," becomes clear when we return to the decision-making process and the demands Tiedeman's theory makes regarding the student as a decider.

Throughout the student's passage from stage to stage in the decision-making process, Tiedeman asserts, he must continually process data. This need to process data makes it essential that the student be aware of one fact about data: in the real world, data are never complete. Indeed, it is precisely this incompleteness that makes decisions necessary in the first place. As one goes through the process of deciding, therefore, he must keep in mind that in one way or another the data with which he is dealing are incomplete. Accepting data on these terms is important to Tiedeman because such an understanding can help to make the student more able to take responsibility for the choices he makes. Once he recognizes that the decisions are not in the data, he has taken the first step toward looking to himself as the responsible agent for choice. The word "responsible" is used here in both its meanings: the student is the one who makes the decisions, not someone or something external to him; he is the one who enjoys or suffers the consequences. To encourage this sense of responsibility, ISVD would "place the student among resources, and enhance his access to them." The project would accomplish this by creating an environment within which the student's access to data would be facilitated, and his understanding of data heightened.

They called this environment an *information system* and its function was to support the student's exercise of the decision-making process. This requires, obviously, that whatever we eventually come to mean by the term "information system" it has got to include more than just a library. When ISVD came to this realization, they began to look to the computer as a possible component of the environment they needed to create. They realized that a library was unsatisfactory in the environment because the time involved in searching is usually more than one can afford. Certainly large amounts of resources, such as occupational descriptions, can be stored, indexed, cross-referenced, and made generally available in a library. On the other hand, they realized that the computer is capable of all of this and, as well, of providing fast access to data so that search time need not hamper decision making. Thus ISVD looked to the computer as a device to store large amounts of occupational data and to make them immediately and selectively available to the individual as he proceeds through the decision-making process. With such accessibility, the project hoped to encourage the individual to feel that he is among resources.

But placing the student among resources is just part of what the ISVD guidance theory requires. It requires, as well, that the student get help as he engages in the decision-making process. Specifically, as the student goes through the various stages of the decision-making process as outlined in the first half of the paradigm—the anticipation phase—an information system must provide him three things which are particularly important.[12] First, he must have the opportunity to browse through a large set of resources within the system, and to obtain cues from the system as he goes. Browsing is an unstructured activity, but it is not an aimless one; and, therefore, the system should facilitate the emergence of

[12]The accommodation phase of the decision-making paradigm was excluded from the ISVD model because it involves *acting* upon choice and, as such, occurs after that aspect of the guidance function with which ISVD was concerned.

order by probing, suggesting, reminding, and generally being at the individual's disposal. Second, the student needs the ability to follow up leads, discard them, go as far as he wishes and then start anew. There should be available to him projections and estimates about himself and about the world of work with which he may compare his own interests and abilities to those of others who have taken certain courses of action. This way he can begin to assess both his chances and his willingness to pay the price involved in particular alternatives. Finally, he needs a way to relive his past in terms of his present orientation and to act out the future or, perhaps, to bring his awareness of the future to bear upon his current need to make a career decision. The system must contain some kind of simulator or game player, therefore, which can process student data within the larger context of data about the world of work so that the student can engage in what amounts to a "career game."

For the information system to provide such assistance to the student, there needs to be between him and the data of the system, some interface—mediator—through which the data are filtered. In some respects a human being—counselor, librarian, teacher, friend—would be the best interface. But, of course, he would not be very good at treating variables in a multivariate way or at the kinds of search, estimation, computation, juxtaposition of data, and recording and presentation of material that the system requires. In these areas ISVD looked to the computer. Yet, as well as they expected the computer to serve as the interface, ISVD did not expect that the computer would replace the counselor. To ISVD, neither counselor nor computer was satisfactory alone, but functioning together they would provide the student the support he needs.

Another factor in the decision-making process that led ISVD to look to the computer is that of *monitoring.* Monitoring consists of keeping track of the student as he goes from stage to stage through the paradigm. Aside from the usual reasons for monitoring a student's behavior—to analyze his performance, select from alternate courses of action, and generally maintain an account of his interaction with the information system—ISVD proposed to present facts of this monitoring to the student himself so that he might use them as additional data. As a result, hopefully, the student would become aware of his patterns of action. This awareness, in turn, encourages a "higher order of understanding of both the decision-making process and the panorama of career choice in which decision points are linked."

In part, therefore, ISVD would provide the student with information about the structure and form of his interaction with the system's data, and about his passage through the decision procedure. Tiedeman conceived of a monitoring and feedback system wherein the student processes data from monitoring on his way to a decision. These demands of monitoring student behavior and of processing the products of such monitoring convinced the ISVD staff that a computer was indispensable to their project. At the very least the time element involved, the manual storing, retrieving, presenting, editing, updating, restoring, and cross-referencing of data indicate that a human being would not be up to the monitoring task. Thus, ISVD concluded that even though the computer cannot be expected to carry the full burden, it is a vital component of the information system called for by Tiedeman's theory.

So, while the ISVD project was an effort totally directed to the consideration and solution of certain guidance problems, Tiedeman and the other project leaders understood that their ability to deal fully with such guidance problems depended upon the computer. This dependence is revealed in Tiedeman's statement that *a computer-based information system would be the mechanism through which the project worked to improve vocational decision making.* The project's first major report states that this computer-based system would serve to help the student

> relate knowledge about himself to data about education, training, and work and thereby create a body of information on which he can base his career decision. The entire program links person, computer, and teacher or counselor in such a way that the student can conduct a dialogue with the computer, while the counselor assists in interpreting and evaluating the results of the dialogue.[13]

The purpose of such a computer-based system is to

> cultivate [in the student] the capacity for and confidence in choosing by giving users almost infinite possibility for the exercise of decision-making among data bases while simultaneously attempting to make the processes of decision-making both explicit and mastered.[14]

The computer was to play a central role, then, in achieving this goal and were we not careful, we might easily make the mistake of looking at ISVD as a computer project.

Why it would be a mistake to consider ISVD to have been a project about computers rather than strictly about guidance may not be obvious. After all, the project spent as much as $15,000 *a month* just for computer time and computer equipment, and of all the people who worked on the ISVD project during its three years, about 25 percent of them were directly involved with programming, operating, or testing the computer. In computer programming alone, ISVD invested the equivalent of twenty-two man-years of work, and when they were done they delivered to the U.S. Office of Education 6,000 feet of computer tapes—that is a little more than a mile of tape—containing programs and data of the

[13]*Annual Report 1966-1967*, Information System for Vocational Decisions, 1967, p. 2.
[14]Ibid.

project's information system. It would not be rash, therefore, to wonder why all of this does not clearly establish ISVD as a full-scale computer project.

The answer to this question, the explanation of the assertion that ISVD was not a project *about* computers, is that the ISVD staff knew what computers are. They knew, as we came to understand in Part I, that a computer is an incomplete machine: not a machine in its own right, but a device with which to build machines. With computers you build machines by describing them, that is, by specifying their behaviors, and this is the crux of the matter: the purpose of ISVD was *to specify how a guidance machine should behave.*

When ISVD researchers said that the computer was to be the interface between the student and the storehouse of data, he really meant that a guidance machine (a computer imitating a guidance machine) would be the interface. ISVD would build a guidance machine; but not with the usual tools, of course. They would build it by describing it. For ISVD the computer was a convenience, a mechanism for talking about procedures. The particular procedures that interested Tiedeman and his associates were guidance procedures. The end product would be a guidance machine, not because anyone thought about it directly, but because a statement about procedures, when unambiguous, contains a description of the machine needed to carry out those procedures. Thus the centrality of the computer in ISVD stemmed from the fact that it enhanced the project's ability to talk sensibly and unambiguously about guidance.

CHAPTER SEVEN: the development

By now the idea that someone might build a guidance machine by describing it to a computer is probably acceptable, at least in a general way. But what about the specifics? How, specifically, does one go about describing a guidance machine to a computer in such a way that, when it operates, the computer behaves as though it were that guidance machine? The technical specifics that answer this question fall outside the scope of this book,[1] but, even so, we can address the question directly and propose some useful answers to it. To find these answers we must begin with a look at some of the things ISVD had to do to get the computer ready to accept a description of a guidance machine.

This last sentence may be a little surprising because up to now we have talked as though computers come ready to accept descriptions of machines. Suddenly we seem to have changed this point of view, saying now that something has to be done to a computer to make it capable of dealing with such descriptions. The apparent inconsistency here comes from the fact that a bare computer, able to understand its own machine language only, is too formidable a device for ordinary people to communicate with. In this bare state, the computer is ready to accept programs, of course, but the task of dealing with machine language is

[1]See David Brewster, "Program Description - DASM: Direct Access Storage Management", Project Report No. 35; Heather Scott, "Program Description - HASM: Hierarchical Access Storage Management", Project Report No. 34; Ann Taylor, "GLURP—Generalized Language for Understanding and Responding to People", Project Report No. 29, Information System for Vocational Decisions, 1970.

tedious, complicated, and it takes more time and effort than usually it is worth. Even computer programming specialists, systems analysts, software designers and other technical experts rarely deal with the bare computer if they can possibly help it. They prefer, instead, to work with a computer that has been prepared in such a way that the programming task is made a lot easier. That is, they prefer to work with a computer that already is programmed. But these are special programs. Their job is to make it easier to write *other* programs. These special programs are usually called *system programs*, or, more generally, *system software*, and were it not for the existence of a rich set of such system software, the computer would not have found its way so deeply into the field of education.

Of course the higher level computer languages—assemblers and compilers—as computer programs whose task it is to facilitate the writing of other computer programs, qualify as system programs. (See Appendix.) Assemblers and compilers make up the primary example of system programs, but there are others. A second example of system programs is often called the "system library," which stands for a collection of programs and routines that one can call up with his own program. When called, these routines—generally routines to perform often used functions such as computing a square root or an arcsine, or accessing some input/output device, or linking several programs together—become a part of one's program just as though he had written them himself. A third example of system software is the executive system, a set of routines that operate "behind the scenes" to oversee the functioning of one's program. In a typical computing center where many people submit their programs, the executive software system keeps track of which program is being run, how much time it is taking, whether or not it is in trouble and needs to be taken off the machine, and the like. It is a computer program that "watches" other computer programs operate.

Many other examples can be cited but, by now, it is probably clear enough that anyone using a computer will depend heavily upon system software. But in the case of ISVD, the system software provided by the computer manufacturer, while extensive, was not enough to do the job. The problem ISVD hoped to solve was so complex, from the computing point of view, that its need for tailor-made system routines was greater than the usual case. Thus before ISVD could begin its effort to describe a guidance machine to a computer, it had to fashion its own network of system programs—its own library, its own data handling routines, its own information retrieval system, even its own programming language. But as we take a brief look at the major components of the ISVD system software, do not let the extensiveness of the effort obscure its sole intention, which was that the ISVD guidance specialists use the various components of this system software as the tools with which to build their guidance machine.

System Software

Most people know that fluorescent lights do not glow continuously while they are turned on. They flicker on and off, but so rapidly that to us it seems that they give off a constant stream of light. The reaction time of human beings is not quick enough to perceive such rapid flickering. Of course, this fact about the reaction time of human beings is not restricted to perceptions of how fluorescent lights behave. Many examples of how man's relatively slow reaction time affects his perceptions can be cited, and the typical introductory text in physics—covering such topics as sound, light, heat, electricity and magnetism—is filled with such cases.

In an interesting way, the computer's speed provides another example of this phenomenon, and this fact was to become very important to ISVD in its considerations about system software. Because a computer is so much faster at doing things than human beings are at reacting, it has become possible for more than one person to use a given computer at what seems to them to be the same time. Much the way the chess master plays chess against seven local champions simultaneously, the computer can process the programs of several users at the same time.

Time Sharing

Having a computer process several different programs at what appears to be the same time is usually called *time sharing.* To see how time sharing might work, imagine, say, sixteen electronic typewriters (or other terminal devices—such as the teletypewriter or the video display terminals pictured in the Appendix), each of which is connected to the same computer by a wire of some sort. Usually this is a telephone wire, and the terminals are located some distance from the computer. But do not worry about the specifics of this connection, just assume that data and programs are input to the computer by "typing" them in at a typewriter, that is, by transmitting the input over one of the wires to the computer. Similarly, the computer sends output over a wire to any of the sixteen typewriters where it is printed or, in the case of a video display terminal, displayed on a television-like screen. Now even though all sixteen terminals are connected to the computer, in the sense that input and output can be sent back and forth over any of the sixteen wires to and from the corresponding terminal, the computer pays attention to only one user at a time. The computer, like the chess master, cycles from one user to the next and then the next, processing the programs of each. During any given cycle, the time the computer spends on a particular user may be no more than one-tenth of a second, but of course, a computer can perform many operations during even such a small slice of time. Besides, the computer will cycle back to each user so quickly, when compared to human reaction time, that often he will not notice he is sharing the computer with anyone. As with the flickering of the fluorescent lamp, the computer's cycling from user to user is not readily perceived.

Time sharing was especially appropriate for ISVD. ISVD theory called for fast access to data and for interaction between the student and the computer routines that comprised the "guidance machine" and a time sharing system would be the appropriate setting for such access and interaction. Furthermore, with a time sharing system, ISVD could accommodate a larger number of students. The ISVD project staff, recognizing these arguments, described their need for a time shared computer facility by saying,

> this project proposes the development of an interactive reckoning environment in which an individual's exercise of a career decision-making procedure will be maximally facilitated. Within this environment, the computer will be used as an approximation to that reckoning device which our theory calls for. Essentially, the computer will be used (1) to store large amounts of vocationally relevant data, such as occupational descriptions, job characteristics, statistical projections of manpower needs, and student data files; and (2) to provide access to these data on demand or as a result of certain interactions with the individual.
>
> At once we draw the obvious conclusion that such a computer should be able to communicate with at least one individual at a time. We mean by this the kind of communication one might have at a teletypewriter or inquiry station connected to a computer. Accepting for the moment the restriction that the computer accommodate only one person at a sitting—that is, that there be only one station "live" at any time and that until the person using that station signs off, no other person can use the system—it is clear, nonetheless, that there will need to be more than one station connected to the computer. It is unreasonable to require all individuals—programmers, researchers, students, counselors, teachers, and the others to whom the system will be made available—to come to a single location to gain access to the system, particularly since it is our intention to provide our model as an integrated part of the various environments in which these individuals function. We conclude then, that the computer should possess the capability of being fed information from a number of remote-inquiry stations. This is what is ordinarily meant by "multi-access computer." Considering next the restriction that the computer accommodate only one person at a sitting: we find this untenable. The trouble of setting up time schedules, allotting individuals pre-arranged amounts of time, rescheduling because of changes of plans or unforeseen circumstances, and the like, would be reason enough for us to reject such a condition. More important than this, however, is the fact that since no individual could ever use the full capacity of the computer for the entire duration of his communication with it, this restriction becomes indefensibly wasteful. Finally, of course, it is inconsistent with the purposes of this project that a person could not have access to the system without excessive delay. It becomes desirable then to require that more than one individual be given access to the computer at what amounts to the same time. That is, that more than one remote-inquiry station—in fact, most or all of them—should function as though they were "live" at the same time. The

> popular term for this condition is "timesharing" (although "time-slicing" is probably less misleading)—a technique of allotting computer time to different remote stations in little quanta or slices so minute when compared to human reaction time that each user has the illusion of having the machine to himself.[2]

So, the first major component of the ISVD system software would be a time sharing system. To write the system programs that will allow a computer to time share is a task of major proportions requiring many man-years of work and extensive resources neither of which ISVD could afford. Fortunately, however, ISVD would not have to build from scratch its own time sharing system. Instead it could use the system a computer manufacturer developed to go with its machine. The particular time sharing system ISVD was to use is called the Basic Time Sharing System (BTSS) developed by the Radio Corporation of America to operate on its RCA Spectra 70/45 computer. But even with the availability of BTSS, the ISVD programmers had considerable work ahead of them in system software development.

BTSS is a time sharing system designed to be used primarily by engineers, technicians, and certain scientists who wish to use the computer to do their various calculations. Because of this orientation, BTSS as it stood, was not strictly appropriate as an educational information retrieval system. Of course, ISVD would be able to use BTSS to perform the basic functions of time sharing for the project, but before ISVD would have the complete system software it needed, major programming changes would have to be made.

Data Handling

The most extensive set of changes ISVD had to make to BTSS concerned the problem of data handling. Massive amounts of data relevant to career choice had to be stored, retrieved, decoded, updated, displayed, and otherwise processed, and BTSS was not up to the task. It was not meant to be; it had been designed to allow a user to write and execute fairly small programs and to store them on the computer in such a way that no other user could get at these programs. But ISVD needed the opposite of this scheme of private files: all the elements of the extensive ISVD data bases had to be "public" and easily accessible by any user of the system.

To this end ISVD designed its own system software for the extensive handling of massive amounts of occupational data.[3] This data handling system is the second major component of the ISVD software. When

[2]Allan B. Ellis and Charles S. Wetherell, "The Computer and Career Decisions," *Technical Memorandum No. 1,* Information System for Vocational Decisions Project, Harvard University, Cambridge, Mass., 1966, pp. 25–26.

[3]This work was done with the assistance of Massachusetts Computer Associates. Especially see their Technical Report CA 6704-0422, April 1967.

completed, this system was "sewn" into BTSS, replacing its more restrictive data storage scheme.

The ISVD data handling system software consists of two components, the first of which is called DASM, which stands for Direct Access Storage Management. The basic and most important function of DASM is to retrieve data from the data bases stored on disk. But, naturally, associated with retrieval is storing, updating, deleting, and, in general, maintaining the data, and DASM was designed to perform all these functions.

DASM's functions become clearer when we consider a portion of the ISVD data handling requirements. The computer ISVD chose to use for the project had connected to it four storage disc drives. Each disc drive stores up to 7.25 million characters, meaning that at any given time, the system software had to keep track of up to 29 million characters worth of data and programs. Not only did these data and programs need to be stored on the disks, as well, they needed to be organized. That is, the data had to be grouped into different *files*—occupational file, educational file, user characteristics file, and the like—and within each file the data needed to be further grouped into *records.* Each record, in turn, had to contain *categories* of data. For example, the occupational file in ISVD consisted of the names and extensive descriptive data for 850 occupations. For each occupation there was a record and within each of these 850 records there were 56 categories of data such as "strength required," "education required," "salaries and wages," "opportunities for promotion," "union membership," and "requirements for travel." (We will look at the data bases more closely further on.)

Given such requirements, the collection of programs that make up the DASM system software set had to perform a number of functions relating to data handling: it had to structure the disks to properly house the data; it had to place the data on the disks, organized according to the ISVD scheme and stored so as to facilitate search and retrieval; it had to update, purge, replace, delete, and manipulate the files of data; and then as its central function, DASM had to retrieve data on demand during a time shared session, searching and locating records on the disk and delivering them to whatever program called for the data.

DASM has a companion called HASM, the second component of the ISVD data handling system software. While DASM is responsible for all aspects of the *physical* organization and retrieval of data, HASM—Hierarchical Access Storage Management—looks after the *logical* aspects of data handling. One such logical aspect is the decoding of data once they have been retrieved. This is a major function of HASM, but its prime responsibility is to serve as a go-between for DASM and the user. When a program or a user makes a request for data, this request ends up in HASM where it is processed. HASM then tells DASM which record to retrieve from which data base. DASM completes its job by passing the record in question back to HASM where it is further processed. When HASM completes the required decoding or analysis, it sends part or all of the record on to the appropriate place either for still more processing or for display.

Here is a simplified example of how HASM and DASM function together. Suppose a user at a terminal types in the question: "How much does a carpenter earn?" Other parts of the ISVD software system—described further on—would process this sentence and determine that the salary category from the carpenter record in the occupational data base had to be retrieved. At this point, the HASM program would be called in to do its first job which is to determine the type of retrieval required—retrieve a datum with decoding, fetch without decoding, fetch a guidance routine for execution, and the like. In this case, its job would be to fetch and decode part of the carpenter record. Determining this, HASM would then check to see if the required data are already in the computer's memory. If not, HASM calls on DASM to retrieve the data from disk storage, giving it the name of the needed record (carpenter). DASM fetches the carpenter record—using a set of procedures to minimize the search time needed to locate the record—and returns it to HASM. HASM then verifies that there is a salary category in the carpenter record, returning an error message to the user otherwise. Finding the salary category, HASM then calls on DASM again, this time to fetch a special table used whenever decoding is required. When it receives this table, HASM looks up the word "salary" to discover the name of yet another table, called a decode table. For each category of data that is coded, there is a decode table that can be used to translate the data into its original form. Finding the name of the decode table needed to translate the coded value of "salary" into the corresponding dollars and cents, HASM again calls on DASM this time to retrieve the relevant decode table. With this table HASM then deciphers the code and passes the value back to the program that made the request, where it is further processed and displayed. All of this may take one-tenth of a second to accomplish.

The ISVD data handling software consisting principally of DASM and HASM constitutes a substantial addition to BTSS and its ability to retrieve and process large storehouses of data. Yet with all of it and with corresponding alterations to BTSS to permit the imbedding of DASM and HASM, still there was a third component of the ISVD system software that had to be designed and implemented. The need for this third element came from the fact that the language of BTSS is FORTRAN. FORTRAN is a sophisticated computer language designed mainly for mathematical and statistical programming. As good a language as FORTRAN is, however, it was not appropriate because the data of ISVD are not numbers, they are words, and thus the language of ISVD would best be one that facilitated the processing of English words, sentences, and paragraphs.

To create such a capacity within ISVD, its staff surveyed the major efforts throughout the country to get computers to deal with complicated English. Because ISVD was to incorporate the fruits of these efforts into its system software, it is relevant for us to turn now to a brief look at some of the work in automated natural language processing they uncovered. As we shall see, the most troubling questions that underlie what it might mean to have a computer "speak English" relate not only to certain technical issues but, as well, go to the heart of the educational questions confronting ISVD. Thus what follows should be read in terms of both the process and the substance of ISVD.

Getting a Guidance Machine to Understand English

Consider this typical conversation between a patient and doctor: (The patient speaks first.)

> *Men are all alike.*
> In what way?
> *They're always bugging us about something or other.*
> Can you think of a specific example?
> *Well, my boyfriend made me come here.*
> Your boyfriend made you come here?
> *He says I'm depressed much of the time.*
> I am sorry to hear you are depressed.
> *It's true. I am unhappy.*
> Do you think coming here will help you not to be unhappy?
> *I need some help, that much seems certain.*
> What would it mean to you if you got some help?
> *Perhaps I could learn to get along with my mother.*
> Tell me more about your family.
> *My mother takes care of me.*
> Who else in your family takes care of you?
> *My father.*
> Your father?
> *You are like my father in some ways.*
> What resemblance do you see?
> *You are not very aggressive but I think you don't want me to notice that.*
> What makes you think I am not very aggressive?
> *You don't argue with me.*
> Why do you think I don't argue with you?
> *You are afraid of me.*
> Does it please you to believe I am afraid of you?
> *My father is afraid of everybody.*
> What else comes to mind when you think of your father?
> *Bullies.*
> Does that have anything to do with the fact that your boyfriend made you come here?

Of the various conversations human beings have with each other, the conversation, such as this one, between a psychiatrist and a patient are, in certain respects, the most difficult ones to have. The patient's words can hide meaning just as often as they reveal what is on his mind. The psychiatrist must listen intently, prod gently, respond to some things and not to others, and, at all times during the conversation, he must exercise great care in his choice of words. This is exactly why such conversations with people are supposed to be left to professionals. Only an expert can handle the subtleties of language and the complexities of meaning involved in such a dialogue.

For the very reason that such dialogues are filled with language difficulties—difficulties of expression, interpretation, and relevance—some computer scientists have come to regard them as a sort of goal. That is, in wondering whether or not computers can be made to deal intelligently with natural language—English, for instance—some computer specialists have aspired to create computational procedures that would specify how a computer could engage a human being in conversation as subtle and complex as that between a psychiatrist and his patient. Before we can see whether or not such a goal is within reach, we must begin by looking at more modest efforts.

Bookkeeping

Probably the most active work, and certainly the most successful, in applying computers to natural language processing could go under the name *language bookkeeping*, but because such work is being done by literary scholars, psychologists, social scientists, educational researchers, statisticians, and other specialists from similarly diverse fields, this work goes under many different names. Among them we find such names as, "stylistic analysis," "content analysis," "attribution studies," "pattern analysis," "automatic indexing," "computer essay grading," "automated concordances," and "automatic inventories." Now, there is nothing about these names that warrants any argument; they all mean something, and, to the expert, each of them is descriptive of a particular concern felt by a particular scholar. Besides, even though they all belong to the same very general area of language data processing, each of the computational procedures represented by these names is sufficiently different from the others to deserve to have its own name. The only trouble is that, to the layman trying to get a beginning grasp of what computers can be made to do with words, these names do little to reveal that many of the procedures involved are simple and understandable. Not all of them, of course. Some of the computer programs involved with language bookkeeping exceed the understanding even of some of the people who use them successfully. But many others are clear enough for us to consider here.

At the base of those language data processing applications which may be grouped under the heading language bookkeeping are computational procedures that involve little more than comparing things and keeping count of the number of times there is a match. Comparing and counting things can provide a sizable amount of basic data useful in quite a few different applications. To see how this might be so, assume that we have keypunched onto data processing cards the text of some book. We would do this in a straightforward manner, just as though we were typing: putting a space after each word; using periods, colons, question marks, and such in their usual places; and not needing to put in any special computer characters anywhere. Having thus put the text in "machine readable" form, we could begin to process the text with computer programs that compare and count. For instance, a program might read in the text character by character, compare each character with a short prestored list of symbols to see if it is a "period" a "question mark" or any one of the other final punctuation marks, and keep count of the number of matches. Obviously, this is a way to count the number of sentences in the text. By the same logic we could count the total number of words in the text; essentially all we need to do is count the spaces, because, in a sense, every word ends in a space. Should our program then divide the word-total by the sentence-total, it would produce for us the "average sentence length"—a measure which, along with the standard deviation of sentence length, has played an important part in many studies attempting to resolve cases of disputed authorship.

Naturally, what we do with the sentence, we can do as well with the paragraph, and the chapter. Chapter size, sentences-per-paragraph, average paragraph length, and similar "counts" are all easily produced. Similarly, the "word" can be the unit of measure. Among the things popularly done with words, there is the *word count.* By comparing and counting, programs easily produce word count lists, containing all the words used in a text and for each word the number of times it appears. Rearranging the output and adding, for each word, reference to the passages in which it occurs produces the *concordance.* Of course, both the word count and the concordance have been important to the literary scholar well before the advent of the computer. No longer, however, is the labor involved excessive.

Other applications of the procedures of language bookkeeping include the comparing of words of a text with words on a prestored list of commonly misspelled words or against a list of commonly used words thereby checking, respectively, spelling and the use of unusual words. This latter measure has been used in "readability formulas" and is one part of the scheme used by Ellis Page in his attempts to grade student essays.[4] Still another language bookkeeping function consisting basically of comparing and counting involves searching texts to locate patterns of

[4]See for example, Ellis Page, "Measurement Frontiers Symposium, Essay Grading by Computer," American Psychological Association, Chicago, 1965.

usage. At the simplest level this entails flagging every use of a specified word or words, while at another level the procedure might call for searching out specific combinations of words.

The General Inquirer

These are just a few examples of automated language bookkeeping tasks that rest upon various forms of comparing and counting. Other, more sophisticated computational procedures are usually involved as well, of course, and the use of the term language bookkeeping is not intended to suggest that this aspect of language data processing is either simple or trivial. Indeed, in some cases, exceedingly powerful computer systems have been constructed out of computational procedures that can be thought of as language bookkeeping procedures.

One such sophisticated computer system, created by Philip J. Stone of Harvard University, goes by the name *The General Inquirer.* The General Inquirer is a collection of computer programs for content analysis, which means it is a system for making inferences by examining texts in certain careful ways. Like many other language bookkeeping programs, the main program of the General Inquirer system contains a dictionary. When some text is read into this program, each word will be compared with the contents of the dictionary—really just a list of words in which the researcher is interested—to find a match. But the intention here is not merely to find out how many times words are used, it is to keep account of how many times *classes* of words are used in a text. Thus the words in the dictionary are grouped into classes of words. For instance, the words "wife," "daughter," "aunt," "mother," "sister," "bride," and "actress," might all be grouped under the category, FEMALE-ROLE. Probably "thesaurus" is a better word to use to describe such collections of words, but through common practice they are called "dictionaries." When using this main program of the General Inquirer system, one may use any one of the various dictionaries that have been developed by Stone and his associates—a psychosociological dictionary, a political dictionary, an anthropological dictionary, and some fourteen others[5]—or, if we wish, we may make up our own dictionary, representing the groupings and the words that interest us. With some text and with a dictionary, we are ready to use the system.

The main program of the system—a "text tagging" program—reads in the text, sentence by sentence, and "looks up" each word in the dictionary. Whenever a word is found to be in the dictionary, the category (or categories) of which that word is a member is noted. When the

[5]For a complete description of these dictionaries, plus a full account of all the details of the design and the use of the General Inquirer, see Philip J. Stone, Dexter C. Dunphy, Marshall S. Smith and Daniel M. Ogilvie, *The General Inquirer: A Computer Approach to Content Analysis*, M.I.T., Cambridge, Mass., 1966.

complete sentence has been thus processed, the sentence is written onto computer tape along with the names of each of the noted categories. When every sentence in the text has been processed in this way, this program's job is completed and the output tape, containing the "tagged" sentences, is ready to become input to other programs in the General Inquirer system.

Usually, the next of these programs to be used is the "text and tag listing" program. The central function of this program is to print each sentence along with its tags (categories), and a count of words is included. The output from this program helps the researcher to get an idea of the distribution of categories within the text. A second program—"tag tally"—serves a similar function, but is organized by document rather than by sentence. Output consists of raw frequencies and percentage frequencies of the appearance of each dictionary category. A third version of category distribution is provided by the "graphing" program, which represents tag tallies as bar graphs. Along with these there are other programs to provide such things as means, standard deviations, frequencies across documents, and various combinations of subtotals.

The programs of the General Inquirer system that have been mentioned by themselves make up a very useful and impressive collection of language bookkeeping procedures. Yet none of them can be said to represent the principal function of the system. They all play important parts in making the General Inquirer a powerful system for content analysis, of course, but of all the functions of the system the central one is that of retrieval. The items retrieved are the sentences, and the ways the General Inquirer permits sentence retrieval accounts, more than anything else, for its power as a sophisticated system for language data processing.

Using the "retrieval" program of the General Inquirer system—which processes the tape produced by the "text tagging" program—it is possible to retrieve for inspection sentences that have characteristics that interest you. You can specify that the sentences retrieved contain certain words, for example, or a certain category or categories of words. You can even specify that the program retrieve sentences containing certain categories and *not* containing others. Such a request may be "retrieve all those sentences containing words from the SELF category and the GOOD category but *not* containing either the word "pool" or the word "billiards" and not containing a word from the MONEY category." It does not require much reflection to begin to see the power such a system offers—even though not all of the things the system can do have been described—and yet even the retrieval portion of the General Inquirer involves little more than comparing and keeping track of matches.

Up to now in this account, computational procedures based upon "comparing and counting" algorithms have held our attention not because they are all that are involved in language bookkeeping, but because concentrating on them makes it easier to see some ways computers can be made to deal with language. One should not be misled by this, however, to think that it is easy, in general, to get computers to process language. Nor, certainly, should one assume that all efforts in the area of language data processing have been completely successful. Indeed, many of the potentially most important applications of computers in language processing are yet to be fully implemented. One such application is that of machine translation of text, an area to which many outstanding language scholars and computer specialists have devoted years of effort. One conclusion these men have drawn from their work—which, incidentally, was not without significant achievement—is that "there is no immediate or predictable prospect of useful machine translation."[6] A second important area of language processing yet to be fully automated, is the area of document abstracting. While work progresses in this field, no solution has been found that makes automatic abstracting sufficiently practicable or economical to supplant the human abstractor. Automatic indexing and classification, and document storage and retrieval are two other areas of language data processing in which work remains "experimental" and where, despite the application of both talent and effort, the prospects for complete implementation are still uncertain.[7]

Thus, while we now have a beginning idea of how computers conceivably can deal with language, we should know also that there are limits. Of course, these limits are not intrinsic to the computer; they are defined by us or, more accurately, by the extent of our understanding of the processes we wish to automate.

Conversation

In October 1950, the late Alan M. Turing—the eminent English mathematician and logician whose pioneer work on automata theory we considered in Chapter Two—published an article entitled "Computing Machinery and Intelligence," in which he proposed to examine the question of whether or not a machine can think.[8] His first step was to replace this question by another one "which is closely related to it and is expressed in relatively unambiguous words." He said:

> The new form of the problem can be described in terms of a game which we call the "imitation game." It is played with three people, a man (A), a woman (B), and an interrogator (C) who may be of either sex. The interrogator is to determine which of the other two is the man and which is the woman. He

[6]Automatic Language Processing Advisory Committee, *Language and Machines*, National Academy of Science, Washington, D.C., 1966, p. 32.
[7]An excellent account of the work in these areas of language data processing is offered by Harold Borko, (ed.), *Automated Language Processing: The State of the Art*, Wiley, New York, 1967.
[8]Alan M. Turing, "Computing Machinery and Intelligence," *Mind*, October 1950, **59**, pp. 433–460.

> knows them by labels X and Y, and at the end of the game he says either "X is A and Y is B" or "X is B and Y is A." The interrogator is allowed to put questions to A and B thus:
>
> C: Will X please tell me the length of his or her hair? Now suppose X is actually A, then A must answer. It is A's object in the game to try to cause C to make the wrong identification. His answer might therefore be, "My hair is shingled, and the longest strands are about nine inches long."
>
> In order that tones of voice may not help the interrogator the answers should be written, or better still, typewritten. The ideal arrangement is to have a teleprinter communicating between the two rooms. Alternatively the question and answers can be repeated by an intermediary. The object of the game for the third player (B) is to help the interrogator. The best strategy for her is probably to give truthful answers. She can add such things as "I am the woman, don't listen to him!" to her answers, but it will avail nothing as the man can make similar remarks.
>
> We now ask the question, "What will happen when a machine takes the part of A in this game?" Will the interrogator decide wrongly as often when the game is played like this as he does when the game is played between a man and a woman? This question replaces our original, "Can machines think?"[9]

This imitation game has interested scholars ever since it was devised, and they have come to refer to this set of "conditions" as "Turing's test." Mostly, their interest has centered on what it would take to get a computer to pass Turing's test. Marvin Minsky and others working in the field called "artificial intelligence" refer to the more general problem as that of "making machines do things that would require intelligence if done by men."[10] Whatever the specific solution, the computer must, in a certain sense, behave like a person. This certain sense is the sense of language behavior. That is, to play the imitation game, a computer must seem to "understand" and "speak" language the way people do, at least well enough to fool everyone into thinking it is a human being.

Now nobody is fooled when he opens his mail and reads:

DEAR ELECTRICITY USER:
OUR RECORDS SHOW THAT YOUR BILL FOR THE MONTH OF MAY IS
STILL OUTSTANDING. IF IT IS NOT PAID BY RETURN MAIL YOUR
SERVICE WILL BE DISCONTINUED.
VERY TRULY YOURS
LIGHT AND POWER CO.

We have been getting notes like this from computers for so long that the pretense that they are communications from some human being no longer works. It is not enough to get a computer to print words. The imitation

[9]Alan M. Turing, op. cit.
[10]Marvin Minsky (ed.), *Semantic Information Processing*, M.I.T., Cambridge, Mass., 1968, p. 4.

game requires that the machine be more convincing than that. It must give the appearance of being, somehow, a personal or individual communication. Consider this communication, for example,

THIS IS A REPORT WRITTEN SO THAT YOU CAN READ ABOUT YOURSELF AND LEARN TO UNDERSTAND YOURSELF BETTER. WE SEND THIS REPORT TO YOUR DOCTOR OR COUNSELOR. HE HAS READ IT BEFORE GIVING IT TO YOU, AND HE WILL DISCUSS IT WITH YOU. HE WILL EXPLAIN THE PARTS THAT MAY NOT BE CLEAR TO YOU.
ANALYSIS OF THIS KIND CAN BE DONE FROM ANY OF SEVERAL PSYCHOLOGICAL TESTS. IN THIS CASE, THE TEST ANSWERED AND SUBMITTED FOR ANALYSIS WAS THE MINNESOTA MULTIPHASIC PERSONALITY INVENTORY.
YOU HAVE TOLD US BOTH GOOD AND BAD THINGS ABOUT YOURSELF. YOU ARE A SOMEWHAT TIMID PERSON. YOU ARE A RATHER COMPLIANT PERSON. YOU USUALLY GOES ALONG WITH THE RULES, AND YOU USUALLY GOES ALONG WITH OTHER PEOPLE'S WISHES. YOU ARE NOT VERY WELL ORGANIZED. YOU ARE A FLEXIBLE AND OBLIGING PERSON. YOU ARE NOT VERY STRONG-WILLED. YOU ARE SPONTANEOUS AND FLEXIBLE, AND NOT RIGID. YOU ARE A RATHER CHANGEABLE AND UNPREDICTABLE PERSON. YOU DO WHAT YOU HAPPEN TO FEEL LIKE AT THE TIME.
AT YOUR BEST YOU ARE GENEROUS, SENTIMENTAL, PEACEFUL, AND COOPERATIVE.
YOU ARE A PERSON WHO FEELS A NEED TO LEAN ON OTHER PEOPLE. YOU ASK THEM TO TAKE CARE OF YOU, TO GIVE YOU ADVICE, AND TO REASSURE YOU. YOU ARE DEPENDENT IN A PASSIVE WAY.

But this does not fool us either. The simple sentences, the misuse of the words "goes" and "send," and such betray the fact that this "letter" was produced by a computer. But, clearly, it is much better than we are used to and, in any case, we should be impressed by the processing involved to produce this letter. Producing such statements is a part of a project called OPTIMUM. The project director, Joseph C. Finney, a psychiatrist at the College of Education, University of Kentucky, and his colleagues are using a computer program that reads in responses to a test such as the MMPI, scores the test, computes the various scale factor scores, performs certain statistical analysis on the results, and then selects the appropriate sentences or phrases from a stored set, resulting in a verbal description—analysis—of the individual based on his test performance.

Protran

Another computer system designed to produce sentences describing a person's performance on some objective test or other is called PRO-

TRAN. PROTRAN was created by Carl E. Helm as a tool with which "to explore the procedures used by psychologists in evaluating a person's performance on a battery of psychological tests."[11] Strictly from the point of view of language data processing techniques, Helm's work is more sophisticated and wider reaching than the work of Finney and his associates. In comparison, for instance, PROTRAN functions less like a computer program and more like a computer language. Input to the system are statement-rules specifying which sentences or phrases are to be combined and printed under which conditions, that is, depending upon the particular subtest involved and the particular test score or range obtained by the student.

Helm's interest in PROTRAN rests in the area of *simulation*—imitating a process in order to better understand it—and, specifically, his goal is to gain insight into the things psychologists do when they interpret a battery of test scores. Helm's procedure was to talk with and observe psychologists over an extended period of time in order to determine as well as possible what rules they were using to analyze test scores. Once he had a set of these rules, he could direct PROTRAN to use them to process a battery of test scores, comparing PROTRAN's output with the written interpretation generated by the psychologist. When the correspondence between the two was poor, Helm went back to the psychologist to see whether there were other rules being used but not yet revealed. Then these new rules were added in another test of PROTRAN. By such a process of successive approximations, characteristic of simulation studies, Helm was able to begin to codify the procedures and rules involved in the process.

There follow excerpts from two interpretations of a particular student's test scores, one generated by a psychologist, the other generated by PROTRAN. It is left to the reader to decide which one is which.

> His abstract reasoning ability is only average, his arithmetic reasoning ability is high average, and his skill in the rapid handling of numerical computations is average. His vocabulary level is poor, his comprehension of narrative material is fair, and a 30-minute essay was fair in quality. He demonstrates poor ability in making interpretations from data presented in chart and graph form. He has poor knowledge of contemporary world affairs.
>
> He has rather poor general verbal ability. His arithmetic reasoning ability is average as is his skill in handling numerical detail. His ability to interpret graphs is much worse than usual. He displays little knowledge of current world events.[12]

The PROTRAN version, whichever one it is, comes pretty close to sounding like a human being. In fact, this example of how PROTRAN

[11]Carl E. Helm, "Simulation Models for Psychometric Theories," *Proceedings of the Fall Joint Computer Conference*, Spartan Books, Washington, D.C., 1965, p. 728.

[12]Both examples are taken from Helm, op. cit., p. 733.

uses language probably qualifies it in Turing's sense as an "intelligent machine." If we take Turing's test literally, however, even PROTRAN would not succeed at the imitation game, because there is something lacking in the things it does with language. This missing element is *conversation*; PROTRAN "talks" to you, conceivably it might correspond with you, but it does not converse with you. But, Helm did not intend PROTRAN to hold up one end of a two-way interchange, because his interests concerned the process of interpretation not the activity of communication, and, thus, Helm was not interested in building a conversational computer.

Eliza

However, getting a computer to engage a human being in an apparently meaningful conversation has captured the interests of quite a few researchers. Products of these interests in conversational computers include such things as "question and answer" systems; programs to solve algebra word problems, natural language systems for storage and retrieval of information, and programs for "Socratic" teaching.[13] Probably the most conversational of all these systems is one created by Joseph Weizenbaum which he calls ELIZA. We will look briefly into ELIZA to see something of how it works and to learn a little of the kinds of conversations it is able to have with human beings. From this look, you will get a good sense of how far researchers have come in their efforts to get computers to deal with language.

ELIZA is a computer program named after Pygmalion's Eliza Doolittle because the program "can be taught to speak increasingly well."[14] ELIZA's function is to hold conversations with human beings, and for those who have not guessed it already, we may reveal that it was ELIZA and not a psychiatrist that had that talk with a "patient" at the beginning of this section.[15] As remarkable as it is that a computer can be programmed to hold such a conversation, probably it is more remarkable that, in general, ELIZA is based on relatively straightforward computational procedures. The program is complex, of course, and just learning how to use it requires study. But, even so, the underlying principle of ELIZA is elegantly simple.

This principle is that you can converse with someone and hold up your end fairly well even if you do not understand everything the

[13]For a review of these and other efforts to develop conversational systems, see, for example, Borko, op. cit.; Minsky, op. cit.; William D. Orr, (ed.), *Conversational Computers*, Wiley, New York, 1968; Benjamin Kleinmuntz, (ed.), *Clinical Information Processing by Computer: An Essay and Selected Readings*, Holt, New York, 1969; John Starkweather, "A Common Language for a Variety of Conversational Programming Needs," in Atkinson and Wilson, (eds.), *Computer-assisted Instruction, A Book of Readings*, Academic Press, New York, 1969.

[14]Joseph Weizenbaum, "Contextual Understanding by Computers," *Communications of the ACM*, vol. **10**, no. 8, August, 1967, p. 474.

[15]The conversation is taken from Weizenbaum, op. cit., p. 475.

conversation is about and even if you do not understand most of what the other speaker is saying to you. Weizenbaum makes this point when he says,

> Consider the sentence "I am very unhappy these days." Suppose a foreigner with only a limited knowledge of English but with a very good ear heard that sentence spoken but understood only the first two words "I am." Wishing to appear interested, perhaps even sympathetic, he may reply "How long have you been very unhappy these days?" What he must have done is to apply a kind of template to the original sentence, one part of which matched the two words "I am" and the remainder isolated the words "very unhappy these days." He must also have a reassembly kit specifically associated with that template, one that specified that any sentence of the form "I am BLAH" can be transformed to "How long have you been BLAH," independently of the meaning of BLAH.[16]

Using ELIZA entails writing a *script*—an overall description of the desired interaction between the foreigner (the machine) and some user of the system. Contained in the script is a list of the words understood by the foreigner (keywords); the various templates he applies to input sentences (decomposition rules), and for each template the "kit" he uses to put the sentence back together (reassembly rules). More specifically, an ELIZA script is divided into two parts: a keyword section and a program section. The keyword section contains keywords and decomposition and reassembly rules. "The keywords provide some hint as to what the student is talking about while decomposition rules provide a way to analyze his sentence to determine what he is saying."[17] The reassembly rules describe how the program is to fashion a response to the student's input, while the program part of the script contains further details of what is to be done when there is a match between a decomposition rule and an inputted sentence. Weizenbaum describes the general procedure of the program as "quite simple," stating that the

> text is read and inspected for the presence of a *keyword.* If such a word is found, the sentence is transformed according to a *rule* associated with the keyword, if not a content-free remark or, under certain conditions, an earlier transformation is retrieved. The text so computed or retrieved is then printed out.[18]

To see something of how this works in practice, take the sentence uttered by the patient near the end of the excerpt

[16]Joseph Weizenbaum, "ELIZA—A Computer Program for the Study of Natural Language Communication Between Man and Machine," *Communications of the ACM,* vol. **9**, no. 1, January, 1966, p. 37.
[17]E. F. Taylor, "The ELIZA Program: Conversational Tutorial," *IEEE International Convention Record,* vol. **6**, part 10, 1967, p. 10.
[18]Weizenbaum, op. cit.

YOU ARE AFRAID OF ME.

The first thing the script does is to replace the word "you" with the word "I" and the word "me" with the word "you." The sentence thus becomes

I ARE AFRAID OF YOU.

Then each word in this sentence is looked up in the KEYWORD list, and it is discovered that "I" has been given the highest ranking in the list. This means the decomposition rules in the script associated with the word "I" will be used to process the input. One of these templates is

(Ø I ARE Ø)
1 2 3 4

which means "check to see if the input sentence is of the general form: any number of words, including no words at all, followed by the words "I" and "ARE" followed by any number of words." If there is no match between the input sentence and this template, then the program goes on to another template. Since there is a match, however, one of the reassembly rules related to this template is used to create an output sentence. For example, a reassembly rule might read

(DOES IT PLEASE YOU TO BELIEVE THAT I AM 4.)

The "4" refers to the fourth component in the input—in this case everything in the input sentence following the "ARE" or literally "afraid of you." Since "afraid of you" is the fourth component, it will be printed in place of the 4 in the reassembly rule producing as a response to the statement

YOU ARE AFRAID OF ME.

DOES IT PLEASE YOU TO BELIEVE I AM AFRAID OF YOU?

So you see that even with ELIZA, the most advanced system for conversation between man and machine, a good portion of the underlying algorithm is based on comparing input to a stored list and keeping track of matches.

ELIZA has played other roles than that of a psychiatrist. Edwin Taylor used ELIZA for instruction in elementary physics, for example.[19] Besides this, Weizenbaum has used ELIZA to explore solving algebra word problems, and problems of "inferential data acquisition," and to teach the computer some German. Clearly, ELIZA is a most sophisticated system for processing natural language.

As with just about all the sophisticated systems for natural language

[19]For further description of Taylor's work, see Edwin Taylor (ed.), *ELIZA: A Skimmable Report on the ELIZA Conversational Tutoring System*, The Educational Research Center, M.I.T., Cambridge, Mass., 1968. The use of ELIZA for guidance is discussed in Allan Ellis, Margaret Pincus, Patricia Yee, "Getting a Guidance Machine to Understand English," Project Report No. 14, The ISVD Project, Harvard University, 1968.

data processing, however, ELIZA remains "experimental." As Taylor has shown, the ELIZA algorithm is just as capable of producing a totally inappropriate (or meaningless) response as it is a convincing one.[20] Thus, while we should not doubt the computer's ability to process language, even to the point of seeming to hold conversations, neither should we consider Turing's test to have been met outside the laboratory.

The Language of ISVD

Now we may return to ISVD and consider the problem it faced of finding a language of the system—to replace BTSS's FORTRAN—which would permit sophisticated processing of English words, sentences, and paragraphs in the ways described in the previous section. After exploring various possibilities, ISVD selected a computer language called TRAC-text reckoning and compiling—designed by Calvin Mooers and Peter Deutsch.[21] TRAC is a *string manipulating* language, which means it treats data as strings of *characters* rather than as sets of values represented by characters. As a string manipulator, TRAC was ready-made for the task of processing natural language text. But it was not its facility at processing text alone that made TRAC an especially appropriate language for ISVD. More generally, its philosophy of design fit well with the overall intentions of ISVD.

> The design goals for the TRAC language and its translating system included: (1) high capability in dealing with back-and-forth communication between a man at a keyboard and his work on the machine, so as to permit him to make insertions and interventions during the running of his work; (2) maximum versatility in the definition and performance of any well-defined procedure on text; (3) ability to define, store and subsequently use such procedures to extend the capabilities of the language; and finally (4) maximum clarity in the language itself so that it could be easily taught to others.[22]

Even though the TRAC language had been meticulously designed and described by Mooers and Deutsch, it was not a simple job to make it a part of the ISVD system software. First, up to that time TRAC had never run on the type of computer ISVD was using. Second, TRAC had to be altered in several ways to permit it to execute guidance routines and to coordinate with the other programs as a new member of BTSS.[23] When this work was accomplished, TRAC functioned not only as the language of the system, but also as the central processor that controlled the overall

[20] Ibid.
[21] TRAC is a trademark of the Rockford Research Institute, Inc., Cambridge, Massachusetts.
[22] Calvin N. Mooers, "TRAC, A Procedure-describing Language for the Reactive Typewriter," *Communications of the ACM*, vol. 9, no. 3, March 1966, p. 215.
[23] This work was performed by Ann Taylor of the ISVD staff.

operation of the other components of the ISVD systems software. Logging users on and off the system, sending retrieval requests to HASM, receiving output from HASM, processing guidance routines, keeping a record of all user interactions with the system, and controlling the display and formatting of data on the terminals are some of the varied functions performed by TRAC.

With TRAC and HASM and DASM and BTSS—along with numerous other program components developed or revised by ISVD—ISVD had a complex of system software capable of performing just about any function necessary for the computer to act like a guidance machine. Indeed when the ISVD prototype was completed, it did not nearly exhaust the power of the system software on which it was built. Yet as it was to turn out, even though this system software was as it stood the most powerful set in use in education it was not enough. If the ISVD guidance staff was to develop a comprehensive description of the behavior of a guidance machine, and if these descriptions were to be turned into computer programs, then still more power and more system software would be needed.

A Language for People

The single fact that made this additional power necessary is that the computer people and the guidance people of the ISVD project had trouble talking to each other. This difficulty did not arise out of any estrangement between the two groups. On the contrary, it was their closeness and their ability to share concerns that had led to the project in the first place. But this communication existed on a fairly general plane, requiring little detail. Suddenly, the project underway, there was a great need for specifics because no computer system can be built without specifics.

The communication problem that faced the ISVD staff during the project's early days stemmed from the fact that each of the principals was a specialist, unaccustomed to any but his own intellectual terrain. The computer programming specialists, systems analysts, software designers, and the other technical experts of the project knew all about the computer, but they were not the ones who knew enough about guidance to stipulate anything much about the behavior of a guidance machine. On the other hand, the guidance specialist knew nothing of the technicalities involved in communicating his description to a computer. That is, he did not know what system programs to use, nor what form and sequence of operations, nor what level of detail. Consequently, the computer expert would ask, "Tell me exactly how you want the computer to behave" and the guidance expert would respond, "You tell me what I can have the computer do."

More and more as each specialist attempted to respond to his colleague's question, the outer reaches of what they sought together became clearer and better formulated. It would seem, therefore, to be an obvious solution to this problem of communication to have the guidance specialist talk to the computer specialist who in turn would translate the conversation to the computer. This way we avoid any requirement that either expert master the other man's discipline. In doing this, however, we run the risk of making the guidance specialist's association with computers a second-hand association thereby denying him the critical asset which the computer offers. This asset is the enhancement of his ability to think directly about guidance procedures. Of course as the two specialists talk to each other there is an enhancement of the guidance expert's ability to think about guidance procedure, but it is diminished by the fact that he is talking to an interpreter. No translation is literal and so the act of translating involves the making of certain decisions about substance. Often these decisions are the very ones that ought to be made by the guidance specialist and by no one else. At such times he should have direct access to the computer, not physical access necessarily, but intellectual access. Without needing to stoop to the computer's level he should be able to speak a language of procedure for which the computer needs no intermediary.

The staff of ISVD took a step in this direction when they decided to establish among themselves a set of *conventions* regarding how they would communicate with each other. The point of these conventions was to structure the way the staff talked about a guidance machine so that this talk would be specific and unambiguous. This way, talk about how the computer was to behave would approach the level of a computational procedure and, as such, would not require interpretation by the computer specialists of the project. Specifically the conventions were designed so that for each desired unit of interaction between a user and the system three questions would be answered.

What exactly does the computer say to the user?
What are the various responses a user can make?
For each conceivable response, what does the computer do next?

These questions would have to be answered for every unit of behavior expected of the guidance machine. Following the practice within the field of programmed instruction, these units of behavior were called *frames.* Writing frames became, for a while, the means through which the ISVD staff communicated with each other. Here is an example of a frame:

```
7.00 JOB1
  1. (CRT) LOOK AT THE PICTURE ON THE SCREEN.
              WHAT IS THE MAN'S OCCUPATION?
  2. (SLIDE) (show picture of dentist)
```

3. (KEYBOARD)
4. ACTION (CRT)

DENTIST/VERY GOOD/JOB2
DOCTOR/YES. BUT WHAT KIND OF DOCTOR?/3
/SORRY, THAT IS INCORRECT/JOB1A

Explanation: This is frame number 7.00, and it has the name JOB1. The first step of this frame says that the computer is to display on the cathode ray tube face of the user's terminal the message, "Look at the picture on the screen. . . ." Step 2 says that the computer is to display a particular slide on the slide screen portion of the terminal. Step 3 means that the system should then expect the student to reply by typing his answer on the terminal keyboard. According to Step 4, if the answer is "dentist," the computer responds with "very good" and then branches to the frame named JOB2. Should the student answer "doctor," the system prints the indicated message and then branches back to Step 3 of this frame to await another answer. Finally, if any other input is received from the terminal, the computer responds with "Sorry, that is incorrect," and then branches to the frame named JOB1A, where, perhaps, the student gets additional help in identifying the dentist.

Collections of frames such as this one were organized into *scripts.* Not unlike the manuscript of a play (from which it gets its name), a script is a set of rules (frames) describing how the computer (guidance machine) is to act. Thus, using the conventions that had been established, the ISVD guidance specialists set out to create a network of scripts covering the various areas of behavior they wished to specify.

A Language for the Computer

Now, these script writing conventions functioned as elements of a language and, consequently, ISVD referred to the set of conventions as a script writing language. This language—called MYNORCA—was used to specify how the computer was to behave, but it was *not* a computer language. MYNORCA was a paper and pencil language used by the guidance specialist, in place of English, to tell the computer specialist, unambiguously, what he wanted the computer to do. The computer specialist was then to take these scripts and turn them into computer programs written in TRAC—the computer language of the system. But then it occurred to some of them that if MYNORCA can be used to produce unambiguous statements of procedure, then a translator could be written allowing the computer to interpret MYNORCA statements directly. It was at this point that ISVD began to create the final component of its system software—a computer language for the interpretation and execution of scripts.

Naturally the first step in the creation of such a computer language was to evaluate how well MYNORCA was serving its purposes. By this time the guidance staff had produced in MYNORCA over two hundred scripts and the experiences attached to this work provided a rich source of data to begin to determine the strengths and weaknesses of the language. As a result of this evaluation, MYNORCA was abandoned.

The concept of "frame" in MYNORCA was unnecessarily restricting, encouraging the script writer to break up his sequence into units of behavior far too small to be comfortable to the user. The idea of the small unit consisting of a stimulus and a response may work well within the domain of programmed instruction, but ISVD was supposed to be an information system that gave the user control and the freedom to roam through the data bases. The notion of controlling his behavior, therefore, was an intrusion to the idea of ISVD. A second way MYNORCA misappropriated aspects of programmed instruction theory was in the idea of reinforcement. In MYNORCA this became an encouragement to the script writer always to respond to the student and with statements such as "Very Good," "O.K.," "Nice Going," and the like. Besides being meaningless, such statements fostered the deceiving notion that the system was approving or disapproving of the user's behavior. MYNORCA fostered such statements because its syntax made it seem as though they were required. But even though MYNORCA fostered such improper "dialogue," its ability to specify natural language interaction between the system and the user was extremely limited, so much so, in fact, that no meaningful language interaction was specified in any of the 200 scripts. Finally, the syntax of MYNORCA was so different from TRAC, that were it computerized it would have to function as a separate language, resulting in considerable duplication of function and effort.

Replacing MYNORCA would be a new language which Ann Taylor—its designer—called GLURP, for Generalized Language for Understanding and Responding to People.[24] GLURP is a language of languages, containing as subsets, ISVD's version of TRAC; a script writing language that can call on TRAC when it needs to, and that no longer contains the restricting ideas of MYNORCA; the routines to decompose English sentence input following Weizenbaum's ELIZA language; the ability adapted from the General Inquirer to perform the basic function of content analysis; the capacity to control the functioning of HASM and DASM; the facility to perform PROTRAN-like substitutions; and the algorithms for executing scripts and keeping track of user interaction with the system.

To have all this power, GLURP had to be a more technical language than MYNORCA. To use GLURP, therefore, the script writer had to learn more about programming than he would have otherwise, but, in the end,

[24]For a complete technical description of GLURP, see Ann Taylor, GLURP—Generalized Language for Understanding and Responding to People, Project Report No. 29, ISVD. For a GLURP user's manual, see Richard Roman, Manual for GLURP: A Computer Assisted Instruction Language, Project Report No. 33, ISVD.

the enhancement of his ability to describe a complex guidance machine seems to have made the extra trouble worthwhile.

With the addition of GLURP, the ISVD system software was complete, and it possessed such versatility and power that it is better thought of as a generalized educational software system since, clearly, its usefulness is not confined to guidance applications. Of course, the system was neither the ultimate version of a computer system for education, nor in every respect superior to other systems that have been constructed for educational applications. Yet, in its final form, the ISVD system software contained several features that made it unusually well suited as the base for an information system. Among these features were

1. a time sharing system allowing different users simultaneously to be doing such different things as taking scripts, writing programs, and retrieving data.

2. a data storage and maintenance system for organizing, updating, deleting, and maintaining over 50 million characters of data.

3. a symbolic data retrieval and decoding system for the logical processing and interpretation of data bases.

4. an extensive script network which constitutes a behavioral description of some education machine—in this case a guidance machine.

5. a rich script writing language which includes the ability to process aspects of natural language input.

6. a system language of which the script language is a part, allowing the user, even when executing a script, to produce his own programs, and allowing the full use of the logical power of the computer.

7. the provision for keeping a complete log or record of the interaction between users and the system.

8. a set of system support programs to permit such things as the preprocessing and loading of scripts, the analysis and statistical summarization of logged interactions, and the tracing of the system's behavior as it functions.

In the face of all of this, one may no longer be persuaded that ISVD was first and foremost a project about guidance. All the description of the ISVD system software may make it appear that the point of the project was to develop an extensive set of computer programs. But remember that the creation of the system software was largely a necessary evil in the sense that its sole function was to create a computer environment which made it feasible and convenient for ISVD to attempt to build a guidance machine.

CHAPTER EIGHT: the workings

Robert Cohen sits down in front of a special table-sized student terminal consisting of a televisionlike device—a Sanders 720 video display (see Appendix, Figure A-25)—a typewriterlike keyboard, a slide projection screen, and a teletypewriter printer.[1] When this terminal is connected to the ISVD computer, twelve miles away, over telephone lines, printed output will appear on the tube-face of the Sanders 720 (CRT), and slides will be projected, under computer control, on the slide screen. Whenever Robert Cohen needs to input a message to the system, he will use the keyboard to type it in, and whenever he wants a copy of what is appearing on the CRT, he can push a button and it will be copied on to the teletypewriter printer. On the terminal, as well, is a Data-phone, and Robert uses it to dial the number of the ISVD computer. When he hears the tone that means the connection has been made, he pushes the data button on the Dataphone and puts down the receiver. He is now on the ISVD system.

SYSTEM: PLEASE TYPE YOUR ID NUMBER SO THAT YOU CAN BEGIN. PRESS THE BUTTON MARKED SEND BLOCK WHEN YOU FINISH. (IT'S ON THE RIGHT SIDE OF THE KEYBOARD.)

COHEN: 20961

SYSTEM: YOUR ID NUMBER HAS BEEN RECEIVED. NOW PLEASE TYPE

[1]This student terminal system was designed and built for ISVD by Sanders Associates who hold the patent on the device.

YOUR PASSWORD. IT WILL BE INVISIBLE SO NO ONE ELSE CAN READ IT. PRESS SEND BLOCK WHEN YOU ARE DONE.

COHEN: (types in password)

SYSTEM: BEFORE BEGINNING WITH THE REST OF THE SYSTEM, WE NEED TO KNOW CERTAIN BASIC FACTS ABOUT YOU. PLEASE TYPE YOUR FIRST AND LAST NAMES. PRESS SEND BLOCK WHEN YOU ARE FINISHED.

COHEN: BOBBY COHEN

SYSTEM: THANKS BOBBY. NOW YOUR AGE IN YEARS. PLEASE USE NUMBERS, NOT WORDS.

COHEN: 16

SYSTEM: ARE YOU A MALE OR FEMALE?

COHEN: MALE

SYSTEM: NOW TYPE YOUR GRADE IN SCHOOL. PLEASE USE NUMBERS, NOT WORDS. SOPHOMORE = 10, JUNIOR = 11, SENIOR = 12.

COHEN: 11

SYSTEM: WELCOME TO ISVD, BOBBY. WHEN YOU SEE THREE ASTERISKS *** AT THE BOTTOM OF THE SCREEN, THE MACHINE IS READY TO RECEIVE YOUR RESPONSE. IF YOU DON'T FEEL LIKE SAYING ANYTHING, SIMPLY PUSH THE "SEND BLOCK" BUTTON. TRY THAT NOW.

COHEN: (pushes send block button)

SYSTEM: SOMETIMES WE WILL ASK A DIRECT QUESTION, BECAUSE WE NEED TO KNOW SOMETHING FROM YOU BEFORE GOING ON. WHEN WE DO, PLEASE TYPE IN WHAT YOU WANT TO SAY AND PRESS SEND BLOCK. IS THIS CLEAR SO FAR?

COHEN: YES

SYSTEM: YOU ARE ALMOST READY TO USE THE SYSTEM. THERE ARE JUST A FEW OTHER THINGS YOU SHOULD KNOW ABOUT. IF YOU SHOULD WANT A PRINTED COPY OF WHAT IS ON THE SCREEN, WAIT UNTIL YOU SEE THE THREE ASTERISKS AND THEN PUSH THE BUTTON MARKED "COPY PAGE." WAIT UNTIL THE MATERIAL HAS BEEN COPIED. THEN TYPE IN YOUR RESPONSE AND "SEND BLOCK." TRY IT NOW.

COHEN: (pushes copy page and send block buttons)

SYSTEM: DID YOU GET A PRINT-OUT OF WHAT WAS ON THE SCREEN?

COHEN: YES

SYSTEM: GOOD. SOMETIMES YOU WILL NOT KNOW HOW TO ANSWER THE SYSTEM WHEN IT ASKS YOU A QUESTION. IN THIS CASE, YOU SHOULD TRY TYPING @ HELP. TRY IT ONCE.

COHEN: HELP

SYSTEM: NO, YOU DID NOT TYPE THAT CORRECTLY. TYPE THE SYMBOL @ AND THEN HELP. DO NOT PUT A SPACE IN BETWEEN.

COHEN: @HELP
SYSTEM: FINE. SOMETIMES THE SYSTEM WILL GIVE YOU A HINT WHEN YOU ASK FOR HELP, BUT NOT ALWAYS. YOU CAN ALWAYS TRY, THOUGH.[2]

The Script System

By this point Robert Cohen has gone through two ISVD scripts and has just begun the third one. This third script serves to introduce a user to the special "commands" that he can use anytime he wishes to interrupt the normal flow of the interaction and exercise a more direct control over the system. He is told that there are available to him nine such commands, which are:

@HELP - when you do not know how to respond.
@STOP - to go on to something else.
@QUIT - to log off the ISVD system.
@DATA - to go into a direct data retrieval mode.
@DATA-COL - to go directly to college data retrieval.
@DATA-JOB - to go directly to occupational data retrieval.
@DATA-TRADE - to go directly to trade school data retrieval.
@DATA-MIL - to go directly to military data retrieval.
@SUMMARY - to get a review of what you have been doing.

Once he learns these commands, the user will be able to explore the system, going directly to various places and avoiding others as he chooses. But for Robert Cohen, this is his first exposure to ISVD so, for the present, he will communicate with the system in English, leaving the command language for another time.

Now, the three scripts Robert has taken thus far are introductory scripts. The first one logs him on the system and determines whether or not he has been "on" before; if not the system elicits certain information about him, otherwise a call to DASM brings the needed basic information into memory. The second script provides a general introduction to the system for the newcomer and a shorter refresher to a returning user. As we have seen, the third script explains the command language to the student. These introductory scripts, along with the one "major" and the various "minor" orientation scripts belong to a class called *system scripts.* The function of the system scripts, in general, is to help determine what part of the ISVD network of scripts and data a particular student wishes to use. Once this is determined, these scripts make the appropriate branches on behalf of the user.

[2]Illustrations of interaction with the ISVD system which appear in this chapter were generated by project personnel from actual print-outs. Most of these examples were kindly provided by Robert Aylmer.

Of course, there are other types of scripts, with other functions. For instance, there are *teaching scripts*, a network of about 160 scripts designed to teach the user things related to career choice. Topics include college choice, job selection, military careers, and trade school selection. Another set consists of the so-called *data scripts.* This set of scripts allows direct exploration of the data bases under user control. He requests a specific datum and obtains an English sentence containing the desired information. There are several ways to reach the data scripts, one way being by the use of a@ DATA command. Yet another group of scripts is called the *template scripts.* A template script resembles a data script except that the user need not be so specific about the data he requests. Instead of a specific fact, he receives a general description of the college or job or military specialty he inquired about. Then there are the *preference scripts,* designed to help the student translate certain preferences relating to work or to school into specific job or school alternatives. Each preference script is associated with an appropriate data base. As a student goes through a preference script, the system keeps track of his stated preferences and when he has completed the script there is filed for him a list of those jobs or schools that meet all the criteria he selected. Finally there are *access scripts* which are constructed to reflect various elements of the Tiedeman-O'Hara paradigm of vocational decision making. These scripts are designed to help the student become aware of himself as a decider and of his decision-making style.

The overall structure of the ISVD script system is depicted in Figure

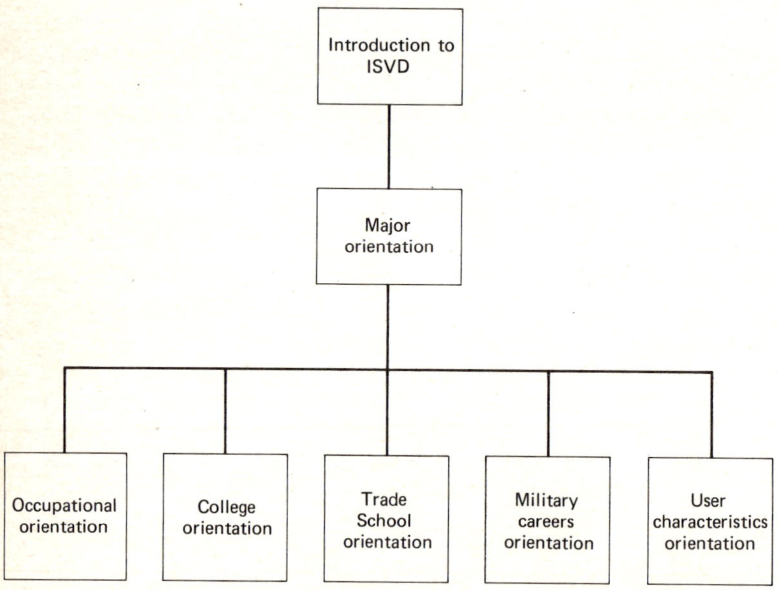

Figure 8-1 Overview of the ISVD script system.

8-1. Within each of the five portions of the script system represented by the five minor orientation boxes there is a network of scripts. In each network all six classes of scripts are represented. For instance, Figure 8-2 represents the script network associated with the occupational portion of ISVD. Similarly, Figure 8-3 depicts the college script network. All together the script networks associated with the various major portions of the ISVD script system—along with such other script subsystems as the Life Career Game, and the self-concept profiling scripts—make up ISVD's description of a guidance machine. Under the control of this script system, the computer functions as the guidance machine so defined.

The Data System

In the most general sense, the overall function of the ISVD guidance machine is to mediate the student's access to vocationally relevant data. These data—stored at the computer and ready for retrieval through DASM and other system software—are organized into four large collections called data bases. Each data base, as we have seen, is further organized into records, where each record consists of the set of facts relating to a particular occupation or college or trade school or the like.

The largest of the four ISVD data bases is the *occupational* data base, containing facts on more than 850 occupations. For each of these occupations, 56 categories of information are available including such things as entry occupations, industries where found, brief verbal description, aptitudes—general, verbal, manual dexterity, form perception—strength required, salaries and wages, required abilities, union membership, hours of work, seasonality, demand for workers, and trend of wages. The data in the occupational data base were taken from two documents published by the U.S. Department of Labor: the *Dictionary of Occupational Titles*, and the *Occupational Outlook Handbook*.

The second major collection of data, the *education* data base, is actually three data files-in-one. First it contains the *secondary school* file, made up of data about the junior and senior high school programs in the Newton, Massachusetts, public schools—these schools were part of the field test of the system—including course descriptions, electives, requirements, and curriculum levels. Second, the education data base contains the *college* file. For each of the 376 colleges and junior colleges included in this college file, there are 80 categories of data covering a range equally as broad as that of the occupational data categories. Because the Newton schools were the sites for the field test of the system and because follow-up studies showed that 90 percent of Newton graduates attend one of 273 junior or senior colleges, it seemed unnecessary to make this data file any larger. The *trade school* data file was restricted in another reasonable way, including only institutions located in New England. The 128 vocational training schools that made up this data file—with 30

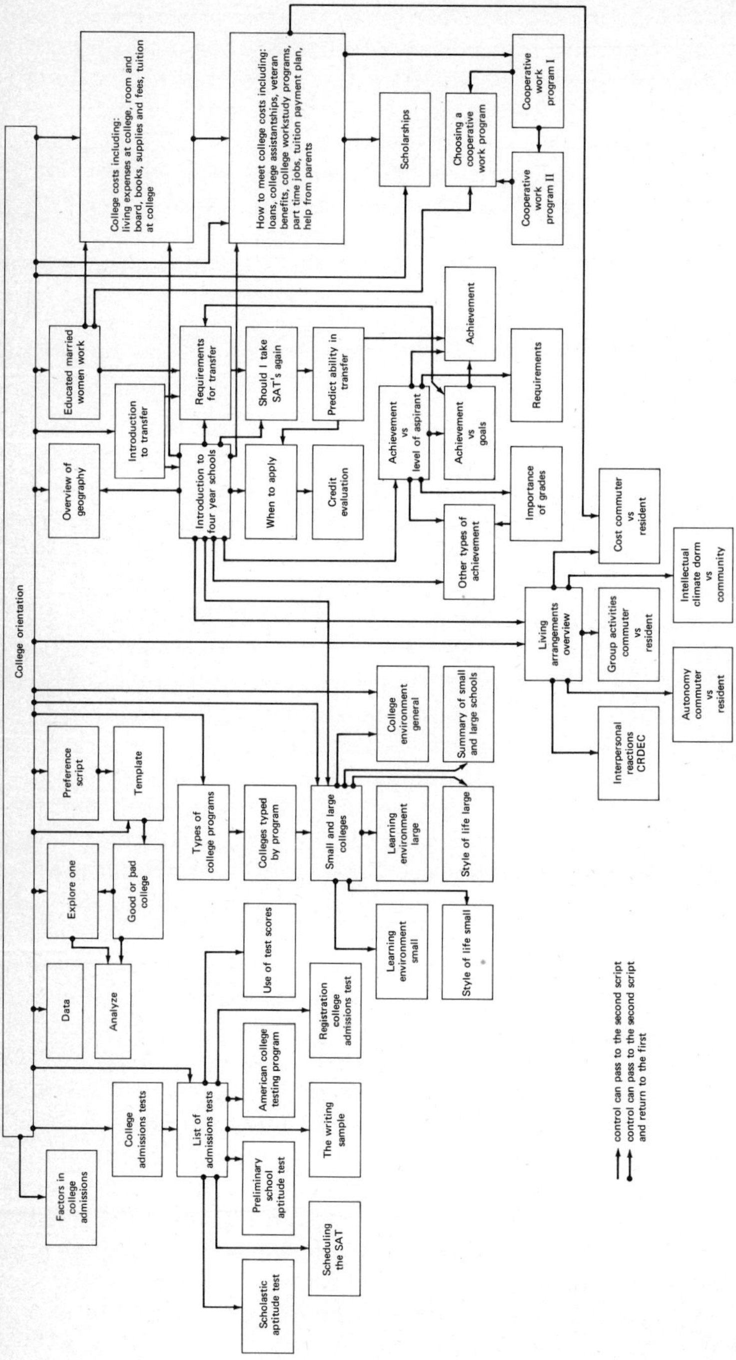

Figure 8-2 The ISVD Occupational Script Network (each box represents a script).

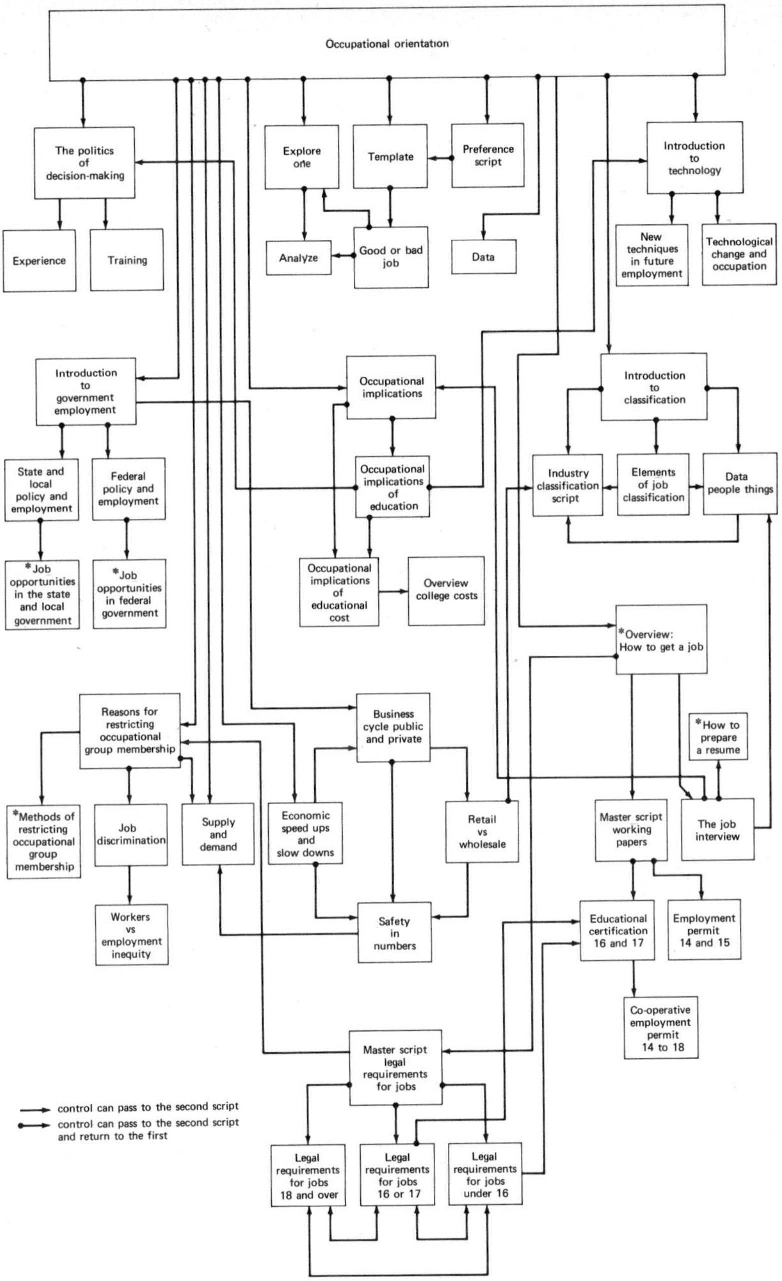

Figure 8-3 The ISVD College Script Network (each box represents a script).

categories of data on each—covered a broad enough range to permit the testing of the ISVD prototype.

The third large collection of data is the *military careers* data base. The data here are broken down into the three major branches of the military and then further grouped by sex and by rank. Overall the military careers data base includes 170 enlisted occupations with thirteen categories of data for each, plus some smaller number of data on officer specialties.

Finally, there is a *user characteristics* data base. When Robert Cohen entered his name, sex, age, and grade they were stored in this data base for later use. As he continues to use ISVD, the system will monitor his activities, making note of such things as scripts taken, times through the system, data files accessed, and other aspects of his interaction with the system. Provided for as well in this data base are student grades, test scores, courses taken, and so forth.

So, ISVD consists of a very large storehouse of vocationally relevant data and a large, complex network of scripts. Together they form the ISVD reckoning environment which the student is invited to enter. When he does, he has the capacity, with the help of the guidance machine, not to counsel himself but to *precounsel* himself. That is, he can begin to explore data, consider alternatives, discard options, and retrieve information without eating into the 3½ hours his counselor has allotted him. Presumably, then, when the time comes to be counseled, he will know already the tuition at Harvard or the courses needed to become a carpenter or the difference between a fire control specialist and a fireman. As well, he will have begun to become aware of the career decision-making process and of himself as a decider. By returning now to Robert Cohen we will get some idea of how all of this happens.

Robert Cohen is at the point of having gone through the first three introductory scripts—LOGIN, INTRODUCTION TO THE SYSTEM, and INTRODUCTION TO COMMANDS. The next script he "takes" will be the one called MAJOR ORIENTATION. Here the system will attempt to discover which portion of the script network it is that Robert wishes to use. Once this is done in a general way he will be transferred to the appropriate MINOR ORIENTATION script for a more specific determination of what he wants to do. Starting now with MAJOR ORIENTATION:

SYSTEM: WHAT WOULD YOU LIKE TO DO?
COHEN: I AM UNCERTAIN ABOUT COLLEGE.

Having processed Robert's input along the lines developed by Weizenbaum in ELIZA, MAJOR ORIENTATION transfers control to the COLLEGE ORIENTATION script and passes along the fact that Robert is "unsure." Robert is now in the college script network and the college data base area, and the first task the system has, through COLLEGE ORIENTATION, is to help Robert decide more specifically what he wants to do.

SYSTEM: THE ACTIVITIES YOU CAN REQUEST ARE: SELECT A SCHOOL, DATA ABOUT CERTAIN SCHOOLS, EXPLORING YOUR INTERESTS, FACTORS COLLEGES USE IN ADMISSION, TESTS, SIZE OF SCHOOL, COLLEGE LIFE, TRANSFER, OR SCHOLARSHIPS. TRY TO BE SPECIFIC, BUT USE SIMPLE WORDS. WHAT WOULD YOU LIKE TO DO NOW?

COHEN: IT IS DIFFICULT TO SAY. WHAT CAN I DO?

SYSTEM:
1. CHOOSE A COLLEGE
2. DIRECT DATA ACCESS
3. EXPLORE COLLEGES
4. TESTS
5. COOPERATIVE PROGRAMS
6. COST OF COLLEGE
7. LIVING ARRANGEMENTS
8. PAYING FOR COLLEGE
9. SIZE OF SCHOOLS

COHEN: I STILL DO NOT KNOW WHICH THING I WANT TO DO.

SYSTEM: A LIST OF THE MORE INTERESTING THINGS TO DO IN THE ISVD FOLLOWS. EACH SUGGESTION WILL BE FOLLOWED BY A CHANCE FOR YOU TO TYPE *YES* AND TRY THAT OR *NO* AND GET ANOTHER SUGGESTION.
WOULD YOU LIKE TO SELECT A COLLEGE BY LISTING YOUR PREFERENCE?

COHEN: I AM NOT READY FOR THAT YET.

SYSTEM: WOULD YOU LIKE TO ASK FOR FACTS ABOUT A SPECIFIC SCHOOL?

COHEN: THAT IS MUCH TOO SPECIFIC.

SYSTEM: ARE YOU INTERESTED IN FACTORS COLLEGES USE IN SELECTING THE FRESHMAN CLASS?

COHEN: YES, THAT IS EXACTLY WHAT I NEED.

The COLLEGE ORIENTATION script now knows what to do with Robert; it transfers him to a teaching script—FACTORS IN COLLEGE ADMISSION—where he learns some things about how colleges select from among their applicants. Let us assume that Robert completes this script and then "signs off" for the day. Three days later, say, Robert returns to the ISVD system and after logging in, proceeds with his thinking about colleges.

SYSTEM: WHAT WOULD YOU LIKE TO DO?

COHEN: I AM INTERESTED IN FINDING A COLLEGE TO GO TO.

SYSTEM: YOU ARE NOW BRANCHING TO THE EDUCATION SECTION. THERE ARE MANY FACTORS THAT WILL HELP US LOCATE COLLEGES IN WHICH YOU MIGHT BE INTERESTED. SOME OF THEM APPEAR IN THE INTERVIEW THAT FOLLOWS. AND SOME WILL DEPEND ON WHAT FACTORS ARE IMPORTANT TO YOU IN CHOOSING A COLLEGE. BASED ON YOUR ANSWERS, THE COMPUTER WILL FINALLY PRINT OUT A LIST OF COLLEGES IN WHICH YOU MIGHT BE INTERESTED. YOU MAY EITHER STOP THE INTERVIEW AT THAT POINT, OR GO ON TO FIND OUT SPECIFIC FACTS ABOUT WHAT FACTORS ARE IMPORTANT TO YOU IN CHOOSING A COLLEGE.

COHEN: (pushes the "send block" button, the signal that he has read the message and is ready to proceed.)

SYSTEM: THERE ARE, OF COURSE, MANY FACTORS THAT WILL INFLUENCE YOUR CHOICE OF COLLEGE. SOME THAT ARE GENERALLY CONSIDERED TO BE IMPORTANT WILL BE LISTED FOR YOU. PLEASE READ THE LIST. THEN PUSH "SEND BLOCK" TO CONTINUE.

COHEN: (pushes "send block" button)

SYSTEM:
A. GEOGRAPHIC LOCATION (AREA OF THE U.S.),
B. PRIVATE, PUBLIC OR RELIGIOUS AFFILIATION,
C. SEX OF STUDENT BODY (ALL MEN, WOMEN),
D. SIZE OF STUDENT BODY,
E. TYPE OF PROGRAM (FOR EXAMPLE, LIBERAL ARTS OR PRE-PROFESSIONAL),
F. AVAILABILITY OF FINANCIAL AID (LOANS AND SCHOLARSHIPS),
G. URBAN, SUBURBAN, OR RURAL ENVIRONMENT,
H. SPECIAL COURSES OF STUDY,
I. TYPES OF EXTRACURRICULAR ACTIVITIES AVAILABLE (ROTC, ATHLETICS, SOCIAL ORGANIZATIONS),
J. ACADEMIC STANDING OF PRESENT FRESHMAN (RANK).

COHEN: A F J

SYSTEM: GEOGRAPHIC LOCATION IS GENERALLY CONSIDERED TO BE AN IMPORTANT FACTOR IN COLLEGE CHOICE. YOU MAY ALREADY HAVE ONE OR TWO SPECIFIC AREAS IN MIND. YOU WILL SEE A SLIDE OF THE VARIOUS GEOGRAPHIC AREAS OF THE COUNTRY. WE HAVE KEYED THE FOLLOWING LIST TO THAT MAP.
PRESS THE RUN BUTTON NOW.

COHEN: (presses the run button and pushes send block)

SYSTEM: (simultaneously displaying slide)
NOW, USING THAT MAP, PLEASE TYPE IN THE LETTER OR LETTERS THAT APPEAL TO YOU.
PRESS THE RUN BUTTON NOW.

YOU BEGIN WITH 376 SCHOOLS
A. NEW ENGLAND COLLEGES,
B. MIDDLE ATLANTIC COLLEGES,
C. MIDWESTERN COLLEGES,
D. SOUTHERN COLLEGES,
E. WESTERN COLLEGES,
F. SOUTHWESTERN COLLEGES.

COHEN: A B

SYSTEM: A SOMETIMES IMPORTANT FACTOR IN CHOOSING A COLLEGE IS THE RELATIONSHIP OF COST TO THE AVAILABILITY OF SCHOLARSHIPS AND LOANS. IN SOME CASES, FOR INSTANCE, IT IS POSSIBLE TO GO TO A FAR MORE EXPENSIVE COLLEGE THAN YOU CAN POSSIBLY AFFORD. IF YOU CAN WIN A SCHOLARSHIP OR GET ADDITIONAL LOANS FROM THE COLLEGE OR FEDERAL GOVERNMENT.
INDICATE WHETHER YOU ARE INTERESTED IN A FINANCIAL AID PROGRAM. YOU HAVE 188 SCHOOLS LEFT.
A. FEDERAL LOANS
B. SCHOLARSHIPS
C. BOTH
D. AT LEAST ONE AVAILABLE
E. DOESN'T MATTER

COHEN: D

SYSTEM: ACADEMIC STANDING IS OF COURSE AN IMPORTANT CRITERION FOR CONSIDERING COLLEGES, ALTHOUGH IT IS NOT NECESSARILY THE MOST IMPORTANT. ONE OF THE BEST WAYS TO USE THIS INFORMATION IN CHOOSING A COLLEGE IS TO LOOK AT SCHOOLS WHERE THE AVERAGE STANDING IS CLOSE TO YOUR OWN AT THIS TIME. YOU HAVE 136 SCHOOLS NOW.

COHEN: (pushes send block)

SYSTEM: IF YOU THINK THIS IS A GOOD WAY TO HELP SELECT YOUR COLLEGE, PLEASE TYPE IN THE LETTER CORRESPONDING TO YOUR PRESENT RANK IN YOUR CLASS. OTHERWISE PUSH SEND BLOCK.
A. TOP TENTH
B. TOP FIFTH
C. TOP QUARTER
D. TOP HALF
E. BOTTOM HALF

COHEN: B

SYSTEM: THERE ARE 11 COLLEGES ON THE LIST.
ON THE BASIS OF YOUR RESPONSES THESE ARE SOME COLLEGES YOU MIGHT CONSIDER. PUSH HARD COPY

BUTTON IF YOU WISH.
COLBY COLLEGE
TUFTS UNIVERSITY
UNIVERSITY OF CONNECTICUT
UNIVERSITY OF MASSACHUSETTS
BABSON INSTITUTE OF BUSINESS ADMINISTRATION
BOSTON COLLEGE
BOSTON UNIVERSITY
BRANDEIS UNIVERSITY
HARVARD UNIVERSITY
CHAMBERLAYNE JUNIOR COLLEGE
LESLEY COLLEGE

COHEN: (pushes send block)

SYSTEM: NOW WOULD YOU LIKE TO:
1. FIND OUT MORE ABOUT SCHOOLS ON YOUR LIST
2. DO THE INTERVIEW OVER AND CHANGE YOUR RESPONSES
3. DO SOMETHING ELSE
4. SEE MORE SCHOOLS ON THE LIST

ISVD also includes Preference scripts for the Occupational, Military, and Trade School data files. In addition, the Occupational file has a different Preference-type script utilizing the classification system of the *Dictionary of Occupational Titles,* or "DOT" (U.S. Department of Labor, 1965).

With the list of colleges meeting his expressed preferences, Robert could go immediately to finding out more about some or all of them. Should he leave the system for the day, however, he could pick it up when he returned since the list is stored in his file. But, as well, he now has a printed copy of this list to refer to, so next time he is on the system he can skip right to the data retrieval portion of ISVD and explore his list that way. Let us say Robert leaves the system and returns a week later. After an abbreviated introduction:

SYSTEM: WHAT WOULD YOU LIKE TO DO?

COHEN: @DATA-COL

Robert decides to try the command language so that he can go directly to finding out about the colleges on his list. Immediately he skips the orientation routines and is transferred directly to the data script associated with the college data base.

SYSTEM: THIS IS THE FIRST TIME YOU HAVE USED THE DATA ROUTINE ACCORDING TO THE RECORDS. IF YOU ARE REALLY AN OLD HAND AND WOULD LIKE TO SKIP THE INTRODUCTION, TYPE SKIP. OTHERWISE, JUST PRESS SEND BLOCK.

COHEN: (presses send block)

SYSTEM: ISVD HAS INFORMATION ABOUT JOBS, COLLEGES, TRADE SCHOOLS, AND MILITARY SERVICE. IN ORDER FOR YOU TO GET ANSWERS TO YOUR QUESTIONS ABOUT COLLEGES, THERE ARE A COUPLE OF GENERAL RULES TO FOLLOW. THE RULE THAT WILL PROBABLY BE MOST TROUBLESOME IS THAT TO GET INFORMATION ABOUT A COLLEGE YOU HAVE TO USE ITS CODE NUMBER OR SPELL IT OUT COMPLETELY. FOR INSTANCE, TO FIND OUT ABOUT BOSTON UNIVERSITY, YOU'D TYPE IN ITS CODE NUMBER 109 OR THE WORDS BOSTON UNIVERSITY. B.U. OR BU WOULDN'T WORK.

COHEN: (pushes send block)

SYSTEM: BECAUSE OF THIS INCONVENIENCE, MOST OF THE SCRIPTS WHICH SUGGEST NAMES OF JOBS OR SCHOOLS TELL YOU TO MAKE A COPY OF THE ONES YOU COME UP WITH. IF YOU DON'T HAVE A LIST WITH YOU, OR IF WE HAVE TROUBLE UNDERSTANDING YOUR REQUESTS, YOU CAN GET LISTS OF COLLEGES BY TYPING @ HELP.

COHEN: (pushes send block)

SYSTEM: IF YOU HAVE LEARNED HOW TO GET A NAME, YOU CAN TYPE SKIP AND THE EXPLANATION WILL NOT BE GIVEN.

COHEN: SKIP

SYSTEM: AFTER YOU TYPE IN THE NUMBER OR FULL NAME OF THE COLLEGE YOU'RE INTERESTED IN, WE'LL ASK WHAT YOU WANT TO KNOW ABOUT IT. AGAIN, IF YOU'RE NOT SURE WHAT SORT OF INFORMATION YOU WANT TO KNOW OR IF WE HAVE TROUBLE FIGURING OUT YOUR QUESTIONS ABOUT THE COLLEGE, TYPE @ HELP.

COHEN: UNIVERSITY OF CONNECTICUT

SYSTEM: WHAT DO YOU WANT TO KNOW ABOUT UNIVERSITY OF CONNECTICUT?

COHEN: LOCATION

SYSTEM: COLLEGE = UNIVERSITY OF CONNECTICUT
VARIABLE = LOCATION
UNIVERSITY OF CONNECTICUT IS LOCATED IN STORRS, CONNECTICUT.

COHEN: (pushes send block)

SYSTEM: TYPE IN THE NAME OF THE COLLEGE YOU WANT INFORMATION ABOUT OR THE IDENTIFICATION NUMBER. JUST PUSH SEND BLOCK IF YOU WANT TO KNOW SOMETHING ELSE ABOUT THE SAME COLLEGE.

COHEN: (pushes send block)

SYSTEM: WHAT DO YOU WANT TO KNOW ABOUT UNIVERSITY OF CONNECTICUT?

COHEN: COST

SYSTEM: COLLEGE = UNIVERSITY OF CONNECTICUT
VARIABLE = COST
THE TUITION AT UNIVERSITY OF CONNECTICUT IS $190 FOR STATE RESIDENTS AND $400 FOR NON RESIDENTS.

By using the @DATA-COL command, Robert is accomplishing something very important. He is skirting parts of the system; he is saying, in effect, "Keep the conversation down to a minimum and just give me the bare facts that I ask for." Robert is in control of the system and this is important. The reasons it is so important to ISVD that Robert be in control is that before he can control the system this way, he must be in control of his own decision process, at least to the extent that he steers it and determines the direction it takes. Of course, the situation will fluctuate—the system sometimes prodding or suggesting, other times, functioning completely under user control. In Robert's case, for instance, he will stay in control throughout the rest of this session getting facts and descriptions about some more of his colleges, but the next time on the system he will return to a point in his decision process where some system prodding will be helpful. Just before he signs off for this time, however, Robert decides to think for a few minutes about a summer job. Having a summer job is part of what going to college would mean for Robert and so he directs his attention to it, through the OCCUPATIONAL TEMPLATE script, for the time he has left in this session.

SYSTEM: YOU WILL BE ASKED FOR AN OCCUPATIONAL TITLE, YOU MUST USE THE NAME PRECISELY AS WE HAVE IT RECORDED. IF YOU DO NOT KNOW ANY JOBS YOU COULD TAKE THE OCCUPATIONAL PREFERENCE SCRIPT WHICH WILL LET YOU SELECT A JOB WELL SUITED TO YOU. WOULD YOU LIKE TO TRY THAT SCRIPT?

COHEN: NO

SYSTEM: YOU MAY NEED HELP GETTING THE NAMES CORRECTLY. WHEN YOU ARE ASKED FOR A JOB TITLE, YOU MAY TYPE A CORRECT JOB TITLE. YOU WILL SEE A BRIEF DESCRIPTION OF THE JOB. THEN YOU WILL BE ALLOWED TO ASK FOR FURTHER INFORMATION.

COHEN: (pushes send block)

SYSTEM: THE AVAILABLE TOPICS ARE
REQUIREMENTS FOR THE JOB
WAGES AND BENEFITS
PERSONAL QUALITIES NEEDED
WORKING CONDITIONS
YOU MAY ASK FOR EACH IN TURN OR @STOP, FOR TECHNICAL REASONS THIS INFORMATION WILL BE COLD AND FORMAL. FOR THIS ISVD APOLOGIZES. AS TIME GOES ON,

IMPROVEMENTS MAY BE POSSIBLE. MEANWHILE PLEASE REMEMBER THAT THIS INFORMATION IS INCOMPLETE. THERE IS MUCH MORE TO KNOW ABOUT A JOB THAT WHAT YOU SEE HERE. IF THE JOB INTERESTS YOU STRONGLY, SEE FURTHER INFORMATION. . .

COHEN: (pushes send block)

SYSTEM: WHAT JOB DO YOU WANT DESCRIBED? YOU MAY TYPE THE NAME OF THE JOB OR ITS NUMBER.

COHEN: INFORMAL WAITER

SYSTEM: AN INFORMAL WAITER IS A SERVICE WORKER. PRIMARILY, AN INFORMAL WAITER IS INVOLVED IN BUSINESS AND DOES CONCRETE AND ORGANIZED WORK. ON THE JOB WAITERS TAKE ORDERS AND SERVE FOOD AND BEVERAGES.

COHEN: (pushes send block)

SYSTEM: IF YOU WOULD LIKE TO LEARN MORE ABOUT THIS JOB, PLEASE INDICATE A TOPIC THAT INTERESTS YOU, LATER YOU CAN PICK ANOTHER. OTHERWISE, YOU MAY RETURN TO YOUR JOB LIST.

1. REQUIREMENTS FOR ENTRANCE AND ADVANCEMENT
2. WAGES AND BENEFITS
3. PERSONAL APTITUDES REQUIRED
4. WORK CONDITIONS AND OTHER DATA
5. TRY ANOTHER JOB
6. GO BACK TO WHAT I WAS DOING

COHEN: 1

SYSTEM: AN INFORMAL WAITER MUST AT LEAST COMPLETE JUNIOR HIGH SCHOOL AND SHOULD PREFERABLY GRADUATE FROM A VOCATIONAL HIGH SCHOOL. AFTER COMPLETING SCHOOLING AN INFORMAL WAITER USUALLY HOLDS ANOTHER JOB. PREVIOUS ACTIVITY MAY INCLUDE SPECIFIC TRAINING FOR THE JOB. UP TO 30 DAYS OF ON-THE-JOB TRAINING MAY BE INCLUDED. LOWER LEVEL JOBS LIKE BUSBOY MAY BE NECESSARY BEFORE BECOMING AN INFORMAL WAITER. HIGHER JOBS INCLUDE WAITER, FORMAL, NO INFORMATION ABOUT ADVANCEMENT.

COHEN: (pushes send block)

SYSTEM: A HIGH SCHOOL STUDENT INTERESTED IN BECOMING AN INFORMAL WAITER SHOULD TRY TO TAKE COURSES IN ENGLISH, SALESMANSHIP, SOCIAL STUDIES.

COHEN: (pushes send block)

SYSTEM: IF YOU WOULD LIKE TO LEARN MORE ABOUT THIS JOB, PLEASE INDICATE A TOPIC THAT INTERESTS YOU.

COHEN: 4 (WORK CONDITIONS AND OTHER DATA)

SYSTEM: OF ALL THE PEOPLE IN THIS OCCUPATION 70-95% ARE WOMEN. AS AN INFORMAL WAITER YOU WOULD PROBABLY

NEVER TRAVEL OVERNIGHT OR LONG DISTANCES. IF YOU WERE AN INFORMAL WAITER YOU WOULD OFTEN WORK WEEK-ENDS. YOU WOULD OFTEN WORK NIGHTS. AN INFORMAL WAITER IS SOMETIMES REQUIRED TO GET A LICENSE. THERE IS NO INFORMATION ABOUT UNION MEMBERSHIP. AS AN INFORMAL WAITER YOU WOULD BE SUBJECT TO NO HAZARDS. IF YOU WOULD LIKE TO LEARN MORE ABOUT THIS JOB, PLEASE INDICATE A TOPIC THAT INTERESTS YOU.

COHEN: @QUIT

SYSTEM: YOU ARE NOW LEAVING ISVD.

Three weeks pass before Robert decides to go back on the ISVD system. He logs in as usual but before the system goes into MAJOR ORIENTATION, something different happens.

SYSTEM: LAST TIME YOU WERE WORKING ON A DECISION ABOUT COLLEGES. YOU HAVE LOOKED AT SCRIPTS ABOUT FACTORS IN COLLEGE ADMISSIONS, COLLEGE PREFERENCES, COLLEGE DESCRIPTIONS, DATA.

COHEN: (pushes send block)

SYSTEM: IN THE COLLEGE PREFERENCE SCRIPT, THE CHOICES YOU MADE SUGGESTED 11 COLLEGES:

COLBY COLLEGE
TUFTS UNIVERSITY
UNIVERSITY OF CONNECTICUT
UNIVERSITY OF MASSACHUSETTS
BABSON INSTITUTE OF BUSINESS ADMINISTRATION
BOSTON COLLEGE
BOSTON UNIVERSITY
BRANDEIS UNIVERSITY
HARVARD UNIVERSITY
CHAMBERLAYNE JUNIOR COLLEGE
LESLEY COLLEGE

COHEN: (pushes send block)

SYSTEM: YOU ASKED TO HAVE THESE COLLEGES DESCRIBED

UNIVERSITY OF CONNECTICUT
UNIVERSITY OF MASSACHUSETTS
TUFTS UNIVERSITY
BOSTON COLLEGE
BOSTON UNIVERSITY
HARVARD UNIVERSITY
CHAMBERLAYNE JUNIOR COLLEGE

COHEN: (pushes send block)

SYSTEM: YOU'VE NOW BEEN WITH THE ISVD FOR A LITTLE WHILE,

HOW WOULD YOU NOW DESCRIBE YOUR EXPERIENCE HERE?

COHEN: PRETTY INTERESTING.

SYSTEM: THE SUMMARY STATEMENT YOU JUST MADE ABOUT THE WAY YOU FEEL ABOUT YOUR TIME WITH ISVD IS BEING SAVED FOR YOU. WHAT DID YOU EXPECT YOUR TIME WITH ISVD TO BE LIKE?

COHEN: I DIDN'T REALLY KNOW.

SYSTEM: THERE ARE TWO NEW COMMANDS (LIKE @DATA, @STOP, ETC.) FOR USE IN THIS SCRIPT ONLY. THESE ARE:

*THEN

AND

*NOW

NOTE THAT THE SPECIAL SYMBOL BEFORE THESE NEW COMMANDS IS

* NOT @

TYPE *THEN WHENEVER YOU WANT TO LOOK AT YOUR STATEMENT ABOUT WHAT YOU EXPECTED YOUR TIME WITH ISVD TO BE LIKE.

TYPE *NOW WHENEVER YOU WANT TO LOOK AT THE STATEMENT YOU JUST MADE ABOUT THE WAY YOU NOW FEEL ABOUT YOUR TIME WITH ISVD.

HOW DOES YOUR EXPERIENCE WITH ISVD COMPARE WITH WHAT YOU EXPECTED?

COHEN: STRANGE.

SYSTEM: SORRY, WE COULDN'T UNDERSTAND YOU. PLEASE TRY AGAIN.

COHEN: PRETTY DIFFERENT.

SYSTEM: THEN YOU FEEL THAT THERE HAVE BEEN SOME CHANGES IN YOUR FEELINGS DURING THIS EXPERIENCE. WHAT ARE SOME OF THE DIFFERENCES BETWEEN WHAT YOU EXPECTED AND WHAT HAPPENED?

COHEN: I DON'T KNOW.

SYSTEM: WHAT WERE THE REASONS FOR THE DIFFERENCES BETWEEN WHAT YOU EXPECTED AND WHAT HAPPENED?

COHEN: I DON'T KNOW.

SYSTEM: ARE THESE DIFFERENCES BETWEEN WHAT YOU EXPECTED AND WHAT HAPPENED IMPORTANT TO YOU?

COHEN: YES.

SYSTEM: WHY ARE THESE DIFFERENCES IMPORTANT TO YOU?

COHEN: BECAUSE I DIDN'T KNOW WHAT TO EXPECT AND NOW I DO.

SYSTEM: WE'VE ASKED YOU MANY QUESTIONS IN THE LAST FEW MINUTES, AND MAYBE YOU'VE ASKED YOURSELF SOME, TOO. YOUR OWN QUESTIONS CAN BE MUCH MORE IMPORTANT THAN ANY WE COULD ASK. IF YOU HAVE ASKED YOURSELF SOME QUESTIONS AS WE'VE GONE ALONG, OR IF

SOME COME TO MIND NOW, YOU CAN SAVE THEM IN YOUR PRIVATE FILE BY TYPING THEM IN. IF THIS ISN'T SOMETHING YOU'D LIKE TO DO NOW, PUSH SEND BLOCK AND WE'LL MOVE ON.

COHEN: (pushes send block)

SYSTEM: NOW LET'S REVIEW WHAT WE'VE BEEN DOING. YOUR STATEMENT ABOUT WHAT YOU EXPECTED YOUR SESSION WITH ISVD TO BE LIKE WAS, "I DIDN'T REALLY KNOW." AFTER YOU HAD BEEN EXPERIENCING ISVD FOR A WHILE, YOU MADE THIS STATEMENT ABOUT WHAT IT WAS LIKE: "PRETTY INTERESTING." THE COMMANDS *THEN AND *NOW ARE STILL AVAILABLE IN CASE YOU WANT TO LOOK AT THESE STATEMENTS AGAIN. YOU COULD ALSO MAKE A HARD COPY OF THEM TO KEEP.

COHEN: *THEN

SYSTEM: YOU SAID, "I DIDN'T REALLY KNOW." AFTER YOU MADE YOUR SECOND STATEMENT, WE ASKED SEVERAL QUESTIONS. FIRST, WE ASKED IF THERE WERE DIFFERENCES BETWEEN WHAT YOU EXPECTED ABOUT ISVD AND WHAT YOU FOUND IT TO BE LIKE. YOU SAID, "I DON'T KNOW." THEN WE ASKED WHY THERE DIDN'T SEEM TO BE DIFFERENCES, AND YOU SEEMED UNSURE.

COHEN: (pushes send block)

SYSTEM: IN GOING THROUGH THIS REVIEW EXERCISE, YOU CHOSE TO LOOK AT YOUR STATEMENT ABOUT WHAT YOU EXPECTED ONCE. YOU CHOSE NOT TO LOOK AT YOUR STATEMENT ABOUT HOW YOU FELT AFTER USING ISVD FOR A WHILE. FINALLY, WE ASKED IF YOU HAD ANY QUESTIONS ABOUT YOUR EXPERIENCES THAT YOU WANTED TO SAVE, AND YOU CHOSE NOT TO SAVE ANY OF YOUR QUESTIONS.

The guidance machine has decided to review a little of the interaction Robert has been having with the ISVD system. More accurately, the introductory system scripts keep count of the number of times Robert has been on the system and will offer such a review summary after every third session. In Robert's case, it has helped him to refresh his memory. This review completed, the system continues normally, transferring to MAJOR ORIENTATION.

In MAJOR ORIENTATION, Robert indicates that he wants to get back to thinking about college. The language he uses alerts the system that Robert should be given the EXPLORE script. This is one of the "monitoring" scripts designed to ascertain certain attitudes or interests of the user for later use. Robert will take this EXPLORE script and then later on in this same session the system will put to use the data it gathers in this script.

SYSTEM: WHAT'S IMPORTANT TO YOU IN THINKING ABOUT COLLEGES?

COHEN: I WANT TO KNOW HOW MUCH IT WILL COST, HOW FAR FROM MY CITY THE SCHOOL IS AND IF I CAN GET IN WITH MY BOARD SCORES.

SYSTEM: WE RECOGNIZED WORDS REFERRING TO URBAN OR RURAL SETTING, ADMISSION REQUIREMENTS, COSTS IN YOUR RESPONSE. IT'S ALMOST CERTAIN THAT THIS LIST DOESN'T INCLUDE ALL OF WHAT'S IMPORTANT TO YOU IN CHOOSING A COLLEGE. THE LIST MAY ALSO INCLUDE SOME MEANINGS THAT AREN'T IN YOUR STATEMENT AS YOU SEE IT.

COHEN: YES, IT DOES.

SYSTEM: IF YOU WANT TO KNOW HOW WE GOT ANY OF THESE MEANINGS OUT OF WHAT YOU SAID, TYPE IN THE MEANING YOU'D LIKE EXPLAINED, OR TYPE NO IF YOU DON'T WANT ANY MORE EXPLANATION. (URBAN OR RURAL SETTING, ADMISSION REQUIREMENTS, COSTS.)

COHEN: ADMISSION REQUIREMENTS.

SYSTEM: IT SEEMED YOU WERE TALKING ABOUT ADMISSION REQUIREMENTS WHEN YOU SAID "GET IN." DID YOU MEAN ADMISSION REQUIREMENTS?

COHEN: OF COURSE.

SYSTEM: ARE THERE ANY OTHERS YOU WANT EXPLAINED? URBAN OR RURAL SETTING, ADMISSION REQUIREMENTS, COSTS.

COHEN: URBAN OR RURAL SETTING.

SYSTEM: IT SEEMED YOU WERE TALKING ABOUT URBAN OR RURAL SETTING WHEN YOU SAID, "FAR FROM MY CITY." DID YOU MEAN URBAN OR RURAL SETTING?

COHEN: NO.

SYSTEM: WHAT DID YOU MEAN WHEN YOU SAID "FAR FROM MY CITY?"

COHEN: I MEANT I DIDN'T WANT TO GO TOO FAR FROM HOME.

SYSTEM: MAYBE WHEN YOU SAID "FAR AWAY FROM MY CITY" YOU'RE TALKING ABOUT GEOGRAPHIC LOCATION INSTEAD OF URBAN OR RURAL SETTING, SINCE YOU NOW SAY "FAR AWAY FROM MY HOME."

COHEN: CORRECT.

SYSTEM: GEOGRAPHIC LOCATION IS NOW ON YOUR LIST INSTEAD OF URBAN OR RURAL SETTING. ARE THERE ANY OTHERS YOU WANT EXPLAINED? GEOGRAPHIC LOCATION, ADMISSION REQUIREMENTS, COST?

COHEN: NO. I WOULD LIKE TO GO TO THE DATA BASE TO GET SOME MORE FACTS ABOUT COLLEGES.

Robert then goes on for a half hour or so to explore some additional facts about the colleges on his list. Each time, after he is finished looking into a particular college and before he gets to look into another one, the system asks him to express an opinion about the college. Is he indifferent about it? Or is one or two of them beginning to look like prospects? When the user has expressed favorable leanings toward three or more colleges, the system transfers him to a CLARIFICATION script. The last time Robert was on the system, he indicated both Tufts University and Boston College to be good prospects. Today he has looked so far into several other colleges and discarded all of them for one reason or another. He has just finished looking into Boston University.

SYSTEM: YOU JUST GOT SOME DATA ABOUT BOSTON UNIVERSITY. DO YOU CONSIDER THE COLLEGE:
GOOD
BAD
NEITHER GOOD NOR BAD?

COHEN: GOOD

SYSTEM: WHY DO YOU CONSIDER BOSTON UNIVERSITY TO BE A GOOD COLLEGE FOR YOU?

COHEN: IT'S CLOSE TO HOME AND I THINK I CAN GET IN AND I HEAR THERE ARE GOOD FRATERNITIES THERE.

SYSTEM: YOU'VE SAID THESE 3 COLLEGES LOOK GOOD TO YOU
1. TUFTS UNIVERSITY
2. BOSTON COLLEGE
3. BOSTON UNIVERSITY
DOES ANY ONE OF THESE COLLEGES STAND OUT AS THE ONE YOU'LL GO TO?

COHEN: YES

SYSTEM: WHICH ONE? (TYPE THE NUMBER.)

COHEN: 1

SYSTEM: YOU SAID TUFTS UNIVERSITY LOOKS GOOD BECAUSE "IT'S NOT FAR FROM HOME AND IT'S NOT TOO EXPENSIVE." IS THERE ANYTHING YOU'D LIKE TO ADD TO YOUR REASONS FOR LIKING TUFTS UNIVERSITY?

COHEN: IT HAS GOOD FRATERNITIES.

At this point, the system retrieves Robert's inputs to the EXPLORE script and compares the factors he mentioned there with the ones he is now using to make up his mind.

SYSTEM: WHEN YOU WERE TALKING ABOUT COLLEGES IN GENERAL, YOU SAID GEOGRAPHIC LOCATION, ADMISSION REQUIREMENTS, COST WERE IMPORTANT. IN DESCRIBING WHY YOU LIKE TUFTS UNIVERSITY, YOU SEEM TO BE TALKING ABOUT GEOGRAPHIC LOCATION, COST, SOCIAL

	ACTIVITIES, WHAT ABOUT ADMISSION REQUIREMENTS, SOCIAL ACTIVITIES?
COHEN:	THEY'RE OKAY.
SYSTEM:	HAVE YOU LOOKED INTO THE ADMISSION REQUIREMENTS, SOCIAL ACTIVITIES OF TUFTS UNIVERSITY?
COHEN:	YES
SYSTEM:	HOW DOES THAT MAKE YOU FEEL ABOUT TUFTS UNIVERSITY? IS IT STILL THE COLLEGE FOR YOU?
COHEN:	YES, IT HAS A GOOD DENTAL SCHOOL.
SYSTEM:	YOU SEEM FAIRLY CERTAIN THAT TUFTS UNIVERSITY IS THE COLLEGE FOR YOU. WHAT DO YOU PLAN ON DOING ABOUT GETTING INTO TUFTS UNIVERSITY?
COHEN:	TALK TO MR. SUREDA, MY COUNSELOR, ABOUT IT AND GET AN APPLICATION FORM FROM HIM.

This extended example of Robert Cohen's experience with ISVD over a supposed two-month period serves three useful purposes. It demonstrates the major components of ISVD, showing various ways in which the script network mediates the student's access to data, and even though the example is confined pretty much to the college scripts and data base, still there is more than enough material in the example to permit one to infer how the occupational and military portions of ISVD function. A second useful purpose served by the example is to show some aspects of a person's movement through the several stages of the vocational decision-making process as depicted by David V. Tiedeman and Robert P. O'Hara, and, thereby, to suggest some of the ways the ISVD guidance machine can support, and, in some cases, enhance the student's passage through these stages. Finally, the example supports the earlier contention that "with the computer we have the potential to make guidance in schools less hurried, less directive, and even less factual." It may be true, of course, that ISVD does not go far enough toward utilizing this potential, but in any case, that there is such potential should be clear.

Yet with all of this and with whatever else there may be in the case of Robert Cohen that persuades us of the values, and benefits, and promises of ISVD, still the example will do injury to your understanding of the computer's role in guidance unless you are clear about what is wrong with the example.

Foremost among its weaknesses is the fact that the example is a first level example, a stick figure representation of the real world. Life and the processes that living things engage in are never so simple, and the complexities of these processes are never just the result of extending the simple cases: the complexities make the real life versions *qualitatively* different from any of our simplified characterizations of them. Regarding the vocational decision process, no one doubts that there is constant interaction among issues about occupation, schooling, military obligations, family, and personal criteria of failure and success and the good life. None of these interactions is depicted in the example and to omit them is, ultimately, to be talking about something entirely different from the vocational decision process. Even the time it took Robert Cohen to get from uncertainty to Tufts and the single mindedness with which he did it are blatant fictions.

A second—and yet from a practical point of view, a decisive—shortcoming of the example is that students are rarely as facile as Robert Cohen in their use of the system. Students do not spell words correctly all the time, and often their words and their syntax cannot be understood by the ISVD scripts. Moreover, as Aylmer's study of ISVD has shown,[3] students are often frustrated by the ISVD guidance machine, not knowing always what is expected of them. Other students are too docile, too deficient in their "sense of agency" to even begin to take advantage of the opportunities for controlling the system. It almost seems that sense of agency, like money, comes to those who already have it.

Robert Cohen, were he to exist, would be an unusual student, one, in fact, who would be likely to come to a decision even without ISVD. The problem, of course, is to accommodate those students who, like Vincent Brown, are too willing to do what they are told to do, or who, like Frank Mullen, never really seem to need to see their counselors.

[3]Robert Aylmer, "A Preliminary Investigation of Computer Involvement in Vocational Decision-Making," unpublished doctoral dissertation, Harvard University, 1970.

epilogue

Dangers, cautions, risks, warnings, minimal and superficial successes, flirtations with failure, and the general abuse and distortion of educational practice are the things we have charted in our exploration into the use of the computer in education. The educational technologist, who knows "what computers *do*," who considers "educational technology a tautology," and who concludes "we can't do without the computer in education" makes necessary such a negative and pessimistic account. There is already too much optimism and concensus regarding the computer's promise for education. More than anything else we need to replace this optimism with doubt.

This is not to suggest, however, that the computer holds no promise for education. On the contrary, our efforts to define a computer, and our consideration of the implications this definition holds for education have made the potential clear. However cautious we may need to be, we have seen that with the computer we have a unique opportunity to meaningfully rethink and reformulate educational practice. Nor is it the case that all the efforts to apply computers in education have been dubious projects. While clearly a minority we found examples of well-grounded efforts at automation in education. For instance, the LOGO project of Seymour Papert comes first to mind, followed by portions of the work of Patrick Suppes and Richard Atkinson. Even the formulations of Victor Bunderson may be cited, for while the unthinking educational technologist has misused such notions, Bunderson's work has itself been careful and well developed. Thus we have seen, with computers there must be a mingling of doubt and promise.

But ISVD which began with this sense of doubt and of promise, led us a step further into a deeper contradiction. Even with our one-dimensional depiction of ISVD we could see the effort was grounded in the thinking, examining, probing, and rethinking both of procedure and of the substance underlying that procedure. But we should have seen, as well, that ISVD led us away from the conventional wisdom that seeks to use the computer to facilitate the individual's integration into a technological society and towards the irony that sees the computer as a means to diminish the individual's dependence on technology and its effects. As early in the development of ISVD as 1968, Jordan Baruch noticed the beginnings of this shift in view when he remarked:

> . . . ISVD has taken a step which I consider the most dangerous one it has ever taken. That is the step of helping the student develop a set of tools not just to discover his abilities and the demands of the world of work, but to deal with, explore, and perhaps even define some of his own values so that he cannot only start matching his abilities with the world of work but can start examining the rewards that the world around him offers and decide how well those rewards match his values. That last step, if pursued, is what will destroy the world as we know it.[1]

Thus ISVD became a computer-based environment whose principal function was to nurture in the student the capacity to question and to alter the values and the premises of that very environment itself.

In this respect ISVD tells us we should think of computers much the way we think of academic freedom. We know that academic freedom is only superficially the freedom to say or think anything we please. More important, academic freedom is a point of view about the things we say or think. It is a view wherein we are willing to assert something, and by the same assertion express doubt. Thus a declarative sentence is at the same time a question. With computers the same view should prevail. At one level, this means we see automation of a process as the delving into that process anew. But, as it has been the purpose of this book to suggest, at another, more general level, to use computers in education should be to question the value of computers in education.

[1]Jordan Baruch, "Synthesis," Paper presented at the Invitational Conference on Systems Under Development for Vocational Guidance, October, 1968, mimeo.

appendix

some facts about computers

This Appendix is offered for the uninitiated who wishes to learn some of the elemental facts about how computers work. Throughout the brief account presented here, there is no assumption of prior knowledge about computers. However, we recommend that the reader complete Part I before coming to this Appendix since, thereby, his understanding will be bolstered by a reconsideration of the common points of view about computers.

It is possible, of course, to understand, analyze, and even define computers without ever seeing one. Automata theorists do not need to visit computing centers or to write computer programs in order to delve into the nature of computers, and we know from Chapter Two that Alan Turing published his paper on Turing machines two years before Howard Aiken began work on the first computer. But the purpose of this book is to help educators imagine how computers might specifically assist them in their work; and since in Part I we have dealt, at least in a beginning way, with those misconceptions that usually stand in the way of such imagination, it is probably safe at this point to look at a computer and some of its components.

Hardware

Although present day, general purpose electronic digital computers come in many shapes and sizes, and are used for many diverse purposes, they are as much alike as they are different. Some computers are small enough to fit on top of a desk while others take up considerable floor space in a

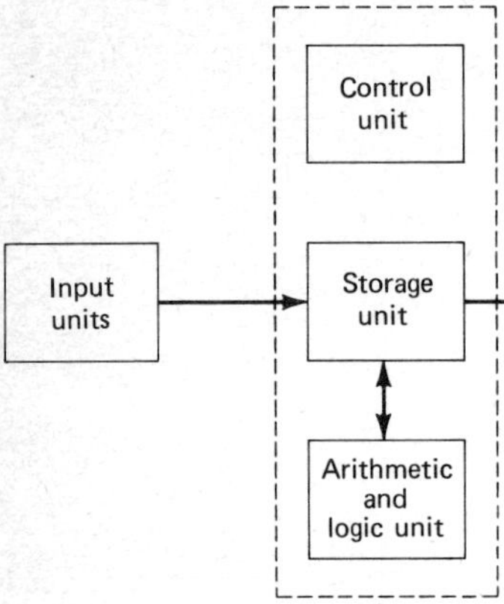

Figure A-1 The functional components of a general purpose computer.

room. Still others, the larger and more powerful computers, fill up the equivalent of a large high school's library. In principle, however, all these machines are similar, having at the most general level the same five functional components. These five functional components, which may be more or less sophisticated and powerful depending upon the particular computer in question, are depicted in Figure A-1 where the arrows represent the flow of information through these components.

Data enter the computer by way of the input units and are placed in storage. When called for by the computer program—which also resides in storage—these data are transferred to the arithmetic and logic unit where they are processed and returned to storage. Finally, when appropriate, the

Figure A-2 IBM System/360 model 40 computer. Courtesy of the International Business Machines Corporation.

Figure A-3 UNIVAC 9400 computer. Courtesy of UNIVAC Division of the Sperry-Rand Corporation.

Figure A-4 IBM System/370 model 135 computer. Courtesy of the International Business Machines Corporation.

Figure A-5 Honeywell series 200 model 200 computer. Courtesy of Honeywell Inc.

Figure A-6 RCA Spectra 70/45 computer. Courtesy of Radio Corporation of America.

Figure A-7 Honeywell 110 computer. Courtesy of Honeywell Inc.

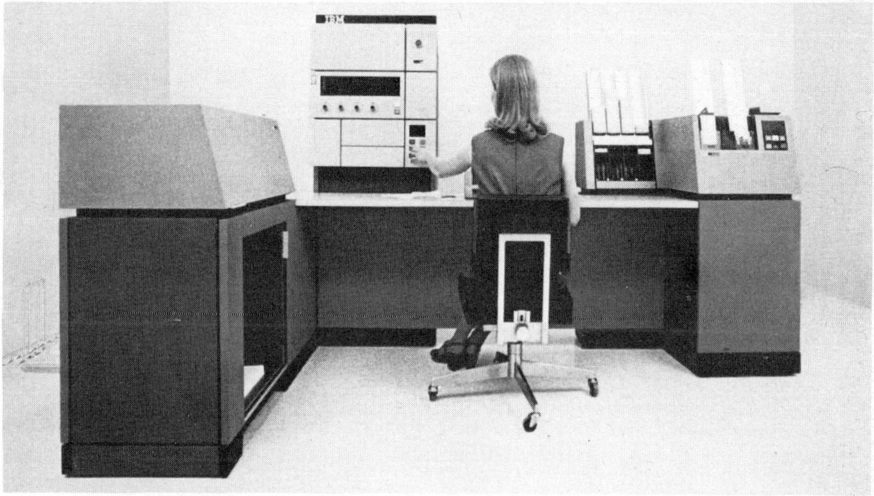

Figure A-8 IBM S/3 card system. Courtesy of the International Business Machines Corporation.

Figure A-9 NCR 100 computer. Courtesy of National Cash Register Corporation.

results of that processing are sent from storage to one of the output units. The entire flow of data through this system, and the corresponding operation of the computer program which dictates the ways information is to be processed, are under the control of the control unit. In this way the four "working units" of the computer's hardware are controlled and made to function harmoniously.

Now, any machine that processes information poses first of all the problem of data input. How will numerals, letters of the alphabet, and other symbols to be processed be put into the machine? Jacquard, remember, used punched cards to represent different patterns for his loom. Similarly Babbage and Hollerith used punched cards as the form of input to their machines. During the 1930s the International Business Machines Corporation (IBM) began to extend the idea of Hollerith's machines to the field of business. Their business machines—often called

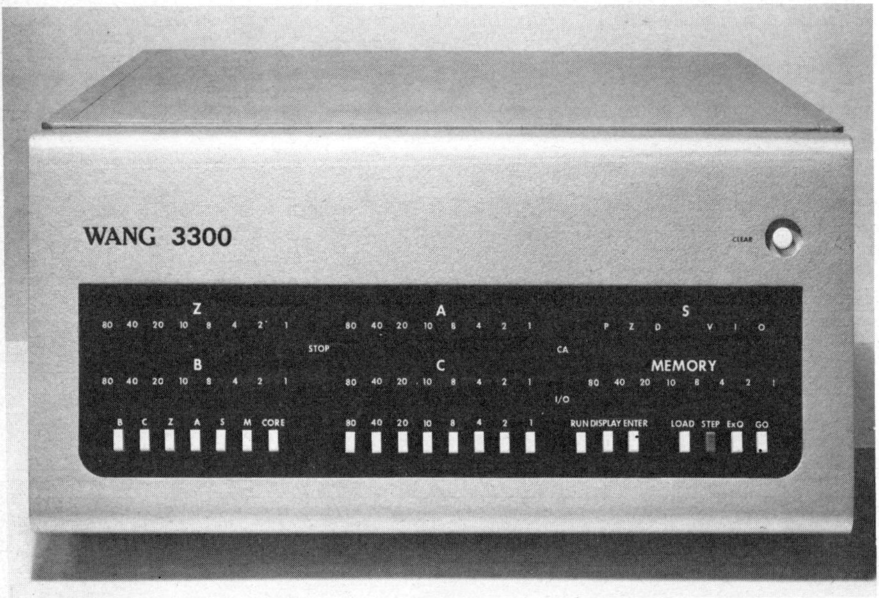

Figure A-10 WANG 3300 mini computer. Courtesy of Wang Laboratories Inc.

Figure A-11 D-112 mini computer. Courtesy of Digital Computer Controls, Inc.

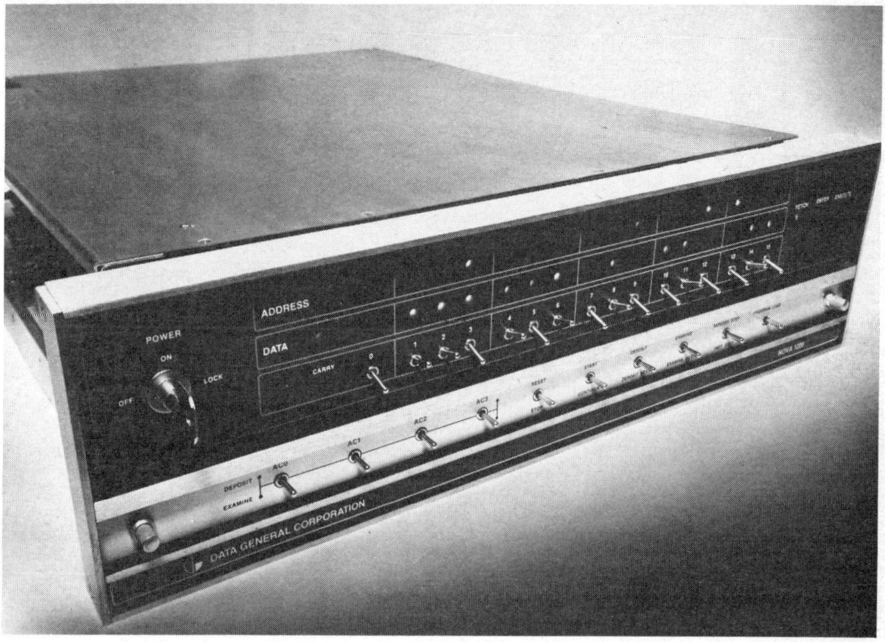

Figure A-12 NOVA 1200 mini computer. Courtesy of Data General Corporation.

unit record machines because a single record can be processed to produce many different reports—were designed to handle punched cards. The development by IBM of machines to sort, collate, print, tabulate, and otherwise deal with punched cards was so extensive that many people erroneously refer to these data processing cards as "IBM cards." Even today, whatever it is called, the punched card remains as in 1801 a basic form of input.

Holes are punched onto a data processing card according to a code devised so that numerals, letters of the alphabet, and other characters can be systematically represented. This code, which has been generally accepted, is essentially the same as the one Herman Hollerith devised in the 1880s and, in fact, is called the Hollerith code.

The Hollerith code is a way of punching holes in data processing cards such that different configurations of holes stand for different characters. A typical data processing card contains twelve rows and eighty columns, and each column can be used to represent just one symbol. Thus up to eighty symbols (characters) can be represented on a card. If you need more columns you can use more cards.

Each of the eighty columns on a data processing card contains twelve positions (rows) where a hole can be punched. The so-called 12-row is at the top of the card and the 9-row is at the bottom. The twelve rows in a

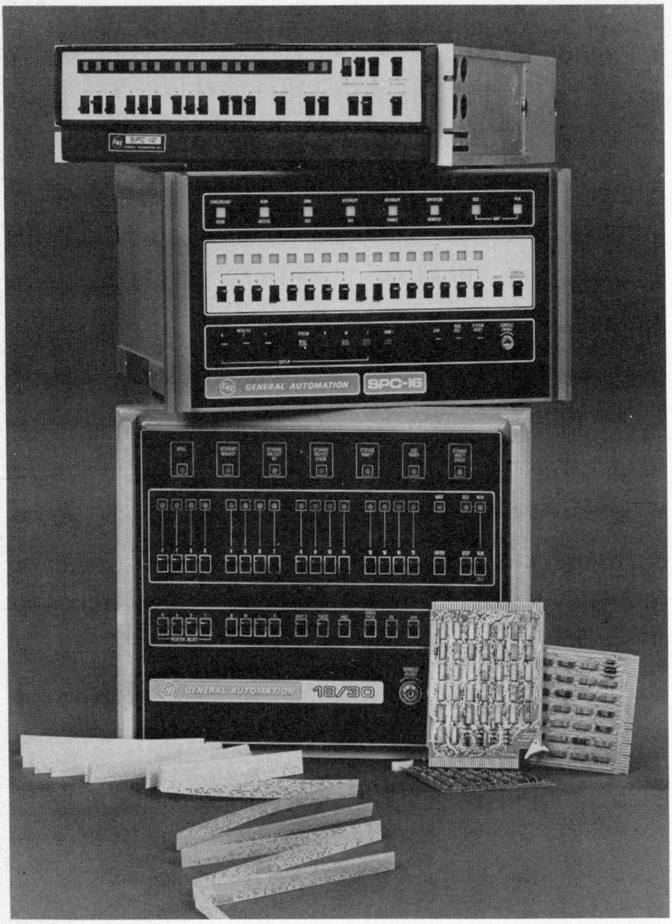

Figure A-13 General Automation mini computers. Courtesy of General Automation, Inc.

given column of a data processing card are in this order: 12
11
0
1
2
3
4
5
6
7
8
9

The Hollerith code divides these rows up into *digit* rows (position 0 through position 9) and *zone* rows (positions 12, 11, 0). Notice that the 0-row is treated as both a digit row and a zone row.

A hole punched in a particular digit row of a column represents the corresponding number. That is, a hole punched in the 3-row of a column represents the number 3, and so on. In this way any one of the numbers 1 through 9 can be represented in a column and in each case, only a single punch is required. Similarly, a hole in the 0-row taken by itself represents a zero. Because the 12-row and the 11-row are never considered digit rows, they are not usually used to represent the numbers 12 and 11. Two columns are needed for this.

The major function of the zone positions—rows 12, 11, 0—is to be used in combination with the digit positions of a column to represent letters of the alphabet and such other characters as parentheses, commas, dollar signs, asterisks, periods, and apostrophes. The letter "A", for example, is represented by a 12-punch *and* a 1-punch in a given column. Thus all the letters of the alphabet, the digits, and many special characters can be represented through the Hollerith code as holes punched on cards. Figure A-14 shows the complete code.

Once they are punched with the appropriate information, data processing cards are read into a computer by a device called a card reader. There are several schemes that might be used to read the card, but they are all in principle the same as that used in the Jacquard loom where the dropping of a needle was either permitted or inhibited depending upon whether or not a hole was punched in a particular place on a card. For instance, some card readers feed the cards one at a time between an electrified surface and a set of metal brushes. The absence of a hole in a

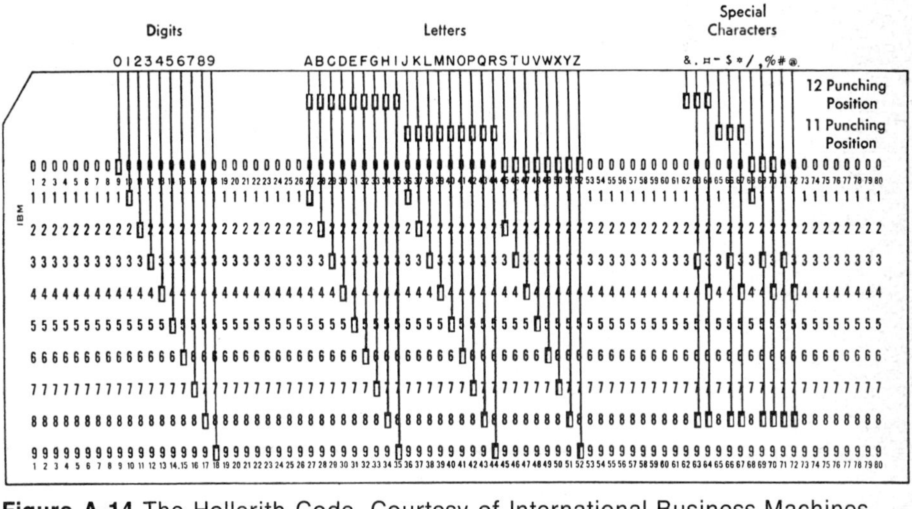

Figure A-14 The Hollerith Code. Courtesy of International Business Machines Corporation.

given position of a card inhibits the completion of an electrical circuit by not allowing the brushes to make contact with the electrified surface. The presence of a hole, on the other hand, permits the completion of this circuit and thus the transmission of an electrical impulse to some other part of the system. In this way the card can be "read" and the data on it recorded within the computer.

Just as a computer can accept punched cards as input, it can provide punched cards as output. By human standards the reading and the punching of cards by computer take place very rapidly indeed. A typical card reading device reads between 600 and 800 cards per minute. That is somewhere between ten and thirteen cards every second. This device can also punch cards at the rate of 250 cards per minute. But, however fast these speeds may seem to us they are painfully slow when compared to the computer's processing speeds. An average computer, for example, can compute the fifty means, the fifty standard deviations, and the 1,225 intercorrelations for fifty measurements on each of 800 people in the same amount of time that it would take to read in the data needed for such an analysis. Making a computer get its input directly from punched cards is thus a gross waste of time. Some other way had to be found to get data in and out of a computer.

A solution which has provided a more reasonable form of input and output is the use of magnetic tape. Much the way we record a speech or a symphony onto tape, we can record the configuration of holes from a punched card onto a magnetic tape especially designed for use with computers. This tape comes, typically, in either 1,200 or 2,400 foot reels, and several hundred characters can be represented in just one inch of tape. Thus many thousands of punched cards can be recorded onto a single reel of magnetic tape. Once the transfer of characters from card to tape is complete, the tape becomes the input medium. Similarly once the

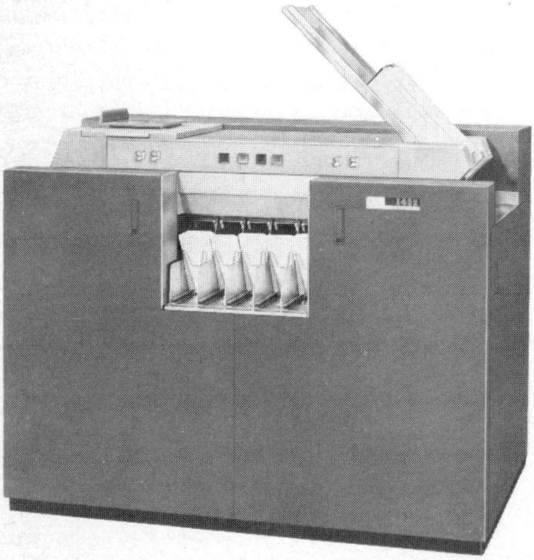

Figure A-15 IBM 1402 card reader/punch. Courtesy of International Business Machines Corporation.

Figure A-16 DOCUMATION M1200 card reader. Courtesy of DOCUMATION Incorporated.

computer has finished its job, the output can be put directly onto tape.

All this trouble to transfer card images onto tape is worth it because computers can read magnetic tape so much faster than punched cards. To get a feeling for the difference, notice that a card reader processing 750 cards per minute will read up to sixty thousand characters every minute. (This maximum is reached when there are eighty characters on each card.) But this is the number of characters a tape unit such as the ones depicted in Figures A-18 and A-19 can read each *second*. Even under conditions where tape reading speeds are reduced—for example, because of the way the data are grouped on the tape—the difference remains large enough to be worth the effort. This difference between cards and tape as forms of input and output is sufficient, and the time of large computers is so valuable that it is common practice at computing centers to use small computers to transfer data from cards to tape. The tape is then used for input to the large computer. For output the process is reversed; the

Figure A-17 RCA 70/237 card reader. Courtesy of Radio Corporation of America.

Figure A-18 RCA 70/442 Magnetic Tape Units. Courtesy of Radio Corporation of America.

Figure A-19 IBM Magnetic Tape Units as part of System/360. Courtesy of International Business Machines Corporation.

Figure A-20 IBM 1403 printer. Courtesy of International Business Machines Corporation.

Figure A-21 RCA 70/243 printer. Courtesy of Radio Corporation of America.

computer uses tape as its output medium and when the computer run is completed the tape is taken to the smaller computer for further processing.

This further processing—often called peripheral processing—may, of course, consist of transferring the data from tape to punched cards, but this is not usually what happens. People most often want to *see* their results and for this reason the common form of output is the printed page. A high speed printer can produce about twelve hundred lines of printed output per minute which is fast enough so that some people have their large computers print the results directly. Others still use tape as an intermediary, leaving to a smaller, peripheral computer the task of printing the contents of the output tape.

Card readers, card punches, tape read and write devices, and printers are the ordinary input/output media, but there are others. Disk storage units, for instance, are input/output devices able to handle large amounts of data. A typical disk storage unit is one manufactured by IBM—called the IBM 2311—which holds up to 7,250,000 characters per unit and which can input data at the rate of 156,000 characters a second. Other machines exist that can read specially marked sheets, translating the marks into characters and either punching the characters on cards or writing them on magnetic tape for input to a computer. Most people have used these as answer sheets for tests, opinion polls, and the census. Still another input device is the optical reader which can read numerals and some printed characters from a sheet. One such device can recognize the full range of typed characters in a variety of fonts. This area of direct input of typed or printed characters is, as one might easily guess, one in which engineers are most active.

One form of input/output that is becoming especially important to the field of education is the communications terminal. These terminals are devices that may be located some distance from a computer, but which can nonetheless communicate—provide input and accept output—with a computer over telephone lines or some similar communications lines. The most commonly known terminal is the teletypewriter depicted in Figures A-22 to A-24. Teletypewriters have typewriter-like keyboards, used for sending data or instructions to a computer, and printers used for receiving output.

Less widespread but potentially more significant for applications to

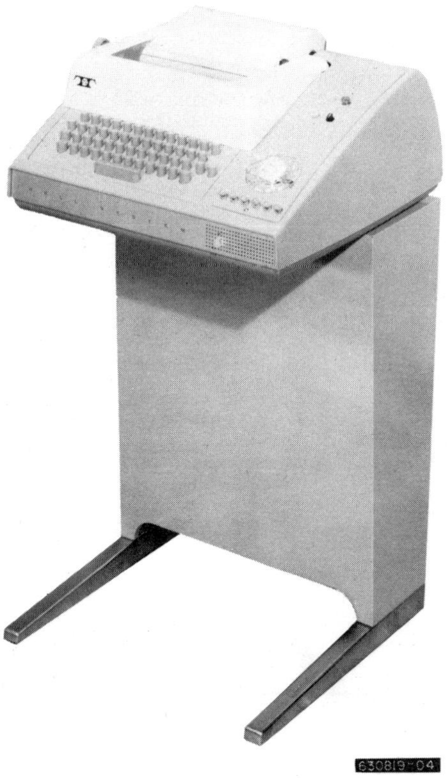

Figure A-22 KSR Model 33 Teletype terminal. Courtesy of Teletype Corporation.

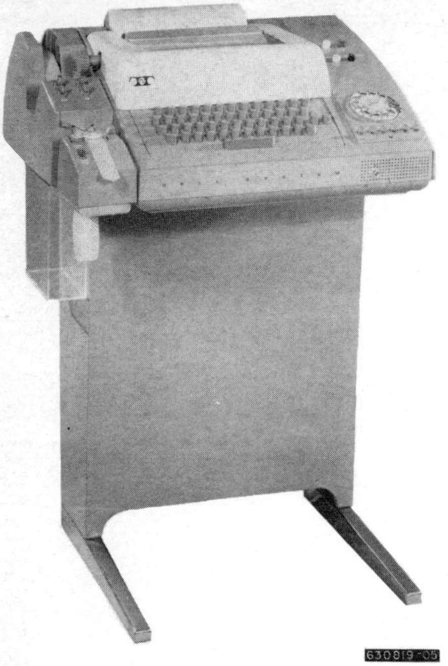

Figure A-23 ASR Model 33 Teletype terminal. Courtesy of Teletype Corporation.

Figure A-24 Teletypes as part of Hewlett Packard time sharing system. Courtesy of Hewlett Packard.

education is the use of a terminal equipped with a television like screen called a cathode ray tube. These video display terminals make it possible to display output on the face of the screen. Display terminals such as those shown in Figures A-25 through A-29 have been combined with such audio-visual devices as film strips, slides, and tape recorders—all under computer control—to provide what some people consider a flexible set of output media useful in education.

Just about all the forms of input and output—cards, tape, disk, even the printed page—may be thought of, as well, as forms of storage. They are the filing cabinets of the computer age. As a form of storage each has its own advantages and disadvantages. Punched cards, for instance, come closest to resembling ordinary office files; they can be stored in drawers, indexed, retrieved manually, individually corrected or updated, and the like. But like office files, cards are bulky, awkward to handle, and perishable. So fragile are they that, often, the slightest nick or fold may render the card unreadable by a card reading device. Magnetic tape on the other hand is more durable as long as strict temperature control is maintained, and disks provide compact storage for millions of characters of data as long as the disk surfaces are kept scrupulously clean. The disadvantage of these two forms of storage, of course, is that one cannot

Figure A-25 Sanders 720 Video Display terminal. Courtesy of Sanders Associates.

Figure A-26 IBM 1510 Instructional Video Display terminal. Courtesy of International Business Machines Corporation.

Figure A-27 INCOTERM SPD 10/20 Programmable CRT Display terminal. Courtesy of INCOTERM Corporation.

Figure A-28 RCA 70/752 Video Display terminal. Courtesy of Radio Corporation of America.

work directly with the data they contain. We cannot look at a tape or a disk and tell what is on it; it must be processed before we can determine its contents. With cards and the printed page we do not have this difficulty, and obviously, therefore, the kinds of storage devices we select depend upon the use we wish to make of data. Whatever their differences in durability, or cost, or appropriateness to our needs, however, these forms of storage belong to the same family, known as *external storage devices.*

Another kind of storage is called *internal storage,* and this is what people are referring to when they talk about the computer's memory. Internal storage is that part of the computer where data are stored for access by the processing components of the computer. When a card or a tape is read by some input device, the data they contain are placed directly into the computer's internal memory. They are kept there until the computer's processing unit is ready for them. When processing is complete, the results are placed back in internal storage where they remain until it is time to either print out the results or to write the results on some other output medium. The input and output of data consists

Figure A-29 Wyle Series 8000 CRT terminal unit. Courtesy of Wyle Computer Products, Division of Wyle Laboratories.

almost exclusively then of sending data to internal storage or taking data from internal storage.

But data are not the only things to be found in the computer's internal memory. Along with data the computer program which describes what the machine is to do with the data is also stored in the computer's memory, and this turns out to be an extremely important fact. Without getting too detailed about it, we can say that a computer program is made up of a list of instructions and that it is the job of the control unit of a computer to take these instructions one at a time and execute them. Now, if these instructions were being fed in from the outside one by one, the computer would have to take them as they come. But, because all the instructions are stored in the computer's memory and thus equally accessible, it becomes possible for one instruction to tell the control unit which instruction to execute next. We saw this principle operating before with Turing machines, where the next state the machine is to be in is indicated by one of the components of its present state.

This ability to jump around instead of having to execute instructions in one and only one prescribed order is called *branching*, and branching accounts for much of the power people ascribe to computers. The interesting thing about branching is that, if we wish, the order in which instructions get executed by the computer can be determined by the very data that are being processed. The example that follows is not a computer program, of course, but it will serve to illustrate how branching can be a function of the data being processed. Suppose we had two numbers and we wished to calculate the absolute difference between them. One way to do this would be to determine which is the smaller number and then subtract it from the other one. It might look like this:

Instruction Number	Instruction
1	Read in the two numbers and call them A and B respectively.
2	Compare A and B, and if A is smaller than B, branch to instruction number 5, otherwise execute instruction number 3.
3	Subtract B from A.
4	Branch to instruction number 6.
5	Subtract A from B.
6	Stop.

The idea of the stored program makes this kind of branching possible, and, because no human intervention is required the computer gives the appearance of making a decision. This apparent ability to make a decision is one of the areas where if we are not careful with our words we can easily fall into those difficulties which are examined in the early parts of Chapter One.

A second interesting thing that comes from the fact that programs are stored in internal memory along with data is that data and instructions are in a sense interchangeable. The only way the computer can tell that something stored in memory is an instruction is if it makes its way to the control unit. As they sit in memory, the computer cannot tell the difference between data and instructions. This means, of course, that a program can purposely send a datum to the control unit, knowing that it will be treated as an instruction. Thus, not only can the sequence of the program be changed, the content of the instructions can be altered during the time of processing.

Realizing now the important role played by the internal storage unit of a computer, it may be interesting to get a closer look at how it works.

A typical storage unit of a computer is made up of an array of tiny, doughnut-shaped things called *ferrite cores*. Ferrite cores exhibit that interesting characteristic that all ferromagnetic materials exhibit, namely that whenever you magnetize them in a given direction they stay

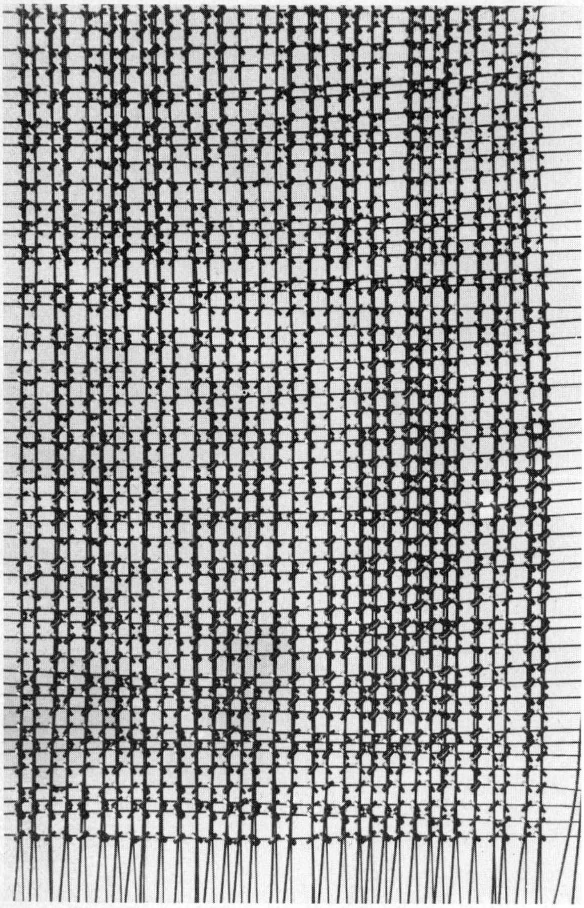

Figure A-30 A matrix of ferromagnetic cores. Courtesy of International Business Machines Corporation.

magnetized that way indefinitely or until you change the direction. A core can be magnetized in either of two directions, clockwise and counterclockwise, and this fits in well with the yes/no or binary logic on which most computers operate. To see how the direction of magnetism might be set, imagine a wire passing through the center of the core. Whenever an electrical current passes through the wire, it sets up a circular magnetic force around the wire which in turn induces a magnetic field within the core. The direction of this circular magnetic force and thus the direction of the magnetic field within the core depends on which way the current is flowing. When current flows one way the core is magnetized in a clockwise direction.

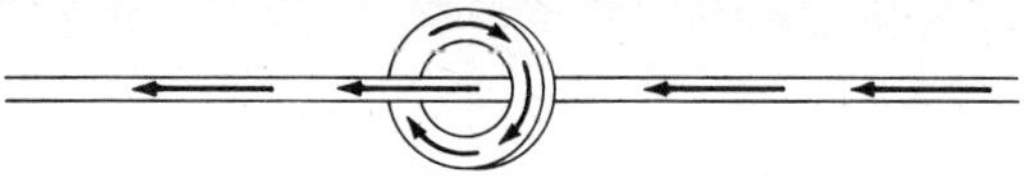

When the direction of the current is reversed, the magnetic field is similarly reversed.

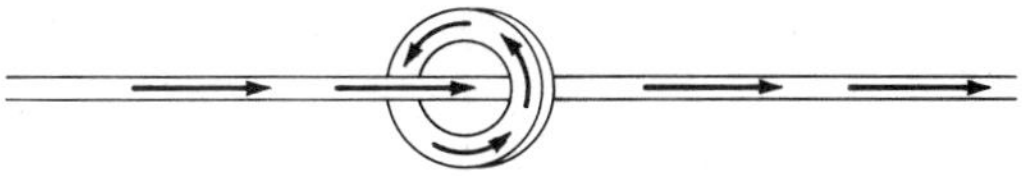

A fair sized—but not oversized—computer memory might have as many as 1,180,000 such magnetic cores. These cores are strung together into groups so that it becomes possible to represent numbers, letters of the alphabet, and other characters. Much like the Hollerith code, different configurations of clockwise and counterclockwise magnetic directions among a group of cores stand for different characters. While this arrangement may seem awkward, it is in fact a very efficient way to store information. Of course, cores are treated in a much more complicated way than is indicated here, but the intention is to provide just a general idea of how information is represented in internal storage.

Along with computer memory there are two additional units which go to make up the central part of the computer. They are the arithmetic and logic unit and the control unit. The arithmetic and logic unit is where the computer's work gets done. Even though the control unit interprets each instruction to be executed and supervises the overall operation of the system, it is in the arithmetic and logic unit that the actual processing takes place.

Because the arithmetic and logic unit does the adding, subtracting, multiplying, dividing, and such logical operations as comparing and branching, some people have come to consider it the essential component of a computer. But this is a mistake. In Chapter Two we defined a computer as a device having certain parts called inputs and other parts called outputs such that what happens at the outputs is in some way related to what happens at the inputs. This statement, as bare and unsatisfying as it is, should suggest, nonetheless, that we cannot single out one component and call it the basic unit. All five components are needed before one can reasonably expect to have a computer.

Software

When a housewife buys a Singer Touch and Sew Special Zig Zag sewing machine Model 603E, she gets a box of twenty-one plastic cams called pattern disks. When inserted properly into its holder, each of these disks makes it possible to automatically sew one of twenty-one fancy or complicated stitch patterns onto her material. Depending on the disk she selects, the housewife can bind her cloth with stitches like the chevron, the thunderbird, the walls of troy, the domino, or the shag, and every time she picks one and snaps it in place she is, in fact, programming her sewing machine. This act of programming is physical, consisting of the exchange of one piece of hardware for another. With computer programming the situation seems to be different, but it really is not.

Computer programs, of course, are statements to a computer of how its basic acts are to be strung together to form procedures. Such programs are called *software*, and because they do not obviously entail the physical exchange or alteration of hardware, they seem to be a different kind of programming from what housewives are used to with their sewing machines. But, even though it is quite clear that *hardware* stands for the physical components of the computer and software stands for the computer programs under which they operate, it is not always easy to tell where hardware leaves off and software begins. Indeed, there is one sense in which it is not meaningful to distinguish between them at all.

When computers were mechanical, people did not make so much of this distinction. Programming a mechanical computer consisted, in part, of using wrenches and pliers to rearrange gears and wheels—adding some, replacing others. Changing programs meant physically changing the machine, and it was clearer then that the value of a computer was not that it was a machine that could do many things but that it was a collection of components that could be reconfigured to become different machines.

None of this changes when computers become electronic and programs become holes punched on cards. It just is not as obvious. Computer programs determine which of the computer's basic acts are to be executed and they determine the sequence of this execution. Affected are the electro-magnetic composition of internal storage, the behavior of the input and output units, and the overall patterns of electrical flow. We cannot see electricity the way we see gears and wheels, of course, but we know, nonetheless, that electrons are material things. Thus computer programs—even though we call them software instead of hardware—affect the machine in certain physical ways.

The significance of this does not rest in an assertion that there is no important distinction between hardware and software. On the contrary, software is the mechanism for the flexibility we have come to expect from computers—a flexibility that would be lost if everything were done with hardware. The point, however, is that the decision of when to accomplish something with hardware and when to do it with software is not always clear-cut.

An example of the ability to accomplish something either way comes from the interesting area where one general purpose computer is made to behave like another general purpose computer. When a business or a university or a research project decides to replace its old computer with a new, more powerful one, it is almost always necessary to rewrite the old computer programs for the new machine. This job often takes one or two years, sometimes even longer, and to conduct business as usual during this period would seem to require that both the old and the new computers be maintained. Because this would be an unreasonable expense, however, another solution has been found. It is to program the new machine so that, when necessary, it can act like the old one, accepting its programs and providing the same output.

Now, this can be accomplished either of two ways. The first way, called *simulation*, consists in writing a computer program which will accept other computer programs written for the old machine and execute them. This is a software solution. The second way is called *emulation* and consists in adding a special piece of hardware to the new machine. This component, called a read-only memory, is wired so that when the new computer reads in a program written for the old machine it can use this special component to determine what the instructions mean.

Between simulation and emulation there are certain differences. The emulator, for instance, is likely to be faster, while the simulator is probably more flexible and can be altered more easily. In either case, however, the results are essentially the same and while there are practical considerations which will help decide the matter, the choice between them, from a theoretical point of view, is arbitrary.

Thus as we now look at some specific things about computer software, we should keep in mind that anything we can do with a computer program we can do, as well, with hardware. The reason we do not is the same as the reason an engineer would be better off making us one Universal Turing machine instead of ten special purpose ones. Indeed, the ability to do with software what would otherwise require hardware is precisely what it takes for a machine to be a general purpose computer.

Still, with all this flexibility there are two things about computers that are awkward for human beings, and these two things are at the base of what we must understand about computer software.

First, the computer's repertory is made up of basic, elemental acts much the same as Turing machines. The computer's set of acts is not as elemental, and there are more of them. But, like those of Turing machines, these acts are not as general as people are used to. "Get the contents of storage location 270," "compare the contents of location 99 with the contents of location 15," "treat the contents of storage location 220 as the next instruction," and "branch to the instruction whose address is equal to the contents of location 21" are just a few examples of the kinds of functions computers execute. People do not usually think of their problems in such detail and specificity, and yet this is the level at which computers expect procedures to be described.

Take, for instance, the simple problem of adding two numbers.

Assume that the two numbers, having been punched on cards and read into the machine, are now stored in memory locations 24 and 25. The part of the program that would prescribe the procedure for addition might say something like:

> Clear the accumulator (a register in the arithmetic and logic unit) and place therein the contents of storage location 24.
>
> Add the contents of storage location 25 to the contents of the accumulator.
>
> Store the present contents of the accumulator in storage location 26.

Clearly this is more cumbersome than saying "add A and B," and even though this is a trivial example, it is enough to suggest how awkward computer programming can be. As the problems to be solved become more sophisticated and more complex then, naturally, the statement one must make to the computer becomes more involved and more difficult.

All of this is confounded by the second awkward thing about computers which is that they do not understand English. As involved and as carefully formulated as our statement of a procedure might be, no computer could understand it when expressed in our language. Thus we must add to the problem of thinking in terms of the computer's basic acts, the need to talk its language when describing our procedures.

The language of computers is a language of ones and zeros. The direction of the magnetic field within the ferrite cores that make up internal memory can be either clockwise or counter-clockwise. These two conditions might be used respectively to represent yes/no, on/off, true/false and the like. It is customary to represent this binary situation within digital computers in terms of ones and zeros. One computer, for example, recognizes

000101000000000000000000000000011000

to mean, "clear the accumulator and place therein the contents of storage location 24." Similarly

000100000000000000000000000000011001

means, "add the contents of storage location 25 to the contents of the accumulator." And,

000110010001000000000000000000011010

means, "store the present contents of the accumulator in storage location 26."

Beside the fact that it is an imposition on human beings to have to think of their problems in the machine's terms and to use the machine's stilted language to express these problems, there are two other difficulties with writing computer programs this way. One obvious difficulty is that all these ones and zeros are confusing and tedious to deal with. Furthermore, we have to keep track of exactly where things are stored in memory, which locations are free for use, and which must be saved for later.

With all these problems and constraints, it does not seem that a computer is worth all the trouble it causes. But even if all the effort that seems to be implied here is justified, it must appear that computer programming is beyond the grasp and the attention span of the educator —researcher or teacher—interested in applying computers to his problems. This is not the case, however, and the reason it is not rests in a basic fact about computers. Since a computer can become any machine we can completely describe to it, it should be possible, if we are clever enough, to write a program that would turn a computer into a translating machine. The input to this program would be another program written this time in a language more familiar to us. The function of the computer would be to translate this second program into its own language. The output would be a translated version of our program in the proper form to be used directly then to solve our problem.

Such translating programs already exist and, as a result, computer programming has become a two-stage affair. First the program is written in a language more comfortable to us and submitted to the translator. Then the output of the translator is used as the machine language program.

Consider our example of adding two numbers. In one computer programming language it would read:

```
CLA  24
ADD  25
STO  26
```

The use of mnemonics frees us from having to remember that "000101000000" means "clear and add to accumulator" or that "000110010001" means "store the contents of the accumulator." The translator program will take care of replacing each mnemonic with its machine language equivalent. Notice, however, that as shown here, we still need to keep track of storage locations even though the specific location of data in storage is a matter of no concern to us as long as things are kept straight and we do not lose data or use one datum when we need another. Indeed a programming language need not require that we bother about storage allocation. At the time the data are read into memory, instead of designating specific locations for each, we need only refer to our data by names we make up for them. Suppose, for instance, we called a datum by the name VAR1. The first time the translator came upon this name in our program it would understand the following to be its instructions: "Here is a datum. I am calling it VAR1. Find any free storage location you like, store this datum there, and keep a record of where you put it. Then anytime I refer to VAR1, go to the appropriate storage location and get the datum in question."

Now in our example, instead of using specific storage locations, we could refer to the data by names, say, A, B, and C, and then we would write:

```
CLA  A
ADD  B
STO  C
```

No longer need we worry about storage allocation, machine language, and the like.

Such languages are called *assemblers* and they have two important characteristics. First, there is a different assembler for each different kind of computer. That is, assemblers are machine specific. The second characteristic is that there is a one to one correspondence between the statements in an assembly language program and the machine language instructions into which they are translated. This means, of course, that whatever benefits we get from the notion of an assembler, we still must conceive our problems in terms of the machine's repertory of acts.

But just as there is no need for human beings to be constrained by a language of ones and zeros, so too there is no reason why they should be forced to rethink their problems to conform to the basic acts of which computers are capable. While assemblers require this conformance, there is another kind of translator—called a *compiler*—which does not. Unlike assemblers, which are oriented to the machine in terms of the formulation and solution of problems, compilers are problem oriented.

A compiler language is one which is developed with respect to some discipline or problem area such as science, business, linguistics, information retrieval, or education. The point with compilers is to let the programmer or researcher state his problems in his own terms. The task of translating these statements into machine language is left to the compiler.

In our example of adding two numbers, you have seen that even with the gains we get from an assembler, we still must think about addition in a more cumbersome way than we are used to. One compiler language, called FORTRAN, allows us to state addition this way:

$$C = A + B$$

The FORTRAN compiler will turn this single, familiar looking statement into the three machine language instructions required to execute it. Thus the constraint of a one to one correspondence between program statements and machine operations is removed, and computer programming becomes less awkward and, as a result, more accessible to the nonspecialist.

This is especially true since a second characteristic of compilers is that they are more or less machine independent. That is, a program written in a compiler language for one computer will, with some qualifications, be acceptable to another computer. One result of this has been that researchers have come to share their programs with each other, thereby extending the influence that computer applications have had on many disciplines. The effect of the development of compilers has been to make the computer no longer the private tool of a small clique of research specialists.

Businessmen, for example, have their own compiler language called COBOL which they use to program computers to solve business problems. Language specialists and researchers into human problem solving behavior use SNOBOL, and LISP. The scientist, the mathematician, the educational statistician rely on FORTRAN and MAD. In high schools where students use computers to solve problems in mathematics or the sciences, the two most prevalent languages are BASIC and APL.

Within the realm of computer software, diversity abounds. But whatever the variety among programming languages, we must remember that all these languages have the same purpose. This purpose is to describe to a computer the machine it is to become. As languages become oriented more to our problem and less to the basic acts that make up a computer's repertory, the risk increases that we will mistake the computer for some godlike patron who knows more than we about these problems and their solution. Here as elsewhere with computers, we must be careful with the words we use and the meanings we derive from them.

bibliography

ALLEN, ROLAND: "Gerbert, Pope Silvester II," *The English Historical Review*, vol. **VII**, 1892.

AMERICAN HISTORICAL ASSOCIATION, (ed.): *The Social Ideas of American Educators*, Littlefield, Adams & Co., 1959.

ANDERSON, ALAN ROSS, (ed.): *Minds and Machines*, Prentice-Hall, Englewood Cliffs, N.J., 1964.

ATKINSON, RICHARD: "CAI-Learning Aspects," in R. Gerard (ed.): *Computers and Education*, McGraw-Hill, New York, 1967.

ATKINSON, RICHARD, AND H. A. WILSON, (eds.): *Computer-assisted Instruction: A Book of Readings*, Academic Press, New York, 1969.

AUTOMATIC LANGUAGE PROCESSING ADVISORY COMMITTEE: *Language and Machines*, National Academy of Science, Washington, D.C., 1966.

AYLMER, ROBERT: "A Preliminary Investigation of Computer Involvement in Vocational Decision-Making," unpublished doctoral dissertation, Harvard University, Cambridge, Mass., 1970.

BABBAGE, CHARLES: *Passages from the Life of a Philosopher*, Longmans, London, 1864.

BARUCH, JORDAN: "Synthesis," Paper presented at the Invitational Conference on Systems for Development for Vocational Guidance, October, 1969. (Mimeographed.)

BEATON, ALBERT: *The Use of Statistical Matrix Operators in Statistical Calculus*, Research Bulletin RB-64-51, Educational Testing Service, Princeton, N.J., 1964.

BECKER, JAMES: "What Ever Happened to the Computer?," *Journal of Educational Data Processing*, vol. **8**, no. 1, 1971.

BELTH, MARC: *Education as a Discipline: A Study of the Role of Models in Thinking*, Allyn and Bacon, Boston, 1965.

BERNSTEIN, JEREMY: *The Analytical Engine*, Random House, New York, 1963.

BITZER, D. L., P. G. BRAUNFELD, AND W. W. LICHTENBERGER: "PLATO-II: A Multiple-Student, Computer-controlled, Automatic Teaching Device," in John E. Coulson (ed.): *Programmed Learning and Computer-based Instruction*, Wiley, New York, 1962.

BOOCOCK, SARANE S., AND E. O. SCHILD, (eds.): *Simulation Games in Learning*, Sage Publications, Beverly Hills, Calif., 1968.

BORKO, HAROLD, (ed.): *Computer Applications in the Behavioral Sciences*, Prentice-Hall, Englewood Cliffs, N.J., 1962.

BORKO, HAROLD, (ed.): *Automated Language Processing. The State of the Art*, Wiley, New York, 1967.

BOWDEN, B. V., (ed.): *Faster than Thought*, Pitman, New York, 1953.

BREWSTER, DAVID: "Program Description—DASM: Direct Access Storage Management," Project Report No. 35, The ISVD Project, Harvard University, Cambridge, Mass., 1970.

BUNDERSON, C. VICTOR: "The Computer and Instructional Design," in W. H. Holtzman (ed.), *Computer Assisted Instruction, Testing, and Guidance*, Harper & Row, New York, 1970.

BUSHNELL, DON D., DWIGHT W. ALLEN, AND SARA S. MITTER (eds.): *The Computer in American Education*, Wiley, New York, 1967.

CARROLL, JOHN B., AND ALLAN B. ELLIS: "Planning and Utilization of a Regional Data Bank for Educational Research Purposes," Harvard University, Cambridge, Mass., 1965.

CIRCLE, DUNCAN, DAVID CLEMENS, ARTHUR KROLL, AND DOROTHEA OVERHOLT: *Career Information Service*, Commonwealth of Massachusetts, Bureau of Vocational Education, Department of Education, 1968.

COMMISSION ON INSTRUCTIONAL TECHNOLOGY: "To Improve Learning," *A Report to the President and the Congress of the United States*, U.S. G.P.O., Washington, D.C., 1970.

CONVENTION REPORTER: *Highlights of the 1971 Annual Meeting of the Association for Educational Data Systems*, Lubbock, Tex., 1971.

COOLEY, WILLIAM W.: "Computer Systems for Guidance," in Alice Scates (ed.): *Computer-based Vocational Guidance Systems*, U.S. Office of Education, Doc. No. FS5.225:25053, Washington, D.C., 1969.

COOLEY, WILLIAM W., AND PAUL R. LOHNES: *Multivariate Procedures for the Behavioral Sciences*, Wiley, New York, 1962.

COUCH, ARTHUR S.: *The Data-Text System. A Computer Language for Social Science Research*, Harvard University, Cambridge, Mass., 1966.

COULSON, JOHN E., (ed.): *Programmed Learning and Computer-based Instruction*, Wiley, New York, 1962.

CURTI, MERLE: "The Last Twenty-five Years," in American Historical Association, Commission on the Social Studies (ed.), *The Social Ideas of American Educators*, Littlefield, Adams & Co., Paterson, N.J., 1959.

ELLIS, ALLAN B.: "New Myths and Old Realities: A Discussion," *Harvard Educational Review*, vol. **38**, no. 4, Fall, 1968.

ELLIS, ALLAN B.: "Regional Data Processing for Schools," in (ed.) Wolf: *Uses and Values of the Computer in Education*, International Review of Education, vol. **XIV**, no. 2, 1968.

ELLIS, ALLAN B.: "Some Characteristics of Educational Data Banks," in D. Bushnell, D. Allen, and Sara Mitter (eds.): *The Computer in American Education*, Wiley, New York, 1967.

ELLIS, ALLAN B., MARGARET PINCUS, AND PATRICIA YEE: "Getting a Guidance Machine to Understand English," Project Report No. 14, The ISVD Project, Harvard University, Cambridge, Mass., 1968.

ELLIS, ALLAN B., AND DAVID V. TIEDEMAN: "Can a Machine Counsel?", Project Report No. 17, The ISVD Project, Harvard University, Cambridge, Mass., 1968.

ELLIS, ALLAN B., AND CHARLES S. WETHERELL: "The Computer and Career Decisions," *Technical Memorandum No. 1*, The Information System for Vocational Decisions Project,

Harvard University, Cambridge, Mass., 1966.

ENGLER, DAVID: "Development, Sharing and Utilization of Technologically Based Instructional Materials: Some Guidelines," in E. L. Morphet and David L. Jesser (eds.), *Designing Education for the Future,* no. 6., Citation Press, New York, 1969.

FATTU, NICHOLAS A., AND STANLEY ELAM, (eds.): *Simulation Models for Education,* Phi Delta Kappa, Bloomington, Ind., 1965.

FEURZEIG, WALLACE: *Educational Potentials of Computer Technology,* Final Report, No. 1672, Bolt, Beranek, & Newman, Cambridge, Mass., 1968.

FEURZEIG, WALLACE: *Programming-Languages as a Conceptual Framework for Teaching Mathematics,* Report No. 2165, Vol. **1**, **2**, **3**, Bolt Beranek and Newman Inc., Cambridge, Mass., June 1971.

FUBINI, EUGENE G.: "Education in Modern Society," in M. Greenberger (ed.): *Computers, Communications, and the Public Interest,* Johns Hopkins, Baltimore, 1971.

GARVIN, PAUL, (ed.): *Natural Language and the Computer,* McGraw-Hill, New York, 1963.

GERARD, RALPH, (ed.): *Computers and Education,* McGraw-Hill, New York, 1967.

GREEN, BERT F., JR.: *Digital Computers in Research,* McGraw-Hill, New York, 1963.

GREENBERGER, MARTIN, (ed.): *Computers, Communications, and the Public Interest,* Johns Hopkins, Baltimore, 1971.

GREENBERGER, MARTIN, (ed.): *Computers and the World of the Future,* M.I.T., Cambridge, Mass., 1962.

HARRIS, SEYMOUR: "The Economics of Technological Advances in Education," in E. Morphet and D. Jesser (eds.): *Designing Education for the Future,* no. 6., Citation Press, New York, 1969.

HAVEN, ROBERT: "Some Results to Date: Project LOCAL," in Dudley L. Post, (ed.): *The Uses of Computers in Secondary School Mathematics,* ENTELEK, Newburyport, Mass., 1970.

HAWKINS, GERALD: *Stonehenge Decoded,* Doubleday, New York, 1965.

HAYS, DAVID G.: *Introduction to Computational Linguistics,* American Elsevier, New York, 1967.

HAYWARD, L. C., (ed.): *BIMD Computer Programs Manual,* University of California, Los Angeles, 1961.

HELM, CARL E.: "Simulation Models for Psychometric Theories," *Proceedings of the Fall Joint Computer Conference,* Spartan Books, Washington, D.C., 1965.

HEYEL, CARL: *Computers, Office Machines, and the New Information Technology,* Macmillan, London, 1969.

HOLTZMAN, W. H., (ed.): *Computer Assisted Instruction, Testing, and Guidance,* Harper & Row, New York, 1970.

HOOK, SIDNEY, (ed.): *Dimensions of Mind,* New York University, New York, 1960.

HORST, PAUL: *Matrix Algebra for Social Scientists,* Holt, New York, 1963.

JONES, KENNETH J.: *The Multivariate Statistical Analyzer,* Harvard University, Cambridge, Mass., 1964.

KAIMANN, RICHARD A., AND ROBERT W. MARKER, (eds.): *Educational Data Processing: New Dimensions and Prospects,* Houghton Mifflin, New York, 1967.

KEMENY, JOHN G., AND THOMAS E. KURTZ: *Basic Programming,* Wiley, New York, 1967.

KENDALL, M. G.: *A Course in Multivariate Analysis,* Griffin, London, 1957.

KLEINMUNTZ, BENJAMIN, (ed.): *Clinical Information Processing by Computer: An Essay and Selected Readings,* Holt, New York, 1969.

KORFHAGE, ROBERT R.: *Logic and Algorithms: with Applications to the Computer and Information Sciences,* Wiley, New York, 1966.

LABRIE, RICHARD: "A Procedure for Performing Least-Squares Analysis when Observations Are Missing," unpublished doctoral dissertation, Harvard University, 1969.

LEEDS, HERBERT D., AND GERALD M. WEINBERG: *Computer-programming Fundamentals,* (2d ed), McGraw-Hill, New York, 1966.

LICKLIDER, J. C. R.: "Preliminary Experiments in Computer-aided Teaching," in John E. Coulson (ed.): *Programmed Learning and Computer-based Instruction,* Wiley, New York, 1962.

LOHNES, PAUL R., AND WILLIAM W. COOLEY: *Introduction to Statistical Procedures: with Computer Exercises,* Wiley, New York, 1968.

MCWILLIAMS, ERIK: "Large Scale CAI-The NSF Project," *Proceedings of the ACM Annual Conference,* August 1972.

MESTHENE, E.: "Computers and the Purposes of Education," in W. Holtzman (ed.): *Computer Assisted Instruction, Texting, and Guidance,* Harper & Row, New York, 1970.

MICHAEL, DONALD: *The Next Generation,* Random House, New York, 1965.

MICHAEL, DONALD: "Some Speculations on the Social Impact of Technology," in Dean Morse and Aaron Warner (eds.): *Technological Innovation and Society,* Columbia, New York, 1966.

MICHAEL, DONALD: "Cybernation and Changing Goals in Education," in D. Bushnell, D. Allen, and Sara Mitter (eds.): *The Computer in American Education,* Wiley, New York, 1967.

MINSKY, MARVIN: *Computation: Finite and Infinite Machines,* Prentice-Hall, Englewood Cliffs, N.J., 1967.

MINSKY, MARVIN, (ed.): *Semantic Information Processing,* M.I.T., Cambridge, Mass., 1968.

MOOERS, CALVIN: "TRAC, A Procedure-describing Language for the Reactive Typewriter," *Communications of the ACM,* vol. 9, no. 3, March, 1966.

MORPHET, E. L., AND DAVID L. JESSER, (eds.): *Designing Education for the Future,* no. 6., Citation Press, New York, 1969.

MORRISON, PHILIP, AND EMILY MORRISON, (eds.): *Charles Babbage and His Calculating Engines,* Dover, New York, 1961.

MORSE, DEAN, AND AARON W. WARNER, (eds.): *Technological Innovation and Society,* Columbia, New York, 1966.

MOSTELLER, FREDERICK, ROBERT ROURKE, AND GEORGE THOMAS, JR.: *Probability, A First Course,* Addison-Wesley, Reading, Mass., 1961.

OETTINGER, ANTHONY, WITH SEMA MARKS: *Run, Computer, Run: The Mythology of Educational Innovation,* Harvard, Cambridge, Mass., 1969.

ORR, WILLIAM D., (ed.): *Conversational Computers,* Wiley, New York, 1968.

PAGE, ELLIS: "Measurement Frontiers Symposium, Essay Grading by Computer," American Psychological Association, Chicago, 1965.

PAPERT, SEYMOUR: "On Making a Theorem for a Child," *Proceedings of the ACM Annual Conference,* August 1972.

PAPERT, SEYMOUR, AND CYNTHIA SOLOMON: "Twenty Things to Do with a Computer," M.I.T. Artificial Intelligence Laboratory, Cambridge, Mass., June 1971. (Mimeographed.)

POOL, ITHIEL DE SOLA, ROBERT P. ABELSON, AND SAMUEL L. POPKIN: *Candidates, Issues, and Strategies. A Computer Simulation of the 1960 Presidential Election,* M.I.T., Cambridge, Mass., 1964.

POST, DUDLEY L., (ed.): *The Uses of Computers in Secondary School Mathematics,* ENTELEK, Newburyport, Mass., 1970.

RICHARDS, I. A.: "The Creative Aim in Instruction," in D. Bushnell, D. Allen, and Sara Mitter, (eds.): *The Computer in American Education,* Wiley, New York, 1967.

ROE, ANNE: *The Psychology of Occupations,* Wiley, New York, 1956.

ROMAN, RICHARD: "Manual for GLURP—A Computer Assisted Instruction Language," Project Report No. 33, The ISVD Project, Harvard University, Cambridge, Mass., 1970.

ROSENBAUM, SEMA M.: *Computer Simulation for High School Students,* Westinghouse Learning Corporation, New York, 1970.

RULON, PHILLIP J., DAVID V. TIEDEMAN, MAURICE M. TATSUOKA, AND CHARLES R. LANGMUIR: *Multivariate Statistics for Personnel Classification,* Wiley, New York, 1967.

SCATES, ALICE, (ed.): *Computer-based Vocational Guidance Systems,* U.S. Office of Education, Doc. No. FS5.255:25053, Washington, D.C., 1969.

SCHEFFLER, ISRAEL, (ed.): *Philosophy and Education,* Allyn and Bacon, Boston, 1966.

SCHEFFLER, ISRAEL: *The Anatomy of Inquiry, Philosophical Studies in the Theory of Science,* Knopf, New York, 1963.

SCHEFFLER, ISRAEL: *The Language of Education,* Charles C. Thomas, Springfield, Ill., 1960.

SCOTT, HEATHER: "Program Description—HASM: Hierarchical Access Storage Management," Project Report No. 34, The ISVD Project, Harvard University, Cambridge, Mass., 1970.

SHARPE, WILLIAM F.: *BASIC. An Introduction to Computer Programming Using the BASIC Language,* Free Press, New York, 1967.

SIEGEL, PAUL: *Understanding Digital Computers,* Wiley, New York, 1961.

SILBERMAN, CHARLES: *Crisis in the Classroom,* Random House, New York, 1970.

SILBERMAN, CHARLES: *The Myths of Automation,* Harper & Row, New York, 1966.

SINGH, JAGJIT: *Great Ideas in Information Theory, Language, and Cybernetics,* Dover, New York, 1966.

SIPPL, CHARLES J.: *Computer Dictionary and Handbook,* Sams, Indianapolis, 1966.

STAKE, ROBERT: "Technologically-based Instruction and Materials," in E. Morphet and D. Jesser (eds.): *Designing Education for the Future,* No. 6., Citation Press, New York, 1969.

STARKWEATHER, JOHN: "A Common Language for a Variety of Conversational Programming Needs," in R. Atkinson, and H. Wilson (eds.): *Computer-assisted Instruction, A Book of Readings,* Academic Press, New York, 1969.

STERLING, T., AND S. POLLACK: *MEDCOMP. Handbook of Computer Applications in Biology and Medicine. Part I. Statistical Systems,* University of Cincinnati, Cincinnati, 1964.

STETTEN, KENNETH: "TICCIT: A Delivery System Designed for Mass Utilization," M71-56, The Mitre Corporation, Washington, D.C., October, 1971.

STONE, PHILIP J., DEXTER C. DUNPHY, MARSHALL S. SMITH, AND DANIEL M. OGILVIE: *The General Inquirer: A Computer Approach to Content Analysis,* M.I.T., Cambridge, Mass., 1966.

STOLUROW, LAWRENCE: "Some Factors in the Design of Systems for Computer-assisted Instruction," in Richard Atkinson, and H. A. Wilson (eds.): *Computer-assisted Instruction, A Book of Readings,* Academic Press, New York, 1969.

SUPER, DONALD, (ed.): *Computer-assisted Counseling,* Teacher's College Press, New York, 1970.

SUPER, DONALD: *The Psychology of Career,* Harper & Row, New York, 1957.

SUPPES, PATRICK: "Computer-assisted Instruction at Stanford," Technical Report No. 174, Stanford University, Stanford, 1971.

SUPPES, PATRICK: "Education in Modern Society," in M. Greenberger, (ed.): *Computers, Communications, and the Public Interest,* Johns Hopkins, Baltimore, 1971.

SUPPES, PATRICK, AND MONA MORNINGSTAR: "Four Programs in Computer-assisted Instruction," in W. Holtzman (ed.): *Computer Assisted Instruction, Testing, and Guidance,* Harper & Row, New York, 1970.

SUPPES, PATRICK: "'New Myths and Old Realities': Six Responses and a Reply: A Discussion," *Harvard Educational Review,* vol. **38,** no. 4, Fall 1968.

SUPPES, PATRICK: "On Using Computers to Individualize Instruction," in D. Bushnell, D. Allen, and S. Mitter (eds.): *The Computer in American Education*, Wiley, New York, 1967.

TAYLOR, ANN: "GLURP—Generalized Language for Understanding and Responding to People," Project Report No. 29, The ISVD Project, Harvard University, Cambridge, Mass., 1970.

TAYLOR, EDWIN F., (ed.): *ELIZA—A Skimmable Report on the ELIZA Conversational Tutoring System*, Education Research Center, M.I.T., Cambridge, Mass., 1968.

TAYLOR, EDWIN F.: "The ELIZA Program: Conversational Tutorial," *IEEE International Convention Record*, vol. **6**, part 10, 1967.

TIEDEMAN, DAVID V., AND ROBERT P. O'HARA: *Career Development: Choice and Adjustment*, College Entrance Examination Board, New York, 1963.

TURING, ALAN M.: "Computing Machinery and Intelligence," *Mind*, **59**, October, 1950.

TURING, ALAN M.: "On Computable Numbers, with an Application to the *Entscheidungsproblem*," *Proceedings of the London Mathematical Society*, vol. **42**, 1937.

WEIZENBAUM, JOSEPH: "Contextual Understanding by Computers," *Communications of the ACM*, vol. **10**, no. 8, August, 1967.

WEIZENBAUM, JOSEPH: "ELIZA—A Computer Program for the Study of Natural Language Communication between Man and Machine," *Communications of the ACM*, vol. **9**, no. 1, January, 1966.

WING, RICHARD L.: "Two Computer-based Economic Games for Sixth Graders," in Sarane S. Boocock and E. O. Schild (eds.): *Simulation Games in Learning*, Sage Publications, Beverly Hills, Calif., 1968.

WOOLDRIDGE, DEAN E.: *Mechanical Man. The Physical Basis of Intelligent Life*, McGraw-Hill, New York, 1968.

WOOLDRIDGE, DEAN E.: *The Machinery of the Brain*, McGraw-Hill, New York, 1963.

YOUNG, GAIL S.: "Comments on Social, Psychological, and Mathematical Aspects of the Suppes-Morningstar Chapter," in W. H. Holtzman (ed.), *Computer Assisted Instruction, Testing, and Guidance*, Harper & Row, New York, 1970.

ZINN, KARL: "A Basic Reference Shelf on Interactive Use of Computers for Instruction," University of Michigan, September 1968. (Mimeographed.)

Index